THE CARLTON SPORTS GUIDE

FORMULA ONE 2017

This edition published in 2017
by Carlton Books Limited
20 Mortimer Street
London W1T 3JW

Reprinted 2017

A CIP catalogue record for this book is available from the British Library.

The publisher has taken reasonable steps to check the accuracy of the facts contained
herein at the time of going to press, but can take no responsibility for any errors.

ISBN 978-1-78097-910-6

Editorial Director: Martin Corteel
Design Manager: Luke Griffin
Designer: Darren Jordan
Assistant Editor: David Ballheimer
Production: Lisa Cook
Picture Research: Paul Langan

Printed in Spain

**Opposite: Lewis Hamilton hoped for victory in Singapore last year, but it went
instead to his Mercedes team-mate Nico Rosberg.**

THE CARLTON SPORTS GUIDE

FORMULA ONE 2017

BRUCE JONES

CARLTON
BOOKS

CONTENTS

Right: Max Verstappen had the most monumental debut for Red Bull Racing last year, winning first time out in Spain to the obvious delight of Red Bull's Helmut Marko.

ANALYSIS OF THE 2017 SEASON

These are interesting times for F1. Discussion was focused on "how to improve the show" and Bernie Ecclestone suggested that the World Championship should run two shorter races at each round. That won't happen yet, but there are many technical changes for 2017, and a new driver at Mercedes. It will be intriguing to see which team manages the changes best.

There have been many and various alterations to the regulations since the World Championship was introduced in 1950. Engines have changed in capacity, with induction permitted from time to time. Hybrids have recently transformed the scene. Throw in, too, the size, shape and number of aerodynamic aids allowed, and the cars are a constantly changing entity, so it's easy to see why the teams have entire divisions devoted to design and engineering. The aim for 2017 is to make the cars both faster and more attractive, to draw in a new generation of fans. *See* Talking Points for details.

Costs are being kept in check too, with the governing body ruling last year that teams would be allowed four power units per

car, down from 2016's allowance of five each. Also, the cost of a power unit supply is to be reduced by €1 million, then by €3m in 2018, meaning that considerable efficiencies must be found.

Traditionally, the ranking of the teams changes when technical changes are introduced, yet it's hard to imagine Mercedes being toppled from the top of the pile, such has been the team's dominance over the last three championships. Lewis Hamilton remains, but Nico Rosberg's surprise decision to retire means a new face in the other car, with Valtteri Bottas arriving from Williams.

Red Bull Racing have kept on Daniel Ricciardo and the extraordinarily impressive teenager Max Verstappen and know

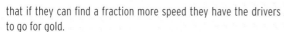

that if they can find a fraction more speed they have the drivers to go for gold.

Ferrari surprised more than a few people when it also stuck with its driver line-up of Sebastian Vettel and Kimi Raikkonen, as it had been expected that the Finn would be replaced, but the team found him easier to manage than Vettel when the German's frustration boiled over. Vettel may have further reason to be angry in 2017, as the removal of the team's technical director wasn't seen as a wise move, especially without a replacement lined up.

Force India's perpetual financial uncertainty led Nico Hulkenberg to take the decision to move on to Renault. This might seem to be a rash move, judging by Renault's weak form in 2016, but investment by the French manufacturer ought to enable this once title-winning team to advance. Sergio Perez is staying on for one more year with Force India, still eyeing up any opening at Ferrari. Hugely promising Esteban Ocon joins from Manor.

Williams has a teenager on its books in its second car in the shape of Lance Stroll, who will be led by the briefly retired Felipe Massa. Headline writers will talk of Stroll as the son of a Canadian billionaire, which he is. However, he is also the dominant European F3 Champion, so expect good things from him.

It will feel strange to look in the McLaren pit this year and not find a car with Jenson Button's name on it, but he opted for retirement. In his place, Stoffel Vandoorne will be Fernando Alonso's team-mate, with the Spaniard sure to be running out of patience unless the team and engine supplier Honda can finally make appreciable progress.

Daniil Kvyat has been given a last chance by Red Bull's driver programme. Dropped by Red Bull Racing back to Scuderia Toro Rosso, he was dispirited and many thought that GP2 frontrunner Pierre Gasly would line up alongside Carlos Sainz Jr, but the Russian was kept on.

Haas will have to fight hard to avoid a second season dip, something that is common after teams have spent the year before their F1 debut concentrating on their first car, only to find less time for its successor. Romain Grosjean stays on and is joined by Kevin Magnussen, a driver who wasn't content with a one-year contract offer from Renault.

Renault can only perform better than last year's half-cocked effort and Hulkenberg will be a capable team leader along with the ever-improving Jolyon Palmer.

Sauber has struggled for years with a lack of money. New ownership will bring stability for Marcus Ericsson and Pascal Wehrlein, but don't expect great strides until 2018.

In the first week of the new year, Manor F1 announced that they had gone into administration. At the time, their chances of appearing on the track in 2017 were slim, leaving ten teams and 20 cars.

MERCEDES AMG PETRONAS

Mercedes' only problem of note in 2016, its third straight title-winning year, was keeping its drivers civil with each other. With Nico Rosberg shocking the team with his sudden retirement announcement, there will be a new dynamic this year.

Nico Rosberg and Lewis Hamilton became used to fighting each other for grand prix wins but Hamilton will have a different team-mate in 2017.

So strong have the past three years been for the Mercedes F1 team, claiming the drivers' and constructors' titles in 2014, 2015 and 2016, that it is becoming increasingly hard to remember that it had a lengthy life before its cars were painted silver after this team with three previous identities was taken over by the German manufacturer.

It broke cover back in 1999 when it entered the World Championship. Unlike many outfits that have made the step up to motor racing's top level, this was an all-new team, not one that had operated previously and won championships at junior levels. This was a team that was the brainchild of 1997 World Champion Jacques Villeneuve and his former ski coach, Craig Pollock, and it started from scratch.

Pollock had worked in sports management in the intervening years and was able to put together the programme by coaxing British American Tobacco to finance a new team: British American Racing.

By buying the Tyrrell team's championship entry, it had a place on the F1 grid for 1999 and so set about raiding the pitlane to handpick the staff that it wanted to operate from its base in Brackley near Silverstone. Ridiculously, the team made overly bold predictions about the impact it would make, making it seem worse than it really was

THE POWER AND THE GLORY

GEOFF WILLIS
Geoff specialised in fluid dynamic research before working in America's Cup yacht racing. His first shot at F1 came with Leyton House in 1990 and this led to a move to Williams in its glory years, where he became chief aerodynamicist after Adrian Newey moved to McLaren in 1996. Appointed technical director by BAR in 2002, he guided the team to second place in 2004, only to be fired in 2006. He made his comeback with Red Bull at Newey's behest in 2007 and, after a spell at HRT, moved to Mercedes in 2011.

ANOTHER YEAR RACING IN A CLASS OF ITS OWN
Try as they might, not one of Mercedes' rivals could raise its game enough to trouble the team last year. With the exception of Max Verstappen's victory in Spain, after Hamilton and Rosberg clashed on lap 1, and a strong challenge from Daniel Ricciardo in the other Red Bull in Singapore, it was all Mercedes and the main focus seemed to be to simply keep its warring drivers apart, and to make it look as though winning wasn't as easy as it proved, for the sake of F1's image.

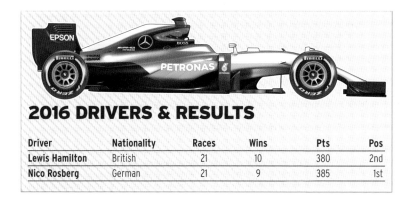

2016 DRIVERS & RESULTS

Driver	Nationality	Races	Wins	Pts	Pos
Lewis Hamilton	British	21	10	380	2nd
Nico Rosberg	German	21	9	385	1st

FOR THE RECORD

Country of origin:	England
Team base:	Brackley, England
Telephone:	(44) 01280 844000
Website:	www.mercedesamgf1.com
Active in Formula One:	As BAR 1999-2005; Honda Racing 2006-08; Brawn GP 2009; Mercedes 2010 on
Grands Prix contested:	324
Wins:	63
Pole positions:	73
Fastest laps:	41

THE TEAM

Non-executive chairman:	Niki Lauda
Executive director, business:	Toto Wolff
Executive director, technical:	James Allison
MD, Mercedes-Benz AMG High Performance powertrains:	Andy Cowell
Technology director:	Geoff Willis
Engineering director:	Aldo Costa
Performance director:	Mark Ellis
Sporting director:	Ron Meadows
Chief designer:	John Owen
Chief race engineer:	Andrew Shovlin
Chief track engineer:	Simon Cole
Test driver:	tba
Chassis:	Mercedes F1 W08
Engine:	Mercedes V6
Tyres:	Pirelli

when it didn't hit these targets. Indeed, neither Villeneuve nor Ricardo Zonta was able to score, with its cars still running at the finish in only 25% of the races.

The 2000 season was an improvement with Honda engines, shown immediately by Villeneuve finishing fourth in the opening round, and the team soared to rank fourth with Benetton. In 2001, Villeneuve raced to third place in the Spanish and German GPs.

For 2003, there was a new face at the top, with Prodrive motorsport engineering company boss David Richards taking over from Pollock and also a new face settling in quickly to outperform Villeneuve to become the team's lead driver: Jenson Button. Race wins started to be a possibility, with Button finishing second from pole position at Imola in 2004. Three more second places left BAR as runners-up to Michael Schumacher-led Ferrari.

For 2006, Honda became more involved, the team being renamed as Honda Racing. This was timely as Button gave the team its first win, in Hungary. So, it was a surprise

when the team's form faded in a major way in 2007, even with a driver as quick as Rubens Barrichello as the second driver.

In 2008, Honda became spooked by its name being on a team that wasn't succeeding, especially as the economic recession was starting to bite and the manufacturer found it harder to justify the expenditure on a racing programme. At the end of the season, the team closed.

It was restored just in time for the start of the 2009 season following a buy-out led by technical director Ross Brawn, after whom the phoenix-like team was renamed. Keeping it alive was achievement enough, but this was a dreamlike year, as the car was designed with a double diffuser, exploiting a loophole in the rules that others would have to follow, as the car was so good that Button won six of the first seven rounds. Barrichello won twice to help Brawn GP land both the drivers' and constructors' titles. With Mercedes looking for a way back into the sport, it's small surprise that it snapped up the team.

For 2010, the cars echoed the Silver Arrows of the 1930s and 1950s, with the attack led by Michael Schumacher on his F1 return. Yet, without the advantage of a technical leap, the team didn't prosper.

Nico Rosberg joined as the team's second driver in 2010. Following seven-time World Champion Schumacher's retirement at the end of 2012, Lewis Hamilton moved across from McLaren, took a year to find his feet, but then bagged the 2014 and 2015 titles as Mercedes, under technical chief Paddy Lowe, pulled clear of all its rivals.

Lowe, Rosberg, Hamilton and Lauda celebrate clinching a third constructors' title in a row.

"It was an unbelievable feeling crossing the finish line in Abu Dhabi. It was my childhood dream come true."
Nico Rosberg

Lewis was thwarted last year in his quest to become a quadruple World Champion, as Nico Rosberg got one over him from within the Mercedes camp. This year, it's clear that he must be 100% on his game all of the year after an inconsistent 2016.

Lewis made it plain from his earliest days in kart racing that he had all the skills needed to aim for the top.

With his father holding down several jobs to finance his racing, the titles rolled in, from cadet karting through the more senior karting categories. Then, a request to McLaren boss Ron Dennis sowed the seeds of one of racing's best patronages.

Lewis stepped up to cars at the end of 2001. British Formula Renault champion at his second attempt with Manor Motorsport, Lewis stepped up to F3 and this category proved to be another two-year programme. In 2005, having moved to the ASM team, he blitzed the European series, winning 15 of the 20 rounds. GP2, F1's immediate feeder formula, was then dispatched with aplomb.

It hasn't always been easy for GP2 champions to land a decent F1 ride, but Lewis had that McLaren seat awaiting him for 2007. He showed immediately that he wasn't bowed by the talents of team-mate Fernando Alonso, then started winning races and, but for a slip-up in China, would have been World Champion. Season two brought the title Lewis craved after a nail-biting finale in Brazil when he clinched the

Lewis had his ups and downs through 2016, and had to raise his game to keep up.

deal with just a few corners to go.

Since then, Lewis endured McLaren's drop in form, but blossomed after moving to Mercedes, taking his second title in 2014 and adding another in 2015 as he twice bettered team-mate Nico Rosberg.

A DISAPPOINTINGLY PATCHY YEAR

Lewis isn't used to being beaten by a team-mate, so the start of last year's championship came as a shock as Nico Rosberg – a driver he had bettered through the previous three years – won the first four races on the trot. A clash at the start of the fifth round put both out of the race in Spain and the atmosphere in the team was toxic. Then the wins came, starting in Monaco, followed by five more in the next six rounds, putting him back into contention. An engine-change penalty meant having to start from the back of the grid in Belgium and a charge through to third, helped by several problems for the frontrunners. A poor start from pole at Monza dropped Lewis to sixth before a charge back to second as Rosberg won again. However, the main blip was to his form when he was lacklustre in Singapore and Rosberg won again. Yet, what floored him was engine failure when in front at Sepang and the fight back from that proved just too much for Lewis.

TRACK NOTES

Nationality:	BRITISH
Born:	7 JANUARY 1985, STEVENAGE, ENGLAND
Website:	www.lewishamilton.com
Teams:	McLAREN 2007-12, MERCEDES 2013-17

CAREER RECORD

First Grand Prix:	2007 AUSTRALIAN GP
Grand Prix starts:	188
Grand Prix wins:	53

2007 Canadian GP, United States GP, Hungarian GP, Japanese GP, 2008 Australian GP, Monaco GP, British GP, German GP, Chinese GP, 2009 Hungarian GP, Singapore GP, 2010 Turkish GP, Canadian GP, Belgian GP, 2011 Chinese GP, German GP, Abu Dhabi GP, 2012 Canadian GP, Hungarian GP, Italian GP, United States GP, 2013 Hungarian GP, 2014 Malaysian GP, Bahrain GP, Chinese GP, Spanish GP, British GP, Italian GP, Singapore GP, Japanese GP, Russian GP, United States GP, Abu Dhabi GP, 2015 Australian GP, Chinese GP, Bahrain GP, Canadian GP, British GP, Belgian GP, Italian GP, Japanese GP, Russian GP, United States GP, 2016 Monaco GP, Canadian GP, Austrian GP, British GP, Hungarian GP, German GP, United States GP, Mexican GP, Brazilian GP, Abu Dhabi GP

Poles:	61
Fastest laps:	31
Points:	2247
Honours:	2008, 2014 & 2015 F1 WORLD CHAMPION, 2007 & 2016 F1 RUNNER-UP, 2006 GP2 CHAMPION, 2005 EUROPEAN F3 CHAMPION, 2003 BRITISH FORMULA RENAULT CHAMPION, 2000 WORLD KART CUP & EUROPEAN FORMULA A KART CHAMPION, 1999 ITALIAN INTERCON A CHAMPION, 1995 BRITISH CADET KARTING CHAMPION

VALTTERI BOTTAS*

Valtteri was all set to continue at Williams for 2017, but then Nico Rosberg rocked the boat by quitting within a few days of becoming World Champion, and so the 27-year-old Finn became the favourite to join Mercedes as his replacement.

JJ Lehto had made a name for Finnish kart racers shining in Formula Ford in the mid-1980s, followed and immediately bettered by Mika Hakkinen. Then, two decades later, through came Valtteri. Fortunately, he was guided through Formula Renault by the Koiranen brothers, finishing third in the Northern European series in 2007, then winning it with Motopark Academy in 2008. More importantly, he also landed the more prestigious European title in 2008, pipping Daniel Ricciardo.

Advancing to F3 in 2009, Valtteri impressed by finishing third in the European championship in a year dominated by his ART Grand Prix team-mate, Jules Bianchi. He won the stand-alone F3 Masters race at Zandvoort. Then history repeated itself in 2010, as he won the F3 Masters again and also repeated his third-placed ranking in European F3.

Most drivers would have then stepped up to GP2 or perhaps the Formula Renault 3.5 series, but Valtteri didn't have the budget for those, so he raced in GP3 instead. He knew that he absolutely had to become champion in this less powerful category, and he did, winning four races for the Lotus

Valtteri knows there are very few winning F1 cars, so 2017 is his golden chance.

ART team. The highlight of his year, though, was the two days of F1 testing with Williams that were part of the champion's prize. Vitally for his career, Valtteri's down-to-earth approach and pace impressed Williams and so started his relationship with the team.

For 2012, Williams gave him a run on the Friday morning at each grand prix. Then, in 2013, he stepped up to a race seat.

After scoring just four points in 2013, Valtteri gathered 186 in 2014 to rank fourth, with six podium finishes. He followed this up in 2015 by ending up fifth overall, clearly showing his talents. However, the vacancy at Ferrari for which he was being tipped failed to materialise as compatriot Kimi Raikkonen stayed on.

After a year of treading water in 2016, the shock retirement of Rosberg opened up a whole new vista. Valtteri's best result last year was third in Canada, but he will be surely ending 2017 with a first win added to his CV.

TRACK NOTES

Nationality:	FINNISH
Born:	28 AUGUST 1989, NASTOLA, FINLAND
Website:	www.valtteribottas.com
Teams:	WILLIAMS 2013-16, MERCEDES 2017

CAREER RECORD

First Grand Prix:	2013 AUSTRALIAN GP
Grand Prix starts:	77
Grand Prix wins:	0
(best result: 2nd, 2014 British & German GPs)	
Poles:	0
Fastest laps:	1
Points:	411
Honours:	2011 GP3 CHAMPION,
	2009 & 2010 FORMULA 3 MASTERS WINNER,
	2008 EUROPEAN & NORTHERN EUROPEAN
	FORMULA RENAULT CHAMPION

GIVING HIS ALL TO STAY NOTICED

All car racing fans know that there is little that even the best driver can do with a car that is not competitive, and there were races in 2016 when Valtteri and team-mate Felipe Massa could do little to make an impression. This must have been incredibly frustrating for this Finn, as there were others when their Mercedes-powered FW38s were quick enough for podiums to be a possibility. Valtteri nailed one in Montreal, but for a driver in his fourth year in F1, with younger drivers coming along all the time, he will have been more than a little aware that you have to be the form driver outside the top teams at the very moment that an opening appears. This is because the next one might be years away and you may never know if you'll have the tools with which to impress. Apart from that third place in Canada in 2016, he raced to fourth place in Sochi and fifth in Barcelona and Malaysia. Valtteri usually had the better of Massa, as you would expect, but results tended to be in the lower half of the top 10 as Mercedes dominated.

13

* Not confirmed at the time of going to press.

There was considerable tension in the Mercedes garage at the penultimate race of 2016, the Brazilian GP at Interlagos, as its drivers aimed for the title.

RED BULL RACING

From looking as though it had no answer to Mercedes' pace at the start of 2016, Red Bull Racing fought back, added Max Verstappen to its attack and, along with Daniel Ricciardo, looks set to have the tools required for success in 2017.

Daniel Ricciardo and Max Verstappen made a formidable pairing in 2016, when they were the best of the rest behind the Mercedes duo.

Sir Jackie Stewart left a considerable mark on Formula 1, winning 27 grands prix from his 99 starts and being crowned World Champion in 1969, 1971 and 1973. A hugely busy man, even decades after his F1 retirement, with a roster of multinational companies to represent, he somehow still found the time to help his older son Paul into racing. He set up a team with which Paul raced in F2000 in 1988, then moved with Paul through F3 into F3000. At this point, Paul realised that there were faster drivers than he, so he stepped back and the pair elected to run a team in F1 instead.

Using Jackie's contacts, especially Ford, Stewart Racing made its debut in 1997, running cars for Rubens Barrichello and Jan Magnussen, and being rewarded when the Brazilian finished second at Monaco. This was a bit of a flash in the pan, and it took until 1999 for this to be improved on when Johnny Herbert mastered changing conditions to win the European GP at the Nurburgring. Perhaps sensing that

its overall ranking of fourth, behind only Ferrari, McLaren and Jordan, would be as good as they could hope for, the Stewarts sold the team to Ford and it re-emerged branded as Jaguar Racing, since Jaguar was then part of the Ford empire.

Sadly, motor manufacturer ownership can lead to interference from those with

THE POWER AND THE GLORY

ADRIAN NEWEY
The most successful F1 designer ever, Adrian took a degree in aeronautics, moving straight into F1 in 1980 with Fittipaldi. His spell at March – in F2, sportscars, then Indycars – helped him develop his craft and he moved ahead of the game with his first F1 design, the March 881. Adrian joined Williams in 1991 and created his first title-winning car in 1992, adding more in 1993, 1996 and 1997. There were no titles for him with McLaren, but David Coulthard coaxed him to Red Bull and this brought four titles in four seasons, 2010-13.

DRIVER CHANGE LEADS TO A TWIN ATTACK
Daniel Ricciardo was always expected to have the upper hand over Daniil Kvyat, but his run of three fourth places in the first three races was topped by the Russian's third place in China. Two races later, though, he had a new team-mate – Max Verstappen – and was fourth to the new boy's first in Spain. Thereafter, though, the Australian's experience showed as he took pole in Monaco and victory at Sepang, giving Verstappen a great role model from whom to learn.

2016 DRIVERS & RESULTS

Driver	Nationality	Races	Wins	Pts	Pos
Daniil Kvyat	Russian	4	0	21	14th
Daniel Ricciardo	Australian	21	1	256	3rd
Max Verstappen	Dutch	17	1	204	5th

little knowledge of motor racing and this proved to be the team's curse over the next few years as first Bobby Rahal and then Niki Lauda were frustrated in their spells as team chief. Mark Webber's form in the cockpit was one of few highlights and Ford sold the Milton Keynes-based team to Dietrich Mateschitz, co-founder of the Red Bull energy drink.

Rebranded again for 2005, and with racer turned F3000 team manager Christian Horner at the helm, Red Bull Racing signed David Coulthard as its lead driver. This was a shrewd choice, as he brought years of experience from McLaren with him. Results didn't improve in that first year, as Red Bull Racing ranked seventh again. However, Coulthard convinced ace designer Adrian Newey to leave McLaren to join the team and that ensured that there would be an upswing in fortune once his cars came on line.

That first win finally arrived in 2009, taken by the team's new signing, Sebastian Vettel, and he and Webber - who had returned in 2007 - set about scoring at almost every race, the team ending the year as runner-up to Brawn GP.

Then the floodgates of success opened. Nine wins in 2010 kept both drivers in the hunt, with Vettel snatching the title at the final round and earning Red Bull Racing its first constructors' title into the bargain.

The next three seasons ended with the same result: another drivers' title for Vettel and the constructors' title for Red Bull Racing. Then Mercedes discovered a winning touch it has yet to lose. Vettel moved on after a 2014 campaign in which he was outscored by new signing Daniel Ricciardo, failing to win a grand prix while the Australian won three times.

In 2015, Ricciardo himself was outscored by a new team-mate, Daniil Kvyat, another driver promoted by Mateschitz's talent spotter Helmut Marko from Scuderia Toro Rosso, Red Bull's junior team. However, although Ricciardo suffered from poor luck and was still very much the team leader, the main problem was that Mercedes had moved on to another plane and the desire to have engines to match Mercedes grew through 2015.

In 2016, the Renault V6, badged as a TAG Heuer, did a good enough job to keep Red Bull Racing as the best of the rest and pitch for further wins to match the one that Max Verstappen landed in the Spanish GP. It was his Red Bull Racing debut, after stepping up from Toro Rosso and swapping drives with Kvyat, albeit coming after the Mercedes had collided with each other.

"We worked tremendously hard last year and to finish second in the championship with two wins was an incredible achievement."
Christian Horner

David Coulthard raced to fourth place in Melbourne on Red Bull Racing's debut in 2005.

DANIEL RICCIARDO

This smiling Australian had every reason to smile last year, as his talents matured yet more and he rose to become the driver most likely to topple the Mercedes drivers, making him Red Bull Racing leader even with Max Verstappen alongside.

Western Australia is an extremely long way from anywhere, with even the rest of Australia thousands of miles away. This made Daniel's early career one that had required patience, and a bigger than usual budget, simply to be able to go out and race against his contemporaries.

After advancing from karting to Formula Ford, he then went overseas in 2006, finishing third in the Asian Formula BMW championship that was won by future Le Mans 24 Hours winner Earl Bamber.

When 17, Daniel moved to Europe to race in Formula Renault, finishing sixth in the Italian championship and then as runner-up to Valtteri Bottas in the European series in 2008 to reward new backers Red Bull.

Then came Daniel's breakthrough as he moved to England and won the 2009 British F3 Championship at a canter for the dominant Carlin team, thus convincing Red Bull to keep him on its roster of stars.

The next step towards F1 was in more powerful Formula Renault 3.5, and Daniel ended up just two points off winning the title in that, finishing just behind Mikhail Aleshin. Looking to nail the title at the second attempt in 2011, his season

Daniel pushed hard through 2016 in pursuit of Mercedes. Will it be any closer this year?

developed a different course when Daniel was moved in to F1 midway through the year when HRT gave him what had been Narain Karthikeyan's drive.

For 2012, Red Bull moved him into its F1 junior team, Scuderia Toro Rosso, and Daniel

put in two strong seasons with the Italian outfit. Then, having just edged out team-mate Jean-Eric Vergne, he became one of Toro Rosso's rare graduates to Red Bull Racing.

Joining as team-mate to Sebastian Vettel - a driver who'd just given the team four consecutive drivers' titles - wasn't expected to be easy, but all pundits were amazed when he took three wins and Vettel none and so ended the year third overall. Looking to improve on that in 2015 proved futile, Red Bull Racing's Renault V6s not offering enough grunt to challenge those powered by Mercedes or Ferrari engines.

TRACK NOTES

Nationality:	AUSTRALIAN
Born:	1 JULY 1989, PERTH, AUSTRALIA
Website:	www.danielricciardo.com
Teams:	HRT 2011, TORO ROSSO 2012-13, RED BULL RACING 2014-17

CAREER RECORD	
First Grand Prix:	2011 BRITISH GP
Grand Prix starts:	109
Grand Prix wins:	4
	2014 Canadian GP, Hungarian GP, Belgian GP, 2016 Malaysian GP
Poles:	1
Fastest laps:	8
Points:	616
Honours:	2010 FORMULA RENAULT 3.5 RUNNER-UP, 2009 BRITISH FORMULA THREE CHAMPION, 2008 EUROPEAN FORMULA RENAULT RUNNER-UP & WESTERN EUROPEAN FORMULA RENAULT CHAMPION

LEADING THE PURSUIT OF MERCEDES

Much as his fellow Australian Alan Jones must have felt in 1979 when Clay Regazzoni beat him to give Williams its first win, so Daniel must have found it tough when Max Verstappen was promoted from Scuderia Toro Rosso and promptly won the Spanish GP on his first outing after the Mercedes drivers clashed. Thereafter, Daniel proved why he was team leader and put in some excellent performances, most notably his chase of Nico Rosberg in Singapore where he went from 25s back to less than half a second. Whereas Ferrari lost its edge in the second half of the year, so Daniel and Red Bull Racing advanced. Three second-place finishes in the four races from Hockenheim to Singapore showed just how well he was racing, with victory coming next time out, at Sepang. There were flashes of prodigious speed in qualifying too, as shown by Daniel taking his first pole, around the streets of Monaco. Third overall behind the Mercedes duo was as good a final ranking as Daniel could have expected.

MAX VERSTAPPEN

Max rewrote the record books last year when he was promoted from Toro Rosso to Red Bull Racing and won on his debut, at just 17 years and 228 days. This year is about using all the experience that he has added since to make a bid for the title.

Max Verstappen's father Jos was a shooting star when he stepped up from kart racing to cars, shocking the racing establishment as he rocketed through the junior single-seater formulae to F1 after just two years, a move all the more remarkable as he had no family behind him. He did it on merit, as in those years he was crowned first as Benelux Formula Opel champion then took the German F3 title. Amazingly, his progress was as nothing, though, when compared to his son's, who took just the one year to go from kart to the sport's top category.

Success in karts for Max was all but guaranteed as not only was Jos a multiple champion up to European level, but so was Max's mother, Sophie Kumpen, meaning that there were plenty of quick genes in his bloodline. Max duly followed suit and took two European titles in 2013 but also, more importantly, landed the World KZ title too.

With nothing left to keep him in karting, Max stepped up to single-seaters in 2014 at the age of 16, bypassing Formula Renault to go straight to Formula 3. Even before the first F3 round, though, Max had proved himself by kicking off his year with the low-key, Ferrari-backed Florida Winter Series in

Max upset a few drivers last year, but he takes no prisoners and is out there to win.

which he took two wins. Racing in F3 for Van Amersfoort Racing, the same team that had run his father in Formula Opel, Max hit the ground running and was a race winner by the end of the second meeting, at Hockenheim.

At the conclusion of this amazing debut year in car racing, which also included victory in the Masters F3 race, Max had added nine more wins to rank third behind Esteban Ocon and Tom Blomqvist. However, of this trio, it was Max who was first to make it into F1, signing a deal to take him into the World Championship with Scuderia Toro Rosso at the age of just 17.

The 2015 season proved to be a major hit as Max's speed was augmented by an ability to overtake where others wouldn't even try. The result, a pair of fourth-place finishes and a ranking of 12th.

TRACK NOTES

Nationality:	DUTCH
Born: 30 SEPTEMBER 1997, HASSELT, BELGIUM	
Website:	www.verstappe.nl
Teams:	TORO ROSSO 2015-16,
	RED BULL RACING 2016-17

CAREER RECORD	
First Grand Prix:	2014 AUSTRALIAN GP
Grand Prix starts:	40
Grand Prix wins:	1
	2016 Spanish GP
Poles:	0
Fastest laps:	1
Points:	253
Honours:	2013 WORLD & EUROPEAN KZ
	KART CHAMPION, 2012 WSK MASTER SERIES
	KF2 CHAMPION, 2011 WSK EURO SERIES
	CHAMPION, 2009 BELGIAN KF5 CHAMPION,
	2008 DUTCH CADET KART CHAMPION, 2007
	& 2008 DUTCH MINIMAX CHAMPION, 2006
	BELGIAN ROTAX MINIMAX CHAMPION

STEPPING UP TO THE BIG TIME

Points scored in the first three races of 2016 suggested that Max's second year of F1 was going to be a step up on the first. Then it was accelerated as, after the first four rounds, Red Bull talent manager Helmut Marko decided that Max might do a better job for Red Bull Racing than Daniil Kvyat and swapped their rides. What happened at the next race amazed everyone, as not only did Max settle in well, but he came away with the victory in the Spanish GP after the Mercedes duo crashed into each other and Red Bull messed up Daniel Ricciardo's strategy. Consecutive second places in Austria then Britain showed that this had been no fluke, but Max came under pressure for some robust driving tactics in the Belgian GP that left the unflappable Kimi Raikkonen less than impressed. The best gauge of Max's progress was of course against team-mate Ricciardo and Max was at first just short of that. Then, through the second half of the season, he began to match the Australia blow for blow, suggesting truly great things lie ahead.

SCUDERIA FERRARI

Ferrari was in the mix again last year, at least to start with, but only to be the best of the rest as Mercedes dominated. Whether it can find the missing ingredient to hit the front again remains to be seen, but messy internal politics have definitely returned.

Sebastian Vettel carried 5 on his Ferrari's nose last year but starts the 2017 World Championship campaign still seeking that fifth F1 title.

Ferrari has been around since before the World Championship commenced in 1950. It is, without doubt, the best-known team and, to millions, the epitome of F1. Yet, Ferrari is seldom the top team, seldom the cutting-edge performer. As shown last year, political elements within its parent company continue to intervene from time to time and upset the applecart. Most recently, technical director James Allison departed last summer, and the break in continuity this upheaval caused is hardly conducive to building a serious attack on the supremacy of Mercedes.

Team founder Enzo Ferrari ran the Alfa Romeo grand prix team in the 1930s, then set up his own team in 1946 to challenge them. After taking its first F1 win in the British GP at Silverstone in 1951, Ferrari dominated in 1952 and 1953 when F2 regulations were adopted and Alberto Ascari took both titles. Juan Manuel Fangio gave the team its third title in 1956 and Mike Hawthorn a fourth in 1958.

Ferrari wasn't quick to change over to the British-influenced ways of moving the engine to the rear of the car, as proved to be the way to go by Cooper when it won the 1959 and 1960 titles. However, not for the last time, the rules were changed in 1961 to benefit Ferrari, with F1 being changed to a 1.5-litre formula. Ferrari scooped the title

THE POWER AND THE GLORY

MATTIA BINOTTO
Ferrari's new chief technical officer is a mechanical engineering graduate who made the short hop from the University of Modena to join Ferrari in 1995, starting as a test engineer. The race team beckoned in 1997, with responsibility for Rubens Barrichello's car. Made chief engineer of race and assembly in 2007, the Swiss national was then promoted a couple of years later to become head of engine operations. Remaining on the engine side of the team, Mattia held the post of chief operating officer of the power unit division from 2014.

FERRARI BREAKS ITS DEVELOPMENT CYCLE
Ferrari started its old blame game routine again last summer when James Allison left the team, to be replaced as Chief Technical Officer by Mattia Binotto. Hopes had been high at the outset of the season, with only a tactical blunder costing it victory in the opening race. After another likely win had been thrown away in Canada, the media attack stepped up. Vettel and Raikkonen gave their all, but now the team is back at the start of another development cycle.

2016 DRIVERS & RESULTS

Driver	Nationality	Races	Wins	Pts	Pos
Kimi Raikkonen	Finnish	21	0	186	6th
Sebastian Vettel	German	21	0	212	4th

FOR THE RECORD

Country of origin:	Italy
Team base:	Maranello, Italy
Telephone:	(39) 536 949111
Website:	www.ferrari.com
Active in Formula One:	From 1950
Grands Prix contested:	910
Wins:	224
Pole positions:	208
Fastest laps:	236

THE TEAM

President:	Sergio Marchionne
Team principal:	Maurizio Arrivabene
Technical director:	Mattia Binotto
Chief designer:	Simone Resta
Chief designer, power unit:	Lorenzo Sassi
Head of aerodynamics:	David Sanchez
Director of aerodynamics:	Loic Bigois
Sporting director:	Massimo Rivola
Operations director:	Diego Ioverno
Reserve driver:	Antonio Giovanazi
Chassis:	Ferrari F17T
Engine:	Ferrari V6
Tyres:	Pirelli

through Phil Hill and repeated the feat in 1964 thanks to John Surtees.

Then the drought began, with a decade of focusing more on sportscar racing than it did on F1, as Ferrari allied more closely to its core product: its road cars. The team was often riven by industrial strife and only became a serious entity again in the mid-1970s, when Niki Lauda combined with team manager Luca di Montezemolo, racing to the 1975 title, missing out narrowly in 1976 – after Lauda had been burned horribly at the German GP – and going top again in 1977.

Lotus caught everyone napping when it adopted ground-effect technology to raise the bar in 1978, but Ferrari took a further title with Jody Scheckter in 1979. Then came a massive hiatus as Ferrari's lack of design expertise led to the British teams – referred to disparagingly as "garagistes" by Enzo – taking over. Williams, McLaren and Benetton all took turns at the top, with Ferrari not reacting quickly enough to changes in technology during Enzo's final years before his death in 1988.

It took the combination of Jean Todt as team principal and Michael Schumacher, after he joined from Benetton in 1996, to turn the team around, and make it truly focused and professional. In other words, Ferrari dropped its "Italian ways" that allowed for lunchbreaks while their British counterparts worked around the clock.

> "I was very happy to sign a contract for 2017 and it gives me pleasure to see disappointed people..."
> **Kimi Raikkonen**

Wins duly started happening that year and, once Mika Hakkinen had stopped winning for McLaren, titles flowed for Schumacher. He was champion each year from 2000 to 2004, with the 2002 campaign being truly dominant as Schumacher and his teammate Rubens Barrichello won all but two of the 17 rounds.

Kimi Raikkonen came from behind to win the 2007 title for the Maranello team. Yet, despite never being short of budget, Ferrari has remained in the shadow of Red Bull Racing and Mercedes since 2010 and proved that it wasn't fully competitive when top-level talents such as Fernando Alonso and Sebastian Vettel have found themselves in a supporting role.

This most famous of teams hasn't looked to be the cream of the crop since Schumacher's days. Indeed, Ferrari is in the chasing pack, taking occasional victories, but Allison's removal from the technical helm may yet confine it to several more years of underachieving. In fact, as long as the parent company continues to place its own people in the racing outfit, this cycle is likely to be repeated.

Second place in the Dutch GP at Zandvoort in 1964 set John Surtees on course for his F1 title.

SEBASTIAN VETTEL

If Ferrari can raise its game for 2017, then Sebastian might have a shot at the title, but his growing frustration became all too obvious last year, notably in Mexico, as he watches the continuing excellence of the Mercedes team and plots how to beat it.

Sebastian has always been a driver who wins races, so the past few years have been tougher for him as Mercedes has risen to dominance. However, glance over his racing career and it's clear that he's one of the drivers who knows how to finish in front.

After a string of karting titles, he stepped up to cars in 2003 in Germany's Formula BMW ADAC series and won five races. Then, with Red Bull backing, he raced to 18 wins from 20 starts to lift the 2004 title.

Sebastian finished fifth in European F3 in 2005, then was second in 2006, but also contested two races in Formula Renault 3.5, winning one and coming second in the other. Staying on in Formula Renault 3.5, he quit after seven rounds when points leader to step up to F1. Already a test driver for BMW Sauber, he got his F1 break when Robert Kubica was injured in Canada. On his debut, Sebastian finished eighth then moved to Scuderia Toro Rosso when it dropped Scott Speed.

Sebastian gave Toro Rosso its first win in 2008, at Monza, then was promoted to Red Bull Racing. He scored its first win and

It will take a major improvement by Ferrari to put a smile back onto Sebastian's face.

ended the year as runner-up to Brawn GP's Jenson Button.

The wins began to flow more freely and, after claiming his first title in a four-way shoot-out in Abu Dhabi in 2010, 11 wins made him a runaway champion in 2011

before adding the next two titles. Failing to score a win in 2014 led to his move to Ferrari.

TRACK NOTES

Nationality:	GERMAN
Born:	3 JULY 1987, HEPPENHEIM, GERMANY
Website:	www.sebastianvettel.de
Teams:	BMW SAUBER 2007, TORO ROSSO 2007-08, RED BULL RACING 2009-14, FERRARI 2015-17

CAREER RECORD

First Grand Prix:	2007 UNITED STATES GP
Grand Prix starts:	179
Grand Prix wins:	42

2008 Italian GP, 2009 Chinese GP, British GP, Japanese GP, Abu Dhabi GP, 2010 Malaysian GP, European GP, Japanese GP, Brazilian GP, Abu Dhabi GP, 2011 Australian GP, Malaysian GP, Turkish GP, Spanish GP, Monaco GP, European GP, Belgian GP, Italian GP, Singapore GP, Korean GP, Indian GP, 2012 Bahrain GP, Singapore GP, Japanese GP, Korean GP, Indian GP, 2013 Malaysian GP, Bahrain GP, Canadian GP, German GP, Belgian GP, Italian GP, Singapore GP, Korean GP, Japanese GP, Indian GP, Abu Dhabi GP, United States GP, Brazilian GP, 2015 Malaysian GP, Hungarian GP, Singapore GP

Poles:	46
Fastest laps:	28
Points:	2103
Honours:	2010, 2011, 2012 & 2013 FORMULA ONE WORLD CHAMPION, 2009 FORMULA ONE RUNNER-UP, 2006 EUROPEAN FORMULA THREE RUNNER-UP, 2004 GERMAN FORMULA BMW ADAC CHAMPION, 2003 GERMAN FORMULA BMW ADAC RUNNER-UP, 2001 EUROPEAN & GERMAN JUNIOR KART CHAMPION

WHEN YOUR ALL ISN'T ENOUGH

Ferrari showed flashes of form last year, but they were just that, suggestions that they could provide a car quick enough to be the pick of the pack and thus able to topple Mercedes. With Mercedes continuing in its position of technical predominance, all Sebastian could do was see whether he could be the best of the rest, only considering whether he might have a shot at victory on the odd occasion. Then Ferrari's form appeared to drop away after the start of summer in Europe, the two Mercedes become ever smaller ahead of him in the races, and increasingly the Red Bulls too, meaning that his five podium finishes in the first eight rounds became something he'd aspire to. For a driver who rattled off four F1 drivers' titles in a row from 2010, when his Red Bull Racing was the car to have, but only by a small margin in the first of these four campaigns, this has been frustrating, but he knows at least that he is Ferrari's go-to driver, with his team-mate Kimi Raikkonen the capable but less than willing number two.

Many thought that 2016 was going to be the Finn's final one in F1, but he has defied his critics and been kept on to do what he does best: collect points while doing nothing at all to help F1's image as he continues to shun public relations activities.

In the decades to come, it may be forgotten how brief Kimi's passage from kart racer to F1 was. It was 23 races. Every contemporary who went on to F1 took considerably longer, until Max Verstappen hit F1 as a 17-year-old in 2015 after a year in F3.

Kimi didn't even get as far as F3, racing only in Formula Renault through part of 1999 then 2000. Crowned British champion in 2000, that ought to have provided his springboard to F3, but Kimi's managers told Sauber that his talent was extra special. Without the budget to bring on drivers of its own, Peter Sauber elected to give him a test, only for Kimi's speed to be so natural that he turned that into a race deal for 2001.

Sixth on his F1 debut in Australia vindicated this risk and first impressions weren't wrong, as he ranked 10th then joined McLaren. With his first win coming at Sepang in 2003, Kimi went on to finish second to Ferrari's Michael Schumacher, then was runner-up again in 2005, this time to Renault's Fernando Alonso.

With Schumacher being lined up for retirement, Kimi was invited to fill the opening at Ferrari and pipped both Alonso and Lewis Hamilton to the 2007 title. An

"Ice Man" Kimi continues to like racing cars and continues to hate performing PR duties.

eternal problem, though, is that Kimi's large wage was not backed up by a desire to help any of his teams to show a public face and he elected to move on after 2009 and to try other forms of motorsport, from contesting the World Rally Championship to

the odd junior-level NASCAR race.

Kimi made his F1 return with Lotus in 2012, winning in Abu Dhabi and ending the year behind only Sebastian Vettel and Alonso, then staying on to be fifth in 2013 before returning to Ferrari.

TRACK NOTES

Nationality:	FINNISH
Born:	17 OCTOBER 1979, ESPOO, FINLAND
Website:	www.kimiraikkonen.com
Teams:	SAUBER 2001, McLAREN 2002-06, FERRARI 2007-09, LOTUS 2012-13, FERRARI 2014-17

CAREER RECORD

First Grand Prix:	2001 AUSTRALIAN GP
Grand Prix starts:	253
Grand Prix wins:	20
	2003 Malaysian GP, 2004 Belgian GP, 2005 Spanish GP, Monaco GP, Canadian GP, Hungarian GP, Turkish GP, Belgian GP, Japanese GP, 2007 Australian GP, French GP, British GP, Belgian GP, Chinese GP, Brazilian GP, 2008 Malaysian GP, Spanish GP, 2009 Belgian GP, 2012 Abu Dhabi GP, 2013 Australian GP
Poles:	16
Fastest laps:	43
Points:	1360
Honours:	2007 FORMULA ONE WORLD CHAMPION, 2003 & 2005 FORMULA ONE RUNNER-UP, 2000 BRITISH FORMULA RENAULT CHAMPION, 1999 BRITISH FORMULA RENAULT WINTER SERIES CHAMPION, 1998 EUROPEAN SUPER A KART RUNNER-UP, FINNISH KART CHAMPION & NORDIC KART CHAMPION

PERFORMING BELOW THE RADAR

Kimi's abhorrence of making an effort in public became more intense than ever in 2016. Yet, out on the track, the raw speed that he has in abundance continued to be obvious. Often close to team-mate Vettel in both qualifying and races, but seldom faster, Kimi did what he has always done: gathered points. There were no wins, and nor were there likely to be as Ferrari was never as competitive as Mercedes. Yet, that relentless and undemonstrative gathering of points proved to be the reason that Kimi was retained for a fourth year by Ferrari. There had been many pushing for a young gun to be given a break with the team, or even for an established F1 driver like Sergio Perez, but it seems that Vettel reckoned it best that Kimi was retained, for the sake of continuity and for not creating a fuss. Indeed, he doesn't. He turns up and drives, and he always drives fast, as shown by his four visits to the podium in the first half of last season when Ferrari enjoyed its strongest form.

Shown here in Mexico, Sebastian Vettel gave chase all season for Ferrari, but he had no answer to the pace of the Mercedes duo or that of Red Bull Racing as the year progressed.

FORCE INDIA

A strong campaign in 2016 could well be repeated this year as midfield regular Force India keeps on Sergio Perez and adds Esteban Ocon to its attack. Last year, it achieved podium finishes and gathered points galore against better-funded rivals.

Sergio Perez stays on as the undisputed team leader for 2017 and will be looking to use the team's Mercedes power to reach the podium again.

Just as Frank Williams set out to take on F1's manufacturer-funded teams, so Eddie Jordan is the man who got this show on the road. Like Williams, he parked his own racing career after F3 to run cars for others. What followed was minor success for Eddie Jordan Racing in F3, then championship honours in F3000 – F1's then feeder formula – in the late 1980s and early 1990s.

Then, in 1991, Eddie made the big move and Jordan stepped up to F1. Not only that, it did so with a beautiful car that was good enough to collect a fastest lap in the Hungarian GP. The team also earned headlines when driver Bertrand Gachot was arrested and later jailed for spraying CS gas at a London taxi driver. His replacement for the Belgian GP was an F1 debutant, Michael Schumacher. Sadly for Jordan, Benetton immediately poached him, for a fee. Fifth place overall for the team was outstanding.

Always chasing a deal was essential to Jordan, as he was attempting the big time on a shoestring. His deal to run Yamaha

engines in 1992 rather than paying for those from Ford backfired and it took a further change to Hart engines to put the team back on track, with fifth place secured again in 1994 and then in 1995, after a change to Peugeot engines, Rubens Barrichello and Eddie Irvine were together on the podium at the Canadian GP in Montreal.

THE POWER AND THE GLORY

OTMAR SZAFNAUER
Born in Romania, Otmar moved to the USA when he was seven and qualified as an electrical engineer. He took a master's degree in business and finance before joining Ford. In 1998, he joined the newly formed British American Racing team as operations director, but a planned move to Jaguar Racing was scuppered when Jaguar fired its F1 boss, Bobby Rahal. Otmar stayed with BAR when it was rebranded as Honda Racing in 2002, becoming director of strategy and business planning. He did move in 2009, becoming Force India's chief operating officer.

RACING STRONGLY ON A MEAGRE BUDGET
Perez and Hulkenberg enjoyed racing for a team free of political intrigue. The budget was small, but the team performed well in the circumstances. Both drivers collected points often enough to fight Williams in the battle for fourth in the constructors' championship. Perez landed podium finishes in Monaco and Baku, while Hulkenberg narrowly missed out on one in Belgium. Team owner Vijay Mallya remained on the sidelines, as he fought to balance his books.

2016 DRIVERS & RESULTS

Driver	Nationality	Races	Wins	Pts	Pos
Nico Hulkenberg	German	21	0	72	9th
Sergio Perez	Mexican	21	0	101	7th

FOR THE RECORD

Country of origin:	England
Team base:	Silverstone, England
Telephone:	(44) 01327 850800
Website:	www.forceindiaf1.com
Active in Formula One:	As Jordan 1991-2004, Midland 2005-06, Spyker 2007; Force India 2008 on
Grands Prix contested:	456
Wins:	4
Pole positions:	3
Fastest laps:	6

THE TEAM

Team principal & managing director:	Vijay Mallya
Deputy team principal:	Robert Fernley
Chief operating officer:	Otmar Szafnauer
Technical director:	Andrew Green
Production director:	Bob Halliwell
Aerodynamics director:	Simon Phillips
Chief designers:	Akio Haga & Ian Hall
Sporting director:	Andy Stevenson
Chief engineer:	Tom McCullough
Test driver:	tba
Chassis:	Force India VJM10
Engine:	Mercedes V6
Tyres:	Pirelli

Reaching the top step took a little longer, but it all came right at the 1998 Belgian GP when Damon Hill was first to the flag, followed home by his team-mate Ralf Schumacher. This was largely due to a change to Mugen engines that were to keep the team right in the picture, with Heinz-Harald Frentzen's two wins in 1999 helping Jordan to rank third overall.

Unfortunately, costs rocketed in the early twenty-first century and Jordan couldn't hang on. Giancarlo Fisichella won in Brazil in 2003, but that was to be the team's last victory.

Eddie Jordan had long been looking to sell the team, and shook on a deal for Russian steel magnate Alex Shnaider to take over in 2005. Renamed Midland, but still operating from its base at Silverstone, the team did little to impress. It was renamed again for 2007 as Shnaider appeared to have little interest in the team and sold it on to become Spyker, named after a Dutch supercar manufacturer. Just one year later, it was bought by Indian industrialist Vijay Mallya and called Force India. Tenth place at the end of 2008 showed that work needed to be done.

What propelled the team towards the front was a deal done for the cars to be powered by Mercedes engines for 2009,

along with technical assistance from McLaren. Pole position and second place for Fisichella in Belgium was the high point.

Since then, Force India's white cars with their Indian orange and green stripes have shown well in the hands most notably of Paul di Resta, Adrian Sutil and more recently Sergio Perez and Nico Hulkenberg. However, money troubles have abounded and it is of considerable credit to them, and the technical side – led first by James Key and more recently by Andrew Green – that they have kept on challenging teams with budgets of which they can only dream. That they have bettered long-time F1 giant McLaren for the past two years is a matter of great pride to a group of individuals who have often wondered how much longer the team can keep going as Mallya is pursued by the Indian tax authorities, yet pressed on regardless.

All talk at the end of 2015 about the team being renamed as Aston Martin Racing for 2016 turned out to be premature.

> "Force India has a tradition of investing in young, talented drivers and Esteban's arrival will bring some fresh energy."
> **Vijay Mallya**

Damon Hill and Ralf Schumacher head for the team's win, and second too, in the 1998 Belgian GP.

SERGIO PEREZ

Two podium visits in 2016 showed what the Mexican can do with competitive equipment and he will be hoping that Force India can provide him with that rather more frequently than last year so that he can line up a top drive for 2018.

Sergio was an early starter in car racing, hitting the single-seater scene shortly after turning 14, a couple of years before such a move is permitted on the European racing scene.

That first year out of karts was spent commuting from Mexico to the United States in 2004 to race Barber Dodge sigle-seaters and he ranked 11th against older rivals in this entry-level category.

Clearly up for the challenge, Sergio transferred to Europe in 2005, racing in Formula BMW. Sixth in the German series at his second attempt, Sergio then gained useful experience racing for Mexico's team in A1GP, learning how to handle these far more powerful single-seaters.

Then it was back down the power range for 2007 and a season in British F3, in which he won the lesser National class title. Remaining with the T-Sport team, he finished fourth overall as Jaime Alguersuari lifted the 2008 title.

The next step was to GP2 and Sergio grabbed two wins in the Asian series before contesting the main FIA series in 2009. He learned well and claimed five

Sergio had his finest year in 2016, although it wasn't always easy to tell as Mercedes won all.

wins in 2010 to end the year as runner-up behind Pastor Maldonado.

With a connection already established with the BMW Sauber team, F1 followed in 2011 and he spent two years with the team,

taking three podium finishes in 2012, the most notable of which was coming close to beating Ferrari's Fernando Alonso at Sepang. This form landed Sergio a ride with McLaren in 2013 but, sadly, the team was on the slide and he moved on after just one campaign to join Force India.

There has been a progression across his years with the team, as 10th overall – matching his 2012 finish – was followed by ninth then eighth last year, but that's as high as anyone with this midfield team can expect to rank. This is why Sergio has been looking to move on, anxious to become a grand prix winner.

TRACK NOTES

Nationality:	MEXICAN
Born:	26 JANUARY 1990, GUADALAJARA, MEXICO
Website:	www.sergioperezf1.com
Teams:	SAUBER 2011-12, McLAREN 2013, FORCE INDIA 2014-17

CAREER RECORD	
First Grand Prix:	2011 AUSTRALIAN GP
Grand Prix starts:	114
Grand Prix wins:	0 (best result: 2nd, 2012 Malaysian GP, 2012 Italian GP)
Poles:	0
Fastest laps:	3
Points:	367
Honours:	2010 GP2 RUNNER-UP, 2007 BRITISH FORMULA THREE NATIONAL CLASS CHAMPION

TWO THIRDS IN A YEAR OF CHASING

It's always strange for a driver to go out to compete with his focus on the future as much as the present, yet this is what Sergio had to do through much of last season as Ferrari's decision to keep Kimi Raikkonen on for a further year blocked his preferred escape route from Force India. Once the Finnish veteran had signed to stay with the team from Maranello, Sergio had to weigh up his options, which was an extremely stressful situation as he knew he had to look as competitive as possible through 2017, and had to be sure that a back-up plan would allow that. There was also the matter of whether Force India could agree on his wage demand but, with that done by autumn, Sergio was finally able to focus fully on each race. Third-place finishes in Monaco and Baku gave him a mid-season boost, but it was the relative frequency with which he was able to score, and score more than team-mate Nico Hulkenberg, that really impressed onlookers and showed that Sergio really deserves a shot with one of F1's top teams.

ESTEBAN OCON

This rising star turned 20 last September and demonstrated in his part-season of F1, after promotion to join Manor, that he's one for the future as he did well enough to be moved on to a superior Mercedes-powered team: Force India.

Formula Three is an exceedingly difficult single-seater formula in which to stand out from the pack, as the cars have limited power and a refined technique has to be achieved to get the most out of the tyres. Do it well, and the vital fractions of a second gained can add up to success, but it can take even talented drivers a year of learning before delivering in this most technical of categories.

Esteban proved in 2014 that he had that ability and it was his remarkable form from the very start of the season with the Prema Powerteam that encouraged Mercedes to snap him up as one of its development drivers as he claimed nine wins and finished well clear of the more experienced Tom Blomqvist and a Dutch novice by the name of Max Verstappen.

This campaign followed two years spent learning about single-seaters in the European Formula Renault Championship after stepping up from kart racing. Third overall behind Pierre Gasly and Oliver Rowland in 2013, this was enough for his step up to Formula Three and the Lotus F1 team had seen enough to sign him on to its books.

Esteban started last year as a touring car racer but ended it by really impressing in F1.

In 2015, Esteban advanced to GP3 with ART Grand Prix and he raced to the title not through winning a lot, as he won only the opening race, but through almost always being on the podium. Indeed, Esteban recorded an extraordinary run of nine second-place finishes as his rivals had more rollercoaster rides.

Without the money to move up to GP2, and with Mercedes offering to pay him to race in the DTM, Esteban took a career swerve for 2016 and, acknowledging how important it is to stick to a manufacturer like Mercedes, Esteban put his single-seater aspirations on hold, with an eye on the bigger picture.

The decision to accept manufacturer support, and not from any old manufacturer at that, but from the one dominating F1, was the right one and Esteban knew that he was one of the lucky ones as Mercedes has the power to take him all the way to the top as long as he continued to impress.

TRACK NOTES

Nationality:	FRENCH
Born:	17 SEPTEMBER 1996, EVREUX, FRANCE
Website:	www.esteban-ocon.com
Teams:	MANOR 2016, FORCE INDIA 2017

CAREER RECORD	
First Grand Prix:	2016 BELGIAN GP
Grand Prix starts:	9
Grand Prix wins:	0 (best result: 12th, 2016 Brazilian GP)
Poles:	0
Fastest laps:	0
Points:	0
Honours:	2015 GP3 CHAMPION, 2014 FIA EUROPEAN FORMULA THREE CHAMPION

NINE RACES IN WHICH TO SHINE

One minute Esteban was competing in the DTM, the German Touring Car series, for the Mercedes-backed ART Grand Prix team, and had just broken into the top 10 at Zandvoort. The next, he was an F1 driver. Being on Mercedes' books had its advantages and the 19-year-old French ace was brought into Manor's F1 line-up from the Belgian GP onwards after Rio Haryanto's money ran dry. With a lack of in-season testing, this was going to be a major ask to hit the ground running, especially with a lack of understanding of how the super-soft compound tyres worked best. So, what particularly impressed F1 paddock insiders was how he got in and got on with it and was soon pressing the team's lead driver, Pascal Wehrlein. Sixteenth place first time out was promising and, by the Japanese GP, he was showing Wehrlein the way, especially an impressive 12th in the Interlagos rain. Yet, driving for Manor, they were only racing for scraps, and could only be as good as the car provided for them by this tail-end team would allow.

WILLIAMS

This most British of teams continues its search to rediscover the winning formula that it enjoyed in the 1980s and 1990s when it seemed to gather F1 titles at will. The key, in its list of requirements, is consistency.

Valtteri Bottas cocks a wheel over the bumps in Baku where he scored points but was far from victory. Will it be the same story for Williams in 2017?

Williams ranks third in the all-time list of grands prix won, pole positions secured and fastest laps set. However, this team, the result of one man's drive to succeed, will on current form be toppled from all three categories by the end of the decade by the best of the current teams: Mercedes.

The quest in 2017 is to make more frequent visits to the podium, to start winning again and so be able to take a tilt at landing its first drivers' or constructors' championship honours since Jacques Villeneuve was World Champion in 1997.

The story of how the team began life goes back to the 1960s when Frank Williams raced in saloons then F3 around Europe. He was average at best and a lack of money was a perennial problem. Frank turned to running cars for others, stepping up to F2 in 1968 with Piers Courage, and entering him in a Brabham under the banner of Frank Williams Racing Cars. The advance to F1, with an ex-works Brabham, in 1969 yielded second-place finishes at

Monaco and Watkins Glen and an eighth-place ranking in the drivers' championship.

Williams landed a works deal with the de Tomaso sportscar company for 1970, but it meant entering Courage in a less competitive car and he crashed to his death in the Dutch GP. Dispirited and in financial turmoil, Frank was back in 1971,

THE POWER AND THE GLORY

ED WOOD
Involved initially in motorbikes, Ed moved across to four-wheeled racing when he joined TWR as a mechanic, working on Jaguar's Le Mans challengers under Ross Brawn. He then did a doctorate in engineering science before becoming an R&D engineer at Ferrari between 1998 and 2000, after which he transferred to be head of engineering at Mitsubishi Ralliart. Ed returned to F1 in 2002, with Renault, before becoming chief designer at Prodrive in 2003. He started his third spell in F1 by joining Williams as chief designer in 2006.

A SEASON OF PROMISE AND FRUSTRATION
A podium finish for third place in the Canadian GP by Valtteri Bottas turned out to be a highlight of 2016 for Williams. The team started off gathering points at will, with both drivers in the points at each of the first five rounds. Then, however, the team appeared to lose its way and its attractive white Mercedes-powered cars simply never looked likely to achieve another podium result. Finance from Canadian billionaire Lawrence Stroll has helped to give Williams improved foundations.

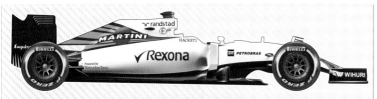

2016 DRIVERS & RESULTS

Driver	Nationality	Races	Wins	Pts	Pos
Valtteri Bottas	Finnish	21	0	85	8th
Felipe Massa	Brazilian	21	0	53	11th

FOR THE RECORD

Country of origin:	England
Team base:	Grove, England
Telephone:	(44) 01235 777700
Website:	www.williamsf1.com
Active in Formula One:	From 1972
Grands Prix contested:	721
Wins:	114
Pole positions:	128
Fastest laps:	133

THE TEAM

Team principal:	Sir Frank Williams
Co-founder:	Patrick Head
Deputy team principal:	Claire Williams
Chief executive officer:	Mike O'Driscoll
Chief technical officer:	tba
Head of performance engineering:	Rob Smedley
Chief designer:	Ed Wood
Head of aerodynamics:	Jason Somerville
Competitor analysis team leader:	Antonio Spagnolo
Chief engineer:	Andrew Murdoch
Race engineers:	Jonathan Eddolls & Dave Robson
Sporting manager:	Steve Nielsen
Test driver:	Alex Lynn
Chassis:	Williams FW40
Engine:	Mercedes V6
Tyres:	Pirelli

running a March for Henri Pescarolo. This was followed by other deals over the next few years, determined more by money than choice. A deal with Canadian oil millionaire Walter Wolf looked to be Frank's turning point, but was not to be.

In 1977, Williams Grand Prix Engineering was founded as Frank brought in Patrick Head as a partner and combined his business acumen with Patrick's engineering excellence. At last, progress was made and Alan Jones started scoring strong results. When Williams got to grips with ground effects, it scored its first win through Clay Regazzoni in the 1979 British GP. Jones dominated the rest of that season and stormed the 1980 title, with Williams also taking the constructors' honours. A far closer title battle in 1982 produced the team's second champion, Keke Rosberg.

Then, with Honda turbo power, Williams really took off in 1985 as wins came streaming in, before the team was denied the 1986 title when Nigel Mansell had a blow-out at the final race in Adelaide. The fact that Williams ran strongly through that season is a tribute to those involved, because Frank broke his neck on his way back from a pre-season test at Paul Ricard, and was left paralysed from the chest down. The show, nonetheless, went on.

Nelson Piquet was champion for Williams in 1987, but Williams hit its highest points when the cars were powered by Renault's wonderful V10 engines. This started in 1992 when Mansell and the FW14B were nigh on unbeatable. Alain Prost replaced Mansell in 1993 and became the team's fifth champion. Damon Hill ought to have made it three titles in three years in 1994 but was beaten by Benetton's Michael Schumacher when the German took him out at the final round. Benetton had the upper hand in 1995, but Williams came good in 1996, with Hill taking the title, a feat that was matched by Villeneuve in 1997.

Then McLaren and Ferrari moved to the fore. Frank was knighted in 1999 and there was an upswing in form when BMW became Williams' engine partner, with three wins for Ralf Schumacher in 2001, but it has been slim pickings since then, with a gap of more than seven years from Juan Pablo Montoya winning the final round in 2004 to Pastor Maldonado's surprise victory in Spain in 2012, a win that hasn't even been close to being repeated.

"Williams has a great record of introducing young drivers to F1 and we hope this will be the start of a long and successful career for Lance."
Claire Williams

Alan Jones - heading for victory at Brands Hatch - was the man to beat for Williams in 1980.

Felipe bade a tearful farewell to F1 at the end of last season and prepared himself for life away from the sport's top stage. Then Nico Rosberg retired and Williams called him back to replace Valtteri Bottas who headed to Mercedes.

Felipe was a driver who made quick work of his passage through from kart racing to Formula One, making his debut just before his 21st birthday. That was with Sauber in 2002 and that now seems a long time ago and he had become one of the old guard by the time he thought he was having his F1 swansong last autumn. Yet, it seems that this might not have been the case following Nico Rosberg's decision to retire and Valtteri Bottas being lined up to replace him, thus Williams' desire to bring Felipe back so that he can be an experienced mentor for the team's new hotshot Lance Stroll.

Fittingly, Felipe himself was a young driver needing as much guidance as he could get when he hit F1. He had won a title each year for three years as he worked his way through the junior single-seater series, winning the Formula Chevrolet series in his native Brazil before two Formula Renault titles in Europe in 2000. Many felt that he was going to step up from the lesser European Formula 3000 title to the FIA Formula 3000 Championship in 2002, yet he didn't bother with that and convinced Sauber to give him his F1 shot.

That first season didn't lead to a further

Felipe was considered the ideal man of experience to come back and bring on Stroll.

year with the Swiss team in 2003, and Felipe was employed instead as a Ferrari test driver thanks to his manager, Nicolas Prost, son of the then Ferrari F1 boss.

Back in F1 with Sauber in 2004, Felipe did enough to land a Ferrari race seat in 2006.

Being Michael Schumacher's team-mate was never easy, but there were days when Felipe matched or even beat him, with Turkey being a happy hunting ground. In all, in eight seasons, he won 11 times but, at the end of 2013, after finishing eighth – team-mate Fernando Alonso was World Championship runner-up – Felipe was encouraged to move on. He joined Williams for 2014 and enjoyed the less political environment there, although for most of 2016, team-mate Valtteri Bottas outperformed him.

TRACK NOTES

Nationality:	BRAZILIAN
Born:	25 APRIL 1981, SAO PAULO, BRAZIL
Website:	www.felipemassa.com
Teams:	SAUBER 2002 & 2004-05, FERRARI 2006-13, WILLIAMS 2014-17

CAREER RECORD

First Grand Prix:	2002 AUSTRALIAN GP
Grand Prix starts:	251
Grand Prix wins:	11

2006 Turkish GP, Brazilian GP, 2007 Bahrain GP, Spanish GP, Turkish GP, 2008 Bahrain GP, Turkish GP, French GP, European GP, Belgian GP, Brazilian GP

Poles:	16
Fastest laps:	15
Points:	1124
Honours:	2008 FORMULA ONE RUNNER-UP, 2001 FORMULA 3000 EURO CHAMPION, 2000 EUROPEAN & ITALIAN FORMULA RENAULT CHAMPION, 1999 BRAZILIAN FORMULA CHEVROLET CHAMPION

LIVING IN BOTTAS'S SHADOW

Having been sixth overall for Williams in 2015, finishing just 14 points behind team-mate Bottas, Felipe was hoping for more of the same, or better, last year. Yet, despite early promise, the season was an erratic one for Williams and Felipe would drop from the top 10 at the final round as McLaren's Fernando Alonso outscored him. Two fifth-place finishes in the opening four rounds and points in each of the first six grands prix suggested that a good season was in the offing, but Felipe scored just one point in the next six rounds and gathered points considerably less frequently in the second half of the year. He ended the season with 28 points and was three places behind Bottas. Feeling certain he was going to be eased out of F1 at the end of the year, he announced his retirement. Felipe hoped to spend more time with his young family or have a full programme in another racing category in 2017. Then Nico Rosberg decided to quit and this set off a chain of events that resulted in Felipe's F1 retirement being put on hold.

LANCE STROLL

So many talented drivers are held back by one thing: a lack of money. With a billionaire father, Lance has never had this problem. Last year, he tempered his wild side and won the European F3 title to line up his shot at F1.

Lance's father Lawrence is passionate about motor racing, dabbling with GT racing and then the North American Ferrari championship a decade ago. He was able to afford this as he is a hugely successful fashion magnate. He assembled a collection of Ferraris, bought the Mont Tremblant circuit in his native Canada, and then turned his sporting aspirations towards son Lance's karting career, one which was soon dotted with titles.

In 2011, at the age of 12, Lance travelled to Europe to contest the Italian Kart Championship. By the following year, he had developed sufficiently to rank fifth in the World Championship before continuing to impress in 2013, becoming the youngest member of the Ferrari Driver Academy.

Lance transferred to car racing when he turned 15, starting with the 2014 Florida Winter Series, a junior single-seater formula set up by Ferrari, then competing in the Italian F4 Championship for the crack Prema Powerteam. After winning seven races and landing the title, he really made his mark by heading down to the Toyota Racing Series that is held each northern hemisphere winter in New Zealand. Four wins from 16 starts gave him the title.

Lance showed the value of extra experience last year and must now learn from Massa.

Keeping this seemingly endless storm of racing going, Lance returned to Europe and took in the full FIA European F3 Championship with Prema Powerteam. The speed was there for all to see, but so were a flurry of accidents. Experienced team-mate

Felix Rosenqvist won the title, but Lance matured sufficiently to score his first win at this level when he won the first of three races at the championship's final round at Hockenheim.

At the end of the 2015 season, with his 50th race of the year completed, he quit the Ferrari Driver Academy and affiliated himself instead with the Williams F1 team ahead of a second year in European F3.

Progress up the racing ladder has been rapid and Lance has been helped by being able to afford to undertake a considerable amount of testings. Look at how he has benefited from this and you have to say that it has been money well spent, even if it does make his rivals jealous.

ADDING JUDGEMENT TO RAW SPEED

Last year saw a sea change in Lance, who added maturity to his abundant natural speed as he contested the FIA European F3 Championship for a second time. Remaining with the Prema Powerteam, he kicked off the year with pole position, fastest lap and victory on the first race of the opening round at Paul Ricard and then built on that through the remainder of the campaign. In fact, by adding 10 more wins, the 2016 title was his with four races to run – and he won all of them too. Lance also raced a sports-prototype, starting his year with fifth place in the Daytona 24 Hours in a one-off for Chip Ganassi Racing. All who have met Lance were enormously impressed with his attitude, as he added a layer of maturity that was missing in 2015 when accidents were too frequent. With good people surrounding him, helping to guide Lance in the right direction, he became a driver fully on top of his game. That he conducted a great deal of F1 testing away from public view added extra experience that will be invaluable preparation for 2017.

TRACK NOTES

Nationality:	CANADIAN
Born:	29 OCTOBER 1998, MONTREAL, CANADA
Website:	www.lancestroll.com
Teams:	WILLIAMS 2017

CAREER RECORD

First Grand Prix:	2017 AUSTRALIAN GP
Grand Prix starts:	0
Grand Prix wins:	0
Poles:	0
Fastest laps:	0
Points:	0
Honours:	2016 FIA EUROPEAN FORMULA THREE CHAMPION, 2015 TOYOTA RACING SERIES CHAMPION, 2014 ITALIAN FORMULA FOUR CHAMPION

McLAREN

It's all change at the top for McLaren as Ron Dennis, the man who took McLaren to the top in the 1980s, has departed. Zak Brown has come in to take over, with the clear brief to get the show back on the road after another disappointing season.

Fernando Alonso knows that, given the right equipment, he can deliver. The big question is whether McLaren and Honda can give him that.

The more that people know about Bruce McLaren, the more they marvel. He was way more than team founder. He was a grand prix winner with an adept mechanical mind who was a motivator extraordinaire. Teams were tiny in the 1960s when he decided to emulate his former Cooper team-mate Jack Brabham and start building his own racing cars. Because there were so few employees, Bruce got involved in everything. Today, with probably 100 times as many employed by each of the leading F1 teams, it would be impossible for any individual to be involved in almost every facet of design and build.

The first McLaren racing car, a sportscar, was built in 1964, and the team's F1 debut came at Monaco in 1966. Bruce coaxed Denny Hulme to become his team-mate in 1968, the year of the marque's first win, when Bruce was surprised to triumph in the Belgian GP. The major success, and earner for McLaren, was the CanAm sportscar championship, though, with McLaren taking the title and associated rich rewards from 1967 to 1971.

A major setback occurred in 1970, however, when Bruce was killed testing the next CanAm challenger at Goodwood. Hulme stayed on and, with team boss Teddy Mayer, kept the team going, adding occasional wins. The Gordon Coppuck-designed M23 – introduced in 1973 – became McLaren's talisman and would help James Hunt win the

THE POWER AND THE GLORY

ZAK BROWN
Last autumn, Zak was being lined up to replace Bernie Ecclestone as F1's impresario, but then Ron Dennis was edged aside from the helm of McLaren and the 44-year-old American filled those shoes instead. Zak raced in the Formula Opel Euroseries in 1991, before spending five years in Formula Atlantic back in the US. He then dabbled in sportscars, but accepted that his parallel career in sports marketing was a better bet and focused on that. Owner of the United Autosports sportscar team, he kept his hand in the racing management business alongside his "serious" job.

FINDING ITS WAY BACK INTO THE POINTS
A glance at McLaren's stunning HQ, and its pair of former World Champions driving for the team, made it hard to understand how McLaren had fallen to such mediocrity. Quite simply, engine partner Honda hasn't shown that it has what it takes to become a champion again. However, there were clear changes in Honda's approach after Yusuke Hasegawa took over from Yasuhisa Arai last March and there appeared to be greater harmony between the parties.

2016 DRIVERS & RESULTS

Driver	Nationality	Races	Wins	Pts	Pos
Fernando Alonso	Spanish	20	0	54	10th
Jenson Button	British	21	0	21	15th
Stoffel Vandoorne	Belgian	1	0	1	20th

FOR THE RECORD

Country of origin:	England
Team base:	Woking, England
Telephone:	(44) 01483 261000
Website:	www.mclaren.com
Active in Formula One:	From 1966
Grands Prix contested:	802
Wins:	181
Pole positions:	154
Fastest laps:	153

THE TEAM

Executive director:	Zak Brown
Chief operating officer:	Jonathan Neale
Head of F1 project Honda:	
	Yusuke Hasegawa
Racing director:	Eric Boullier
Director of design & development:	
	Neil Oatley
Technical director:	Tim Goss
Operations director:	Simon Roberts
Director of engineering:	Matt Morris
Team manager:	David Redding
Chief engineer:	Peter Prodromou
Chief aerodynamicist:	tba
Test drivers:	Oliver Turvey
	& Nobuharu Matsushita
Chassis:	McLaren MP4-32
Engine:	Honda V6
Tyres:	Pirelli

1976 drivers' title. Sadly, when Lotus made ground effects work, McLaren lost ground when it couldn't.

Fortunately, McLaren's greatest days were to come, after Ron Dennis stepped up from running a team in F2 to give it an ultra-professional approach that led to its first constructors' title in 1984, when Niki Lauda was drivers' champion. Alain Prost repeated the feat in 1985. However, when Ayrton Senna joined Prost in 1988 McLaren truly became the gold standard, as the pair won 15 of the 16 rounds. The partnership was too explosive, combining the two top drivers in the best cars, so no one could get close enough to dilute their battle. It became too personal and meant that the team's most successful time was its least happy. That said, Prost took the 1989 title, then left the team, and Senna claimed the following two.

Williams eclipsed McLaren in 1992 and both the team and Senna slipped down the order. When Williams offered Senna a drive for 1994, he jumped at it. Without Senna and

without Honda engines, inserting Peugeot units instead, the team dipped.

A new chapter began in 1995, with McLaren welcoming Mercedes power. The engine became more potent and, in 1998, it was placed in an Adrian Newey-designed chassis. The results were a title for Mika Hakkinen and constructors' honours for the team. Hakkinen added another title in 1999.

With plentiful backing and the most incredible high-tech base, McLaren should have continued racking up the titles, but it didn't as Michael Schumacher put Ferrari back on the map. Although Kimi Raikkonen came close to beating Schumacher to the 2003 title, McLaren tended to underachieve.

In 2007, this looked set to be put right, as reigning World Champion Fernando Alonso arrived, with team protégé Lewis Hamilton joining him. Their competitive animosity unsettled the team, allowing both to be pipped by Raikkonen, now a Ferrari driver.

In 2008, with Alonso having moved on, Hamilton delivered. Yet, Mercedes had plans

to start a team of its own and McLaren lost its way as Red Bull Racing with its Renault-powered racers became the ones to beat.

All hopes that the return of Honda as engine partner would bring back the glory days were thwarted in 2015, showing how F1 had moved on and left Honda behind. McLaren is a big beast now, and some feel that its other activities in building supercars have taken its eye off the ball, but expect more progress in 2017, as long as the team handles the tech changes successfully.

"Stoffel has been well educated in the world of F1 – learning from two world champions. He's determined, so we'll see how it goes."
Jenson Button

James Hunt joined McLaren in 1976 and raced to that year's title after an epic scrap with Lauda.

The last two years have been tough for Fernando, as it's extra hard for a former World Champion to try his heart out simply to scrape into the top 10. Yet, Fernando stuck at it through 2016, found a few positives and this year ought to bring reward.

Keeping an eye on racing's junior categories is a rewarding pastime, offering a chance to see who might make it. Occasionally, a driver comes along who makes it look easy. Such was Fernando's pace on stepping up from a stellar karting career that, in its own right, indicated that he was one of the best.

Armed with Spanish titles galore topped by the World crown in 1997, Fernando entered the largely Spain-based Open by Nissan single-seater formula when he was 17 and won that for the team entered by former F1 racer Adrian Campos. Stepping directly to F3000, Fernando developed his craft through the year, then scored a runaway victory at Spa-Francorchamps to rank fourth. That drive alone was enough to get him into F1 with Minardi.

This tail-end Italian team wasn't good enough for points but, after spending 2002 testing for Jaguar and Renault, he was back in F1 in 2003, taking his maiden win in Hungary and ending the year sixth overall. Fourth in 2004, Fernando then ended Michael Schumacher's run of titles with Ferrari by beating McLaren racer Kimi Raikkonen to the 2005 title and then doubling up in 2006 ahead of Schumacher,

How Fernando has kept smiling through the past two campaigns remains a mystery.

winning seven times in each of these years.

A move to McLaren for 2007 could have made it three titles, but he and team-mate Lewis Hamilton ended up a point behind Ferrari's Raikkonen in an unhappy year.

Returning to Renault wasn't a great move, but Ferrari beckoned for 2010 and he was edged out by Red Bull's Sebastian Vettel, as he would be in 2012. Indeed, that has been as close as he has got to a third title, with his move to McLaren in 2015 leaving him in the midfield.

TRACK NOTES

Nationality:	SPANISH
Born:	29 JULY 1981, OVIEDO, SPAIN
Website:	www.fernandoalonso.com
Teams:	MINARDI 2001, RENAULT 2003-06, McLAREN 2007, RENAULT 2008-09, FERRARI 2010-14, McLAREN 2015-17

CAREER RECORD

First Grand Prix:	2001 AUSTRALIAN GP
Grand Prix starts:	274
Grand Prix wins:	32

2003 Hungarian GP, 2005 Malaysian GP, Bahrain GP, San Marino GP, European GP, French GP, German GP, Chinese GP, 2006 Bahrain GP, Australian GP, Spanish GP, Monaco GP, British GP, Canadian GP, Japanese GP, 2007 Malaysian GP, Monaco GP, European GP, Italian GP, 2008 Singapore GP, Japanese GP, 2010 Australian GP, German GP, Italian GP, Singapore GP, Korean GP, 2011 British GP, 2012 Malaysian GP, European GP, German GP, 2013 Chinese GP, Spanish GP

Poles:	22
Fastest laps:	22
Points:	1832
Honours:	2005 & 2006 FORMULA ONE WORLD CHAMPION, 2010, 2012 & 2013 FORMULA ONE RUNNER-UP, 1999 FORMULA NISSAN CHAMPION, 1997 ITALIAN & SPANISH KART CHAMPION, 1996 WORLD & SPANISH KART CHAMPION, 1994 & 1995 SPANISH JUNIOR KART CHAMPION

SCRAPPING TO GET INTO THE POINTS

Fernando's 2016 campaign started with a bang in Australia when he clipped Esteban Gutierrez's Haas and had an aerobatic accident at Turn 3. This forced him to miss the next round, but it was the fact that he's been scrapping over 11th that put into perspective the struggle that the McLaren drivers had to contend with as the team and Honda attempted to get up to speed. After a disastrous first year together in 2015, it had been hoped that McLaren and in particular Honda would have been swifter to find the strides that needed to be taken to get to the pace. Through the year, the gap came down, but it was still a yawning gap to Mercedes and Fernando's best result of fifth place came at Monaco, where outright power isn't such a requirement. His results later in the year for the minor points were more indicative of real progress, with fifth in the USA. Yet, for a 35-year-old driver with two F1 titles to his name, a life outside F1 must have been becoming more appealing as the year went on.

STOFFEL VANDOORNE

McLaren has put a lot of investment into this young Belgian and, after a surprise debut in Bahrain last year, he's lined up and ready to go for a full campaign after honing his craft in 2016 on McLaren's simulator and racing in Japan's Super Formula.

Christoph Vandoorne, known as "Stoffel", had a notably strong career in karts, finishing 2009 as runner-up in the World Kart Championship.

Stoffel was then given a useful boost at the end of that season when he won the Royal Automobile Club of Belgium's young drivers' programme. This eased him into car racing for 2010 and Stoffel did the rest, winning the F4 Eurocup with a useful tally of six wins in the 14 races.

Formula Renault came next with the long-running Belgian KTR team and Stoffel ranked fifth in the European championship behind three drivers – Carlos Sainz Jr, Daniil Kvyat and Will Stevens – who would go on to race in F1, and third in the lesser Northern European series. Signed by Josef Kaufmann Racing to lead its attack in 2012, Stoffel became European Formula Renault champion, just ahead of Kvyat.

However, Stoffel didn't have Red Bull sponsorship behind him and so F1 still seemed only a distant possibility as he looked to 2013. Having elected to contest the Formula Renault 3.5 championship, Stoffel spent the year with Fortec Motorsports fighting with and eventually

Stoffel scored on his one F1 start and is back to expand through a full campaign.

losing out to Kevin Magnussen, despite taking four wins.

Electing to make his mark next in GP2, which has the added advantage of holding its races on the grand prix support package, thus giving useful track time at almost all of

the venues he'd be racing on if he reached F1, Stoffel joined the crack ART Grand Prix team and ranked second to fourth-year GP2 racer Jolyon Palmer.

Stoffel also became part of McLaren's Young Driver programme in 2014. Not only has this enabled him to spend time at the team's outstanding headquarters outside Woking, working on the simulator and mixing with the team, but he has had track time with the cars and also attended grands prix as the team's reserve driver.

Stoffel became a dominant GP2 champion in 2015, his seven wins leaving him way clear of Alexander Rossi.

TRACK NOTES

Nationality:	BELGIAN
Born:	26 MARCH 1992, KORTRIJK, BELGIUM
Website:	www.stoffelvandoorne.com
Teams:	McLAREN 2016-17

CAREER RECORD	
First Grand Prix:	2016 BAHRAIN GP
Grand Prix starts:	1
Grand Prix wins:	0
(best result: 10th, 2016 Bahrain GP)	
Poles:	0
Fastest laps:	0
Points:	1
Honours:	2015 GP2 CHAMPION, 2014 GP2 RUNNER-UP, 2013 FORMULA RENAULT 3.5 RUNNER-UP, 2012 EUROPEAN FORMULA RENAULT CHAMPION, 2010 F4 EUROCUP CHAMPION, 2009 WORLD KART RUNNER-UP, 2008 BELGIAN KF2 KART CHAMPION

WAITING FOR HIS TURN TO COME

Last March, with his focus entirely on the forthcoming Super Formula season in Japan, his head full of knowledge being picked up through pre-season testing, Stoffel realised that he had a pivotal job to do before the first round: make his F1 debut. This came about due to Fernando Alonso being injured in the opening grand prix in Australia and then not being cleared to compete at Sakhir. Rushed to Bahrain, Stoffel started 12th and finished 10th. Then he flew back to Japan and performed with aplomb in its GP2-equivalent formula. He finished third at the opening round at Suzuka, qualified on pole for the third at Fuji and then won the fifth for Team Dandelion at TI Aida, venue for the Pacific GP in 1994 and 1995. The year in Japan was at Honda's behest, as it kept him race-sharp, with the benefit of Super Formula providing a base not just for developing a chassis on critical tyres through longer races but also in often wet conditions in a way that more spec-formula GP2 does not.

It was clear from the first day of the season in Melbourne that McLaren still had speed to find for Fernando Alonso and Jenson Button. Race day in round 1 was even worse for Alonso as he exited after a spectacular accident.

SCUDERIA TORO ROSSO

There's a reversion to Renault power after a year with Ferrari and it remains to be seen whether this change of engine supplier will help the team be more consistent, as its flashes of pace in 2016 were not continued throughout the whole campaign.

Carlos Sainz Jr was a frequent scorer through 2016. The question for 2017 will be whether Renault power offers the team the same opportunities.

For 21 World Championship seasons, a small Italian team charmed fans as it kept on plugging away at the tail of the field, chasing points but not often expecting to score them. This was Minardi and it has already been somewhat forgotten, as 11 years have passed since its cars last appeared on the grid. Since then, of course, the team from Faenza has had a budget of which it could only have dreamed, and a different identity.

When Red Bull co-founder Dietrich Mateschitz took over Jaguar Racing and turned it into Red Bull Racing, he decided that this wasn't enough, so he bought another team – Minardi – and turned it into his training academy, calling it Scuderia Toro Rosso. This is a way to test the rising stars in a grand prix situation and, if good enough, promote them to Red Bull Racing.

In a funny way, that's precisely what Minardi achieved over the years, albeit without a well-funded parent overseeing its activities. Instead, team owner Giancarlo

Minardi simply picked the best drivers he could find and gave them their F1 break, usually funded by a pay-driver in the other car. Among the list of drivers who made it into F1 this way are Alessandro Nannini (1986), Giancarlo Fisichella (1996), Jarno Trulli (1997), Fernando Alonso (2001) and Mark Webber (2002).

THE POWER AND THE GLORY

JOHN BOOTH
Appointed as racing director of the team at the start of last season, John bounced back from having walked out of the Manor F1 team near the end of the 2015 season after a disagreement over the team's direction. A former Formula Ford racer, John formed Manor Motorsport in 1990, and ran teams in both Formula Renault and F3 with distinction – Kimi Raikkonen and Lewis Hamilton were his two most distinguished graduates. Ever ambitious, Manor advanced to F1 in 2001 when three new teams were invited into the World Championship.

REGULAR POINTS SCORERS UNTIL LATE IN THE YEAR
Getting both cars into the points at the first of last year's races suggested that 2016 would be good for Toro Rosso, with Verstappen sixth next time out. However, Kvyat didn't last the course at Red Bull Racing and swapped rides with Verstappen. Cruelly for Kvyat, Verstappen won first time out, while Verstappen's race engineer, Xevi Pujolar, left at the same time for Sauber. Carlos Sainz Jr was both quick and consistent, while Kvyat lost confidence before bouncing back.

2016 DRIVERS & RESULTS

Driver	Nationality	Races	Wins	Pts	Pos
Daniil Kvyat	Russian	17	0	25	14th
Carlos Sainz Jr	Spanish	21	0	46	12th
Max Verstappen	Dutch	4	0	204	5th

FOR THE RECORD

Country of origin:	Italy
Team base:	Faenza, Italy
Telephone:	(39) 546 696111
Website:	www.scuderiatororosso.com
Active in Formula One:	As Minardi
	1985-2005; Toro Rosso 2006 on
Grands Prix contested:	547
Wins:	11
Pole positions:	0
Fastest laps:	1

THE TEAM

Team owner:	Dietrich Mateschitz
Team principal:	Franz Tost
Racing director:	John Booth
Technical director:	James Key
Deputy technical director:	Ben Waterhouse
Chief designers:	Paolo Marabini
	& Matteo Piraccini
Head of aerodynamics:	Brendan Gilhome
Team manager:	Graham Watson
Technical co-ordinator:	Sandro Parrini
Chief engineer:	Phil Charles
Test driver:	tba
Chassis:	Toro Rosso STR12
Engine:	Renault V6
Tyres:	Pirelli

Since then, after becoming Scuderia Toro Rosso, Sebastian Vettel was signed by the team early in his F1 career, going on to give the team its day of days when he mastered wet conditions to take pole for the 2008 Italian GP and then was quickest in the rain the following day to give Toro Rosso its first and, so far, only win.

Back in the early days, after Minardi stepped up from F2 in 1985, Pierluigi Martini led the attack, but the team was hampered by running Motori Moderni engines. He moved on and Alessandro Nannini was promoted from its F2 team to lead the attack, but it was a blunt one full of retirements. Martini returned in 1988 and scored the team's first point by finishing sixth in the United States GP, then added a flurry of points late in 1989, even leading for a lap of the Portuguese GP. The greatest day for Minardi came in the opening race of 1990 when, aided by Pirelli tyres that were superior for a qualifying blast to their rivals'

Goodyears, Martini qualified second at Phoenix to McLaren's Gerhard Berger before fading to seventh as Ayrton Senna won.

By 2005, with F1 becoming ever more expensive, Minardi struggled to keep up, so it made sense for Mateschitz - wanting a junior team - to take over. The cars were given a new livery for 2006, looking not dissimilar to the Red Bulls. Although the team base continued to be in Faenza, the management was changed, with Franz Tost being inserted as team principal.

One advantage for the team, helping to keep costs in check, was being able to use the previous year's Red Bull chassis. This transformed the team's fortunes, with Vettel finishing fourth in the Chinese GP. The following year, again using Ferrari engines, Toro Rosso stole Red Bull Racing's thunder by beating it to achieve its first F1 win, in that race at Monza. This helped the team to rank sixth. However, the next few years were weak before an improvement in 2011 when

Jaime Alguersuari and Sebastien Buemi got into the points more regularly. The idea was that good form would lead to promotion to Red Bull Racing, but this was yet another pair to be shown the door.

For 2012, Scuderia Toro Rosso ran Daniel Ricciardo and Jean-Eric Vergne, keeping them on for 2013 before the Australian got the nod to be promoted.

Then, in 2015, Scuderia Toro Rosso found its next star in Max Verstappen, who was only 17 when he started the year, but came away with two fourth-place finishes. His inevitable promotion, however, came earlier than expected, after four races in 2016, with Daniil Kvyat being demoted.

Vitantonio Liuzzi was one of Scuderia Toro Rosso's drivers in its first season, 2006.

"I aways told Daniil that his future with us was in his hands and he has stepped up to the mark and delivered."
Franz Tost

Kept on for his third year in F1 with Toro Rosso, this son of a rallying great did nothing wrong last year except be eclipsed by Max Verstappen. He is a much underestimated talent but knows that this is sure to be a crucial year for his career.

Motor sport fans in the 1990s will have been extremely familiar with the name Carlos Sainz, for he was twice World Rally Champion, in 1990 and 1992 for Toyota, often seemingly untouchable in the white and red machines, whatever the road surface. Indeed, Carlos was at the front of the field at rallying's highest level for a decade and more.

Because children tend to follow in the footsteps of their sporting parents, it was always expected that Carlos Jr would follow his father into the world of excess on gravel, ice, snow and asphalt. However, unusually, he didn't.

Instead, Carlos Jr started in karts at the age of 11, and soon showed good form, picking up titles at home and abroad. Then, as soon as he was old enough to do so, he moved on to race cars. That was in 2010, when he was 15, making his debut in the European Formula BMW championship and finishing fourth overall as Robin Frijns was crowned champion. As a member of the Red Bull junior team, he was already being backed by the energy drink giant.

In 2011, Carlos Jr moved on to Formula Renault and proved that his sporting genes were good ones by winning Formula

Carlos Jr produced some excellent drives last year and should certainly not be overlooked.

Renault's Northern European championship and finishing as runner-up to Frijns in the full European series.

Having tried a few F3 races in 2011, Carlos Jr had a full season in this traditional stepping-stone category in his third year

of car racing, ranking fifth in the European series and sixth in the British for Carlin.

GP3 was Carlos Jr's main focus in 2013, and he finished 10th in this as future team-mate Daniil Kvyat dominated the series, but he also contested several races in the more powerful Formula Renault 3.5 series, peaking with a sixth-place finish at Monaco.

Returning in 2014, Carlos Jr took seven wins and the title, earning his F1 break with Toro Rosso for 2015. His best finish that year was seventh place in the US GP.

TRACK NOTES

Nationality:	SPANISH
Born:	1 SEPTEMBER 1994, MADRID, SPAIN
Website:	www.carlossainzjr.com
Teams:	TORO ROSSO 2015-17

CAREER RECORD

First Grand Prix:	2015 AUSTRALIAN GP
Grand Prix starts:	40
Grand Prix wins:	0
	(best result: 6th, 2016 Spanish GP, 2016 United States GP, 2016 Brazilian GP)
Poles:	0
Fastest laps:	0
Points:	64
Honours:	2014 FORMULA RENAULT 3.5 CHAMPION, 2011 EUROPEAN FORMULA RENAULT RUNNER-UP & NORTHERN EUROPEAN FORMULA RENAULT CHAMPION, 2009 MONACO KART CUP WINNER, 2008 ASIA/PACIFIC JUNIOR KART CHAMPION, 2006 MADRID CADET KART CHAMPION

IN THE POINTS WHENEVER POSSIBLE

Last year was a strange one for Carlos. He was matched, as in 2015, with hotshot Max Verstappen as a team-mate. But that was only for four races, as the Dutch teenager outscored him and then got what every Scuderia Toro Rosso racer wishes for: promotion to Red Bull Racing. Although the 21-year-old Spaniard continued to rack up good results, notably against Daniil Kvyat who had been demoted from Red Bull Racing, he must have felt that any hope he had of graduating to Red Bull's front-running team was gone for the next few years, perhaps reducing his chances of an F1 future, as staying on with Toro Rosso for year after year isn't how talent manager Helmut Marko views the team's role in the sport. Carlos Jr kept his head down and kept on hitting the top 10 finishing positions for valuable points for the team, with a best result of sixth place in his home race, the Spanish GP, and also in the US GP. After a late summer drop in form, the team came back towards the end of the year, as shown in the USA.

DANIIL KVYAT

Demoted from Red Bull Racing back to Scuderia Toro Rosso after just four races last year, then out of form, it seemed as though Daniil's F1 days were behind him, but a late upswing in form earned him a reprieve.

Like so many of his contemporaries, Daniil used his karting experience to good effect to rocket through the junior single-seater formulae.

Distances were always great from his Russian base, especially as Daniil took in Asian and even New Zealand racing series in the winter alongside European campaigns through spring, summer and autumn. His speed was evident from his first season of car racing, 2010, when Daniil, aged just 16, justified his Red Bull backing as he gained experience in Formula BMW with the EuroInternational team. Ranked 10th at season's end, he advanced to Formula Renault with Koiranen Motorsport in 2011 and was third in the European championship and runner-up in the lesser North European series. A second campaign with the same team resulted in second place behind Stoffel Vandoorne, with everyone else far behind, and the title in the ALPS (middle European) series.

With plenty of pressure to succeed being applied by Red Bull driver scholarship chief Helmut Marko, Daniil knew that continued backing from the energy drink giant needed

Daniil is back for more in 2017 and hopes to be able to demonstrate rejuvenated form.

a title. Stepping up to GP3 for 2013, he did just that by racing to three wins for the MW Arden team to land the crown. Daniil also was given his first taste of F1, having a run out with Scuderia Toro Rosso, and these

endeavours combined landed him his F1 break for 2014 alongside Jean-Eric Vergne. Ninth place first time out was a great start and there were four other point-scoring drives, results which Marko decided were enough to give him the nod over the more experienced Vergne for promotion to Red Bull Racing for 2015 at the age of 20.

Second place in Hungary was the highlight of his year and Daniil outscored Daniel Ricciardo 95 to 92, suggesting a long, fruitful career at RBR, but it didn't prove to be the case for him.

TRACK NOTES

Nationality:	RUSSIAN
Born:	26 APRIL 1994, UFA, RUSSIA
Website:	www.daniilkvyat.com
Teams:	TORO ROSSO 2014, RED BULL RACING
	2015-16, TORO ROSSO 2016-17

CAREER RECORD

First Grand Prix:	2014 AUSTRALIAN GP
Grand Prix starts:	59
Grand Prix wins:	0
	(best result: 2nd, 2015 Hungarian GP)
Poles:	0
Fastest laps:	0
Points:	128
Honours:	2013 GP3 CHAMPION,
	2012 FORMULA RENAULT RUNNER-UP &
	ALPS CHAMPION, 2011 FORMULA RENAULT
	NORTHERN EUROPE RUNNER-UP,
	2009 WSK KART RUNNER-UP

GETTING IT BACK TOGETHER AGAIN

A rollercoaster ride has ups as well as downs, but Daniil's 2016 journey was principally in one direction, and it wasn't up. There was an early boost, with third place in the third round of his second campaign for Red Bull Racing, at Shanghai. Then, the show went down and down. That he was replaced at Red Bull Racing by Jos Verstappen after just four races was painful enough, but the fact that the Dutch teenager won first time out added salt to the wound. Then came the hard task of fighting for glory, or even the odd point, for Toro Rosso. That he was outperformed by his new team-mate Carlos Sainz Jr through the summer reduced the level of his stock further, and it's safe to say that there wasn't a more dispirited driver in the paddock. Such is the modern way of promoting young guns that it seemed that the 22-year-old would have to find other employment. GP2 frontrunner Pierre Gasly was tipped to take his place, then autumn brought better form and Red Bull's talent scouts elected to let him race on in 2017.

HAAS F1

Back for a second season of F1, this American team floored doubters by scoring not just in the first race but the second too. Its aim in building on this is to be inside the top 10, thus in the points, at all rounds, rather than just outside it as for much of 2016.

Romain Grosjean delivered superbly well for the new team last year, but Haas F1 will need to keep developing all year to keep up in 2017.

Despite there being just 22 cars on the grid, no one expected Haas F1 to get into the top 10 to score points at any point in its first season. Everyone would have been delighted had it done so, as the World Championship really needs an American team that can do well. Indeed, even a single point at the end of the 21-grand prix campaign would have been seen as a job extremely well done.

So, when Romain Grosjean raced to sixth place first time out at the Australian GP in Melbourne, F1 insiders had to reappraise their expectations for F1's newest team considerably. Then, even more so next time out when the French racer collected the 10 points for fifth place in Bahrain.

To understand how Haas F1 got to this point, one needs to go back to how it came to be competing in F1. This is all down to Gene Haas, a man who made a fortune through Haas Automation, his machine tooling company that became the largest of its kind in the United States. Its success enabled him to become involved in racing to spread its name. His vehicle for this was NASCAR, the American stock car racing circus that criss-crosses the United States all the way from February to November.

Haas CNC Racing was set up to compete in NASCAR's premier division in 2002 and it gradually picked its way towards the front

THE POWER AND THE GLORY

BEN AGATHANGELOU
Like Adrian Newey, this Anglo-Greek aerodynamicist graduated in aeronautics and astronautics from Southampton University. His first job in racing was with McLaren in 1994, followed by a spell at Tyrrell. He joined Honda F1, but that programme folded following project leader Harvey Postlethwaite's death. Ben kept moving, working for Benetton, then Jaguar Racing, where he stayed after it became Red Bull Racing. He did leave after Newey arrived and had spells with HRT and Ferrari, before joining Manor as chief aerodynamicist in 2015.

HITTING THE GROUND RUNNING
Everyone thought that the target for Haas F1 in its maiden season would be to score a point. This would be aiming high, but it had to be a goal. Any finish in the teens would be respectable. Then Romain Grosjean rocked F1, not only by finishing sixth at the first race, but by backing it up with fifth place in the second. That the points didn't stop there was a huge credit to Haas's team, with its second driver Esteban Gutierrez making major strides too.

2016 DRIVERS & RESULTS

Driver	Nationality	Races	Wins	Pts	Pos
Romain Grosjean	French	21	0	29	13th
Esteban Gutierrez	Mexican	21	0	0	21st

FOR THE RECORD

Country of origin:	USA
Team base:	Kannapolis, USA
Telephone:	(001) 704 652 4227
Website:	www.haasf1team.com
Active in Formula One:	From 2016
Grands Prix contested:	21
Wins:	0
Pole positions:	0
Fastest laps:	0

THE TEAM

Team owner:	Gene Haas
Team principal:	Gunther Steiner
Chief operating officer:	Joe Custer
Technical director:	Rob Taylor
Vice-president of technology:	tba
Chief aerodynamicist:	Ben Agathangelou
Team manager:	Dave O'Neill
Chief engineer:	Ayao Komatsu
Head of logistics:	Peter Crolla
Test driver:	tba
Chassis:	Haas VF-17
Engine:	Ferrari V6
Tyres:	Pirelli

of the field, doing well enough to come to the attention of two-time champion Tony Stewart, and they went into partnership to form Stewart-Haas Racing in 2009. This was truly a springboard to greater things, and Stewart took his third drivers' title in 2011.

All of this, of course, gave considerable publicity to Haas's machine tools in front of an audience of blue-collar fans, many of whom work in manufacturing industries. The team went on to help Kevin Harvick to win the title in 2014 and finish as runner-up the following year, but its ambitions became more global, which is how F1 came into its consideration.

So, the plans started to hatch and Haas determined to go against considered advice that all F1 teams must be based in Europe if they want to succeed. Keen to be as American as possible, he went his own way and set up his F1 team's base in the building next door to its NASCAR

headquarters in Kannapolis, North Carolina. There's an operational base as well at Banbury in England, but the team's brains trust works out of the USA.

While there was some transfer of technology between his two teams, overseen by Matt Borland, Haas staffed his F1 team with former Jaguar Racing technical director Gunther Steiner as team principal. Usefully, Steiner could also talk the language of NASCAR as he moved from Red Bull's F1 team to its NASCAR outfit in 2006 and remained in NASCAR until offered this opportunity to return to F1. The Manor F1 team was raided for the services of Rob Taylor as technical director and Ben Agathangelou as chief aerodynamicist.

Signing Grosjean to lead the driving attack was a great move, and one that wouldn't have been possible had Renault got its offer in first to keep him in the line-up of its squad as it took over the

Lotus team. Esteban Gutierrez brought the experience of two years of racing for Sauber and was anxious to cement his place in F1.

The F1 world waits to see what Haas F1 can manage second time around and whether it really has the tools required to go on to emulate American F1 teams Penske and Shadow that won a grand prix each in 1976 and 1977 respectively. In many ways, the second year can be every bit as tough as the first, as the whole of 2016 was spent going racing rather than having free time to focus on the year ahead.

No smiles were broader in Melbourne last year than those of Gene Haas and Romain Grosjean.

"From the time we began looking at drivers, Kevin was always on our short list. We feel he can accomplish a lot."
Gene Haas

ROMAIN GROSJEAN

There would have been no way in the world that Romain expected to score many or even any points with all-new Haas F1 in 2016, and certainly not to collect them in three of the first four races, but life certainly got harder and his frustration grew.

Some careers are peppered with great results, even titles, and yet never the biggest prizes. Through no fault of his own, this appears to sum up Romain's career.

Look back to the beginning and Romain was clearly quick from the moment that he began racing cars, winning the junior Formula Masters title in his first year - the Swiss Formula Renault 1600 championship - then added a second title in 2005, being crowned French Formula Renault champion. Anyone winning multiple titles in single-seaters is worth watching and Romain was signed to be part of Renault's Driver Development programme. He then kept this career momentum going with title number three in 2007 when he became European Formula 3 champion ahead of Sebastian Buemi and Nico Hulkenberg.

Romain won the Asian GP2 series in 2008 but although he won twice in the main FIA championship, he ranked only fourth. Returning for a second bid for the title, he was behind Hulkenberg on points when his F1 break came after Nelson Piquet Jr was dropped by the Renault team and he stepped in. It didn't prove to be a good

Romain will be hoping that the frustrations of the second half of 2016 are behind him.

move as he failed to score any points in his seven outings.

Romain then took the risk of stepping down a level in 2010, but won the Auto GP title and landed a plum GP2 ride for 2011

when he did what he absolutely had to do: he became champion.

F1 second time around happened with Lotus and he was better prepared, three times finishing on the podium. He ruffled a few feathers with his wild approach and rivals were happier when he cooled it a little for 2013. This was an even better season, with seven podium visits en route to ranking seventh. Then points became harder to find as Lotus lost its edge through 2014 and 2015.

TRACK NOTES

Nationality:	FRENCH
Born:	17 APRIL 1986, GENEVA, SWITZERLAND
Website:	www.romaingrosjean.com
Teams:	RENAULT 2009, LOTUS 2012-15, HAAS F1 2016-17

CAREER RECORD	
First Grand Prix:	2009 EUROPEAN GP
Grand Prix starts:	104
Grand Prix wins:	0
	(best result: 2nd, 2012 Canadian GP, 2013 United States GP)
Poles:	0
Fastest laps:	1
Points:	316
Honours:	2012 RACE OF CHAMPIONS CHAMPION; 2011 GP2 CHAMPION & GP2 ASIA CHAMPION, 2010 AUTO GP CHAMPION, 2008 GP2 ASIA CHAMPION, 2007 FORMULA THREE EUROSERIES CHAMPION, 2005 FRENCH FORMULA RENAULT CHAMPION, 2003 SWISS FORMULA RENAULT 1600 CHAMPION

EXCEEDING ALL EXPECTATIONS

After spending four years driving for Lotus, but not being sure about the team's future as the supply of money dried to a trickle, Romain jumped ship late last year to join new Haas F1. Soon after the deal was done, he must have felt a pang of disquiet when Renault took over the Lotus F1 attack to supply the works backing it had so desperately needed. However, Romain came out ahead as Haas impressed and Renault didn't. There were frustrations, for sure, notably in the second half of the year, including having to retire with brake failure at the Malaysian GP. Yet, as a driver who has had to bounce back, he bounced back and has to be content that his form was good enough next time out, in Japan, to match the Williams duo. Such was his form, with plenty of speed from team-mate Esteban Gutierrez to keep him on his toes, that it was hard to remember some of the time that this was an all-new team, from America no less, attacking F1's midfield with such aplomb, albeit too often just outside the points.

KEVIN MAGNUSSEN

Last season was a tough one for the Dane as, after a year on the sidelines, he made his F1 return with a team that was in decline. It was far from easy, especially when Renault wouldn't commit for more than 2017, so he swapped to Haas F1.

Kevin's father Jan was the hotshot of his age. Nurtured by Jackie Stewart, he dominated the British F3 Championship by winning 14 of the 18 races. F1 beckoned, first with a drive for McLaren as a stand-in for Mika Hakkinen in 1995 and then a year and a half with Stewart GP, but a lack of application meant that he never hit the levels that his ability merited and his career turned away from F1.

With this experience part of Magnussen family folklore, Kevin was forewarned about what is required to reach the top, aware of the pitfalls that can sidetrack careers. After showing good speed in karts, Kevin stepped up to car racing as soon as he was old enough, winning the Danish Formula Ford title aged only 15.

Second place behind Antonio Felix da Costa in the 2009 North European Formula Renault series reiterated his talents. Moving swiftly through the junior formulae, Kevin tried F3 in 2010, ending the year third overall in the German series. He also contested one European series round and took a win in one of the two races. Clearly suited to F3, Kevin signed up for a

Kevin decided that Renault might not hit form so has banked on further Haas F1 progress.

full season in British F3 in 2011 and ended the year as runner-up to Carlin team-mate Felipe Nasr as they took seven wins apiece.

Kevin advanced to Formula Renault 3.5 in 2012, ranked seventh, then returned after joining DAMS to win five races and land the 2013 title.

This opened the door to his F1 break, with no less a team than McLaren, and Kevin had a dream debut when he finished second in the Australian GP. However, he took only one other top-six finish – fifth in Russia. Then, with Fernando Alonso being signed to coincide with Honda's arrival, Kevin stepped down to be a test driver in 2015. Of course, this route is a risky one, as there's no guarantee that the F1 door will open again, but Kevin had no option other than to accept the move. Fortunately, it worked out for him for the 2016 season.

CHASING AFTER ELUSIVE POINTS

Kevin's second spell in F1 was tricky in the extreme last year. There was certainly no repeat of the second place that he scored on his F1 debut in 2014, nothing close. Instead, he raced for a Renault team that was in disarray and was forced to drive a car that spent the middle part of the season in particular making no progress in its level of competitiveness as rivals strode forwards. Having finished in seventh place fourth time out, in the Russian GP, Kevin would have expected more points would follow, but they didn't until he claimed the single point for 10th place fully 11 rounds later, on the streets of Singapore. As with team-mate Jolyon Palmer, both were unsettled by Renault's F1 management constantly deferring the date on which they would tell them whether they would be staying on for 2017 or be replaced by other drivers that Renault thought might do a better job. Losing control through Eau Rouge and crashing out of the Belgian GP was seen as the wrong result at very much the wrong time, certainly not helping his cause.

TRACK NOTES

Nationality:	DANISH
Born:	5 OCTOBER 1992, ROSKILDE, DENMARK
Website:	www.kevinmagnussen.com
Teams:	McLAREN 2014, RENAULT 2016, HAAS 2017

CAREER RECORD	
First Grand Prix:	2014 AUSTRALIAN GP
Grand Prix starts:	40
Grand Prix wins:	0
	(best result: 2nd, 2014 Australian GP)
Poles:	0
Fastest laps:	0
Points:	62
Honours:	2013 FORMULA RENAULT 3.5 CHAMPION, 2011 BRITISH FORMULA THREE RUNNER-UP, 2009 FORMULA RENAULT NORTHERN EUROPE RUNNER-UP, 2008 DANISH FORMULA FORD CHAMPION

RENAULT

This was a team in freefall last year after it became branded as Renault for a second time and lost form due to a lack of investment through 2015. It's now going through a further transition as Renault looks to bring in a hotshot to develop for the future.

Kevin Magnussen and Jolyon Palmer gave their all last year, but the going was tough and this year's drivers will be praying for superior machinery.

Ted Toleman became a millionaire through transporting cars for manufacturers. With this wealth, he indulged in his love of cars and boats, his team growing through F2 to the point that its drivers Brian Henton and Derek Warwick finished first and second in F1's feeder championship in 1980.

Wasting no time, Toleman dipped its toe in the F1 pond in 1981. With chassis penned by Rory Byrne and turbocharged engines from Hart, they became increasingly competitive and then beat other teams to sign Ayrton Senna from F3 for 1984. He almost won the Monaco GP for them, but left for Lotus and the team dipped in form before being bought by Benetton for 1986.

The biggest change for 1986, though, was that the sleek B186 was fitted with a turbocharged BMW engine, and this offered prodigious power in qualifying trim, enabling Teo Fabi to take two poles before Gerhard Berger rounded out the year with the team's first victory, in Mexico.

A change to Ford power for 1987 didn't improve the team's form, but the wins started again when Alessandro Nannini inherited victory in Japan from Senna in 1989. Then, in 1990, Nelson Piquet added two more wins, helping Benetton to finish third behind only McLaren and Ferrari. However, what changed the team's fortunes most was the arrival of Michael Schumacher. He

THE POWER AND THE GLORY

BOB BELL
A doctorate in aeronautical engineering landed this Ulsterman a job as an aerodynamicist at McLaren in 1982. After promotion to head of research and development, Bob worked at Benetton until he was enticed to Jordan in 1999. In 2001, he returned to the team no longer known as Benetton, it had been renamed Renault, and he became technical director when Mike Gascoyne left. Two titles for Fernando Alonso in 2005 and 2006 were an accolade. Bob joined Mercedes in 2011, but left in 2014 to guide Manor, before returning to Renault in 2016.

DROPPING AWAY FROM THE PACE
Bob Bell arrived from Manor last February to take charge of technical matters, so the fruits of his labours won't be seen until 2017, but last season was a struggle as the team had to contend with a lack of development through the autumn of 2015 when its ownership was in the balance before Renault stepped in. Neither Kevin Magnussen nor Jolyon Palmer had the chance to make an impression, with pressure heaped on both as Renault said it was looking for new talent for 2017.

2016 DRIVERS & RESULTS

Driver	Nationality	Races	Wins	Pts	Pos
Kevin Magnussen	Danish	21	0	7	16th
Jolyon Palmer	British	21	0	1	18th

FOR THE RECORD

Country of origin:	England
Team base:	Enstone, England
Telephone:	(44) 01608 678000
Website:	www.renaultsport.com
Active in Formula One:	As Toleman 1981-85, Benetton 1986-2001, Renault 2002-11 & 2016 on, Lotus 2012-15
Grands Prix contested:	593
Wins:	48
Pole positions:	34
Fastest laps:	54

THE TEAM

Managing director:	Cyril Abiteboul
Racing director:	tba
Deputy team principal:	Federico Gastaldi
Chief technical officer:	Bob Bell
Technical director:	Nick Chester
Technical director, engine:	Remi Taffin
Operations director:	Alan Permane
Chief designer:	Martin Tolliday
Head of aerodynamics:	Nicolas Hennel de Beaupreau
Chief engineer:	Mark Slade
Team manager:	Paul Seaby
Chief mechanic:	Greg Baker
Test driver:	tba
Chassis:	Renault RS17
Engine:	Renault V6
Tyres:	Pirelli

joined towards the end of 1991 and was a winner a year later before he, technical director Ross Brawn and designer Byrne combined to win five races in 1993 and then eight in 1994, when Schumacher edged his damaged car into title rival Damon Hill's Williams at the Adelaide finale to ensure that he landed the title.

A change to Renault engines brought another drivers' title in 1995 and the constructors' title too as Johnny Herbert added two wins to Schumacher's nine.

Then Schumacher headed to Ferrari, soon to be followed by Brawn and Byrne. Benetton endured a relative loss of form and only began again to look like a championship challenger some years after it had been rebadged as Renault in 2002 and Fernando Alonso gave it a boost. Keeping its base at Enstone near Oxford, the new team name was just that, a name, and the team had no association with the Renault F1 team that had operated from France from 1977 to 1985.

Alonso won a race in 2003 and Renault progressed to the point that it was there to pounce when Ferrari finally stumbled. This came in 2005, and Alonso's seven wins - combined with Giancarlo Fisichella's one - were enough for the Spaniard to be World Champion and the team to take its second constructors' crown. Alonso did it again in 2006 and Renault also just edged out Ferrari to make it two wins on the trot.

Losing Alonso to McLaren for 2007 was a blow, but he was unhappy there and so returned for 2008, only to find the team's form less than the best. Indeed, desperate measures were taken to ensure that he won in Singapore, with team-mate Nelson Piquet Jr being instructed to crash to bring out the safety car to ensure it. Team principal Flavio Briatore and technical chief Pat Symonds took the rap for that.

The 2012 season marked a third change of name as it became Lotus - the team Tony Fernandes entered F1 in 2010 had been ordered not to use Lotus as its name, and so he renamed his team Caterham Racing instead. Form improved, as Lotus rose to rank fourth overall, and again in 2013, but Red Bull Racing was dominant.

A lack of budget relative to the front-running teams hampered the next couple of campaigns, until, late in 2015, Renault bought a 65 per cent stake in the team, so it started its second spell bearing the name of the French manufacturer.

The current Renault F1 team started life as Toleman and ran Ayrton Senna in its fourth year, 1984.

NICO HULKENBERG

There were plenty of flashes of speed from Nico with Force India through 2016, but a desire to lead a manufacturer's attack has coaxed him to cross over to a team that has been great in the past but was poor last year. It may prove to be a shrewd move.

Some drivers make their journey up racing's ladder to F1 look easy. Of course, Max Verstappen's recent rise has trumped all speedy ascents, but Nico's was one of the exemplary ones until the meteoric Dutch teenager did it in the blink of an eye.

Key to a speedy ascent is winning championship titles, and this is what Nico did, year in, year out. In karting, he won both the junior and senior German titles before moving up to cars at the age of 17. Racing in Formula BMW ADAC, he and Sebastien Buemi dominated, with Nico just taking the title.

Without family wealth, Nico raced the little-fancied Ligier chassis in German F3 in 2006 and did well to finish fifth. Yet, his form earned him a test with the German A1GP team and Nico repaid their faith by winning the German team this nation-versus-nation series and landing a superior F3 deal with ASM for the European championship in 2007, finishing third behind Romain Grosjean and Buemi, and winning the F3 Masters race.

Back with ART Grand Prix for 2008, Nico scored seven wins to be a dominant champion. Then, in 2009, he won the GP2 title as a rookie, winning five races for ART

Nico has signed a multi-year deal and must hope that this former title-winning team can recover.

to leave his more experienced team-mate Pastor Maldonado in the shade.

Having shown good form through that year as a test driver for Williams, Nico was advanced into an F1 race seat with the team

for 2010, snatching pole position in Brazil. Then, as Williams needed money for 2011, he lost his ride to Maldonado.

Force India gave him a race seat for 2012, with Nico running as well as the equipment has allowed ever since. There has been talk of front-end F1 teams, including Ferrari and McLaren, wanting to sign him, but Nico's lanky height and weight have counted against him and now it's up to him to prove them wrong as he leads Renault's attack.

TRACK NOTES

Nationality:	GERMAN
Born:	19 AUGUST 1987, EMMERICH, GERMANY
Website:	www.nicohulkenberg.net
Teams:	WILLIAMS 2010, FORCE INDIA 2012 & 2014-16, SAUBER 2013, RENAULT 2017

CAREER RECORD

First Grand Prix:	2010 BAHRAIN GP
Grand Prix starts:	117
Grand Prix wins:	0 (best result: 4th. 2012 Belgian GP, 2013 Korean GP, 2016 Belgian GP)
Poles:	1
Fastest laps:	2
Points:	362
Honours:	2015 LE MANS 24 HOURS WINNER, 2009 GP2 CHAMPION, 2008 EUROPEAN F3 CHAMPION, 2007 F3 MASTERS WINNER, 2006/07 A1GP CHAMPION, 2005 GERMAN FORMULA BMW ADAC CHAMPION, 2003 GERMAN KART CHAMPION, 2002 GERMAN JUNIOR KART CHAMPION

BURSTS OF SPEED APLENTY

It would have been extremely hard for Nico not to feel that it simply wasn't his year when Max Verstappen was slow away at the start in Singapore and caused Carlos Sainz Jr to move across just as Nico was diving between the Spaniard and his Scuderia Toro Rosso team-mate Daniil Kvyat. In an instant, what could have been an eighth-to-fourth move became a retirement against the wall before the first corner and the end to a run of five consecutive point-scoring drives. Fourth place two races earlier, at Spa-Francorchamps, demonstrated how Force India had found extra pace through the year, making this all the more frustrating as Nico gunned for his first F1 podium and fell short, while team-mate Sergio Perez managed it twice for the underfunded team. He will also still be kicking himself for wasting his mastery of changing conditions to qualify on the outside of the front row in Austria by then making a dreadful start. In short, it was a season in which both drivers delivered, but there were times that Nico didn't master his tyres as well as Sergio did.

JOLYON PALMER

Strong form through the closing stages of 2016 helped Jolyon to recover from a tricky start to his F1 career with a difficult car. He showed in GP2 that he's a driver who keeps on learning, so deserves this second opportunity.

Having a father who was a grand prix and sportscar racer before going on to own and run the majority of British racing circuits meant that it was always likely that Jonathan Palmer's elder son would have a go at racing. Indeed, not only did Jolyon do just that, but his younger brother Will has followed in his wheeltracks.

Jolyon transferred from kart racing to cars when he was 14, in 2005, competing in the T-Car championship, a series for silhouette mini touring cars for junior racers.

A step up to single-seaters followed in 2007, when Jolyon advanced to Formula Palmer Audi, a slicks and wings series created by his father. Finishing 10th in his first campaign, then third in his second, didn't suggest anything other than average talent. Yet, Jolyon progressed, trying the more powerful Formula Two category in 2009, then winning five rounds to end the 2010 season as runner-up to Dean Stoneman.

One of the problems at this point was comparing him to his contemporaries, as most of these were advancing by the

By accepting a one-year deal, Jolyon was the driver chosen to stay on with Renault.

more traditional route though F3. The first true comparison came in 2011 when Jolyon moved up to GP2. Driving for Arden International, almost all the circuits were

new to him and he failed to score a point. In 2012, though, Jolyon scored a first win, at Monaco no less, but could rank only 11th for iSport International as Davide Valsecchi stormed the title. In 2013, Jolyon won twice to be seventh for Carlin.

Back for an almost unheard-of fourth crack at GP2 in 2014, Jolyon knew that only the title would suffice as his climb up the ladder was taking years. His move to DAMS worked, though, and this is precisely what he delivered.

With no F1 seat available, he spent 2015 as test driver for Lotus F1. After those four years in GP2, Jolyon would have been nervous to have reached F1's waiting room with no guarantee for the future, but his father Jonathan pushed hard and landed a race seat for him for 2016.

BIG ENDEAVOUR, LITTLE REWARD

The first marker that Jolyon put down was to outqualify his more experienced team-mate Kevin Magnussen at the opening race. Then his achievement dipped as he struggled to find a way to make the Renault work. As Magnussen could relax thanks to finishing seventh in Sochi, Jolyon became desperate to score his first points, and was chastened by spinning out of a likely point-scoring drive at the Hungaroring. At this point, there were many suggesting that this ought to be Jolyon's first and last season in F1, his results not meriting a second one. Yet, whatever the level of Renault's performance, Jolyon then started to do all he could to prove his worth: he began to equal Magnussen's pace, scored a point at Sepang and even started getting his nose in front in the closing races. Then, with Renault keeping them both hanging and running past deadline dates, it was a battle of who would keep their nerve, who would be happy with the one-year deal that Renault was offering. Jolyon was the one who kept his seat and will benefit when Renault finds better form in 2017.

TRACK NOTES

Nationality:	BRITISH
Born:	20 JANUARY 1991, HORSHAM, ENGLAND
Website:	www.jolyonpalmer.com
Teams:	RENAULT 2016-17

CAREER RECORD

First Grand Prix:	2016 AUSTRALIAN GP
Grand Prix starts:	21
Grand Prix wins:	0
Poles:	0
	(best result: 10th, 2016 Malaysian GP)
Fastest laps:	0
Points:	1
Honours:	2014 GP2 CHAMPION, 2010 FORMULA TWO RUNNER-UP

SAUBER

Sauber starts the 2017 under new ownership following a deal struck last July for a Swiss investment firm, Longbow Holdings, to take the majority share in the Swiss outfit. The finance will be welcome, but don't expect instant results.

Marcus Ericsson came on strong through last year, but the fact that points eluded the team's drivers shows how much work needs to be done.

While everyone welcomes the fact that this Swiss team finally has the money to invest in the year-round development it needs to keep up, even to catch up, with its former midfield rivals, it will feel strange not to have team founder Peter Sauber involved with the show.

Sauber was a racing driver in the 1970s, but he made his mark more thanks to building his own cars. These were sportscars and they attracted a good deal of favourable comment, notably in the late 1980s when he did a deal to fit them with Mercedes engines. From works support in the World Sports-Prototype Championship in 1988, when the team finished second to Jaguar, Sauber became the *de facto* Mercedes sportscar team the following year, with the cars painted silver, to echo the Silver Arrows, Mercedes' racing team in the 1930s and 1950s. Mercedes was clearly onto a good thing, as it won the Le Mans 24 Hours, dominated the teams' championship and its drivers Jean-Louis Schlesser, Jochen Mass,

Mauro Baldi and Kenneth Acheson filled the top four places in the drivers' championship.

In 1990, Mercedes did something different and put forward young single-seater stars alongside the regulars, including Michael Schumacher, Heinz-Harald Frentzen and Karl Wendlinger, taking both titles again.

At this point, Sauber set its sights on

THE POWER AND THE GLORY

NICOLAS HENNEL DE BEAUPREAU
Nicolas Hennel de Beaupreau joined Sauber midway through last year, taking over as head of aerodynamics from Willem Toet. He has worked in F1 since 1997, starting with Benetton. In 2000, Hennel de Beaupreau moved to Ferrari but, after three years, returned to Grove, with Benetton now operating as the Renault F1 team. Keeping with the three-year pattern, he left for McLaren in 2006 and returned to Ferrari in 2009. His last spell before Sauber was from 2013 with Lotus, his third spell with the team from Grove.

RACING FOR LITTLE REWARD
Back for a second year, Marcus Ericsson and Felipe Nasr can't have expected to tilt for glory in 2016, as nothing had changed in terms of the package, and there had been no influx of cash in 2015 to boost the cars' development. Indeed, even their best finishes were outside the points. The continuing quest for an investor at least came to an end, but the drivers know that it's going to take money and years of a stable design team line-up to get Sauber closer to the front again.

2016 DRIVERS & RESULTS

Driver	Nationality	Races	Wins	Pts	Pos
Marcus Ericsson	Swedish	21	0	0	22nd
Felipe Nasr	Brazilian	21	0	2	17th

FOR THE RECORD

Country of origin:	Switzerland
Team base:	Hinwil, Switzerland
Telephone:	(41) 44 937 9000
Website:	www.sauberf1team.com
Active in Formula One:	From 1993
	(as BMW Sauber 2006-10)
Grands Prix contested:	423
Wins:	1
Pole positions:	1
Fastest laps:	5

THE TEAM

Chairman:	Pascal Picci
Team principal:	Monisha Kaltenborn
Operations director:	Axel Kruse
Technical director:	Jorg Zander
Chief designer:	Eric Gandelin
Head of aerodynamics:	
	Nicolas Hennel de Beaupreau
Head of engineering:	Giampaolo Dall'ara
Head of track engineering:	Xevi Pujolar
Head of aerodynamic development:	
	Mariano Alperin-Bruvera
Head of aerodynamic research:	
	Seamus Mullarkey
Head of vehicle performance:	
	Elliot Dason-Barber
Head of performance integration:	
	Paul Russell
Head of systems engineering:	
	Damiano Mofetta
Team manager:	Beat Zehnder
Head of track operations:	Timothy Guerin
Race strategist:	Ruth Buscombe
Test driver:	tba
Chassis:	Sauber C36
Engine:	Ferrari V6
Tyres:	Pirelli

crossing over to F1, doing so in 1993, albeit without hoped-for Mercedes involvement. Impressively, JJ Lehto raced to fifth place on the team's debut in South Africa, then claimed fourth at Imola, a result equalled by Wendlinger at Monza, leaving the team sixth at year's end. Encouraged by this, Mercedes supplied engines for 1994, but moved them on to McLaren for 1995, leaving the cigar-smoking team principal to find a customer deal with Ford. From 1997, Sauber did a deal for Ferrari engines.

Third place for Frentzen in the wet in the 2003 United States GP was a highlight, but it took a change of direction to finally yield Sauber's first F1 win. This came after BMW got involved and brought investment that greatly improved the facilities at Sauber's headquarters in Hinwil. Nick Heidfeld delivered Sauber's first podium when he finished third in the 2006 Hungarian GP, a result matched by Robert Kubica at Monza, having joined the team midway through the year to replace Jacques Villeneuve.

Following a great campaign in 2007 in which BMW Sauber ranked a best-ever second overall, behind the dominant Ferrari, thanks to the driving of Heidfeld and Kubica, the team's greatest day came when Kubica led Heidfeld home in a one-two finish in the 2008 Canadian GP. Only Ferrari and McLaren outscored the team that year.

The BMW deal came to an end after 2009 and Sauber reverted to Ferrari motors, with the team's head of corporate and legal matters, Monisha Kaltenborn, being promoted to be Chief Executive Officer. These changes didn't lead to a boost in form, but it nearly produced another win, when Sergio Perez found himself right on the pace at the 2012 Malaysian GP and even lined up a passing manoeuvre on Fernando Alonso's Ferrari. It didn't come off, and he had to settle for second place.

That year marked a change at the top, as Peter Sauber transferred one third of the team to Kaltenborn and, that October, he stepped back and let Kaltenborn become team principal.

Sadly, a failure to keep up with F1 budget inflation led to the team's decline, with 2014 marking a low point, as neither Adrian Sutil nor Esteban Gutierrez managed to score a point. Felipe Nasr brought a welcome tranche of money from Banco do Brasil for 2015, with Marcus Ericsson also arriving as a second pay-driver. However, finances were only adequate and that is why this deal with Longbow Finance could be the impetus that Sauber has needed.

"We're convinced that Longbow Finance is the perfect partner to make the team competitive again."
Monisha Kaltenborn

Heinz-Harald Frentzen remains one the most successful of Sauber's drivers. This is him in 1993.

MARCUS ERICSSON

Back for a third season with Sauber, Marcus will be hoping that the new investment in the team by Longbow Finance that arrived midway through 2016 can help keep the car development going throughout the season to keep him in touch with his rivals.

Marcus has received considerable support through his career from some of Sweden's former racing stars, guiding both him and his faithful backers up the racing ladder.

Touring car racer Fredrik Ekblom was the one who spotted him first and he and 1998 Indycar champion Kenny Brack then helped Marcus to advance from karts to single-seaters.

His first season in cars was in Formula BMW in 2007, this entry-level category's inaugural season, and Marcus did very well, landing the British championship title for the Fortec Motorsport team.

Staying on with Fortec, Marcus contested the British F3 Championship in 2008 and found the going a little tougher in this notoriously testing arena, ending the year ranked fifth as Jaime Alguersuari took the title for Carlin.

Realising that he might stand a better chance of winning a title in a different arena, Brack directed him to Japan in 2009 and this resulted in the F3 title with the leading TOM'S team. What really showed his progress, though, was when Marcus finished in fourth place in the well-

Marcus made notable progress through 2016 but will require a much better car this year.

supported Macau F3 street race at the end of the season.

After taking in a few GP2 tests, Marcus stepped up to GP2, running in the Asian series before advancing to

the FIA GP2 series in 2010. Brack guided him towards Super Nova, the team with which he himself had been pipped to the 1996 F3000 title by Jorg Muller. Although Marcus won at Valencia, his season was extremely patchy and he ended up ranked 17th overall. So, more GP2 was required and, although he was often on the podium, it took four years at this level before Marcus was able to do well enough to finally climb to F1.

His break came with Caterham in 2014, when the budget that he brought was a huge attraction. Sadly, the team was always strapped for cash, so the equipment was less than the best. A move to Sauber for 2015 started with his first points first time out, but life was never this easy again.

TRACK NOTES

Nationality:	SWEDISH
Born:	2 SEPTEMBER 1990, KUMLA, SWEDEN
Website:	www.marcusericssonracing.com
Teams:	CATERHAM 2014, SAUBER 2015-17

CAREER RECORD

First Grand Prix:	2014 AUSTRALIAN GP
Grand Prix starts:	56
Grand Prix wins:	0
	(best result: 8th, 2015 Australian GP)
Poles:	0
Fastest laps:	0
Points:	9
Honours:	2009 JAPANESE FORMULA 3 CHAMPION, 2007 BRITISH FORMULA BMW CHAMPION

POINTS WERE LIKE THE HOLY GRAIL

It didn't seem to matter what Marcus and team-mate Felipe Nasr did last year, but points always remained just out of reach as the Ferrari-powered Sauber C35 wasn't good enough. As is increasingly the case for the teams neither supported by manufacturers nor with rich histories, money for development is but a dream, making their relative disadvantage all the greater through the course of the year, leaving the drivers ever further from their goal of points. Marcus's best result in 2016 was 11th place and he achieved this at the Mexican GP to augment the three 12th-place finishes he'd already achieved, including two in the first five rounds, at Sakhir and at Barcelona's Circuit de Catalunya. Perhaps Marcus's most impressive run of the year, though, was in qualifying in Singapore when he wrestled his way into the second qualifying session, which was a rarity through the season, and made all the more pleasurable as Sauber had, by this late stage in the season, suffered from its now traditional relative loss of competitiveness.

PASCAL WEHRLEIN*

Extremely impressive from the start of his first year of F1, Pascal is back for another learning year, this time with Sauber, as Mercedes develops his talents for a possible works ride in the near future, after considering him as a replacement for Rosberg.

Pascal was marked out from early on in his karting career as one to watch. This was with good reason too as he started driving karts as soon as he could, at the age of eight, and began his racing career two years later. By 2009, at the age of 14, he was German KF2 champion.

Then came cars, with two years spent in the ADAC Formel Masters series. Sixth overall at his first attempt in 2010, when Richie Stanaway won the title, Pascal racked up eight wins in 2011 to become champion after a year-long battle with Emil Bernstorff and Sven Muller.

Staying on with Mucke Motorsport, Pascal moved up to F3 in 2012 and finished fourth in the European Championship as Daniel Juncadella won the title. It was impressive for a rookie season in this exacting category. Fifth place in the one-off F3 Masters race augmented this, as did his fourth-place finish in the end of season street race in Macau.

Yet, for 2013, there was a change of tack. With Mercedes anxious to snap up young talent and develop it, Pascal was placed in the DTM after impressing in the opening European F3 series round. He collected a

There were some impressive speeds from Pascal in his first year of F1, so expect more in 2017.

trio of 10th-place finishes in this touring car category before demonstrating in 2014 how much he'd learned to take a win in the DTM at the Lausitzring to help him rank eighth at year's end as Marco Wittmann took the title.

The highlight of Pascal's year, though, was when Mercedes gave him his first F1 test.

Then came 2015 and Pascal confounded the critics and he won at the Norisring and in Moscow to beat all the longstanding DTM frontrunners to land the title for Mercedes ahead of Audi's Jamie Green. After showing increasing pace in F1 tests for Mercedes and Force India, Pascal received a late nod to step up to F1 with the revamped and revived Manor team for 2016, thus showing how serious Mercedes is about bringing on young drivers, especially German drivers, to become champions of the future.

TRACK NOTES

Nationality:	GERMAN
Born:	18 OCTOBER 1994, WORNDORF, GERMANY
Website:	www.pascal-wehrlein.de
Teams:	MANOR 2016, SAUBER 2017

CAREER RECORD

First Grand Prix:	2016 AUSTRALIAN GP
Grand Prix starts:	21
Grand Prix wins:	0
	(best result: 10th, 2016 Austrian GP)
Poles:	0
Fastest laps:	0
Points:	1
Honours:	2015 DTM CHAMPION, 2012 EUROPEAN F3 RUNNER-UP & TOP ROOKIE, 2011 ADAC FORMEL MASTERS CHAMPION, 2009 GERMAN KF2 KART CHAMPION

HITTING THE POINTS FOR MANOR

Having finished last at the opening grand prix in Australia, Pascal demonstrated next time out that he is a special talent, one worthy of Mercedes' support, by finishing 13th for little-fancied Manor in the Bahrain GP. This, don't forget, was seen as a team that was expected to break into the top 20 only when others failed. That he finished ahead of a Sauber and both Force India cars was a feather in his cap. However, that proved to be just the arm-up as Pascal then peaked midway through the season when he came home in 10th place in the Austrian GP. He had starred in qualifying to be less than 0.2s off making the final session for the top 10. At race's end, he was right with Williams' Valtteri Bottas, which reflected very well on Pascal. Not only was this fantastic for Pascal's reputation, but it was worth millions of pounds for Manor as it moved it above Sauber, thus up to 10th place in the World Championship, making it eligible for prize money, until this was cruelly reversed when Sauber took a ninth at the penultimate round.

Max Verstappen could hardly have packed any more excitement into his Brazilian GP, earning new fans across the globe with his charge to third place in the treacherous conditions.

TALKING POINT:
ALL CHANGE FOR 2017

The cars have been changed with the aim of making them faster. Given wider front and rear wings, much wider tyres, raked sidepods to accommodate larger bargeboards and a bigger diffuser, they will fly, but will the racing be any better?

Formula 1 has chopped and changed considerably through its 67-year history. Engines have been enlarged, reduced, supercharged and turbocharged. The cars have been allowed to develop unhindered, yet at other times kept on a tight rein. Now, with the aim of making F1 more spectacular, to entice new fans and keep established ones, it's being changed again.

The idea is to make the cars more exciting to behold, and faster by up to 6s per lap. This seems a considerable amount but study of lap records shows that last year's fastest race laps at most venues were down on the records set before 2005, when F1 slashed the amount of downforce that the cars could have by raising their noses and bringing their rear wings forward, as well as increasing engine life and so cutting horsepower. Then, in 2006, lap times increased considerably when 3.0-litre V10s were outlawed and replaced by 2.4-litre V8s. So, it's clear that the tracks can contain cars lapping at that speed.

So, the question was how to achieve this return to power and speed and, hopefully, spectacle. Car dimensions have been expanded, with maximum width up from 1800mm to 2000mm, and the width of the floor extended from 1400mm to 1600mm.

However, it's more what's happening to the wings that tells the story, as they're designed to produce more downforce with front wing width up from 1650mm to 1800mm, the rear wing increased from 800mm to 950mm width and lowered from 950mm to 800mm to put it in a position where it will harness downforce without causing as much drag.

In addition, 2017-spec diffusers are much longer, up from 3500mm to 5250mm, with their trailing edge raised from 125mm to 155mm. In order to help airflow around the sides, the fronts of the sidepods have been angled back, allowing more space for the bargeboards. One cost of this upsizing, though, is that the cars will be around 20kg heavier.

To hit the lap reduction target requires help from another source: the tyres. These have ballooned to offer more grip and a retro look. Front tyre widths are up from 245mm to 305mm, with a view to also giving the cars less lateral weight transfer and so reducing the loss of grip mid corner. Rear tyre widths are up from 325mm to 405mm and Pirelli's Paul Hembery reckons the new cars will drive like they are "on rails".

Not surprisingly, the drivers are keen to try the new-spec cars. Jenson Button enthused about the 2017-spec cars to journalists at the Belgian GP, saying: "I remember going through Jerez's Turn 5 on to the back straight [in those earlier cars] and you'd have one eye closed thinking, 'is this thing going to hold'?

"You couldn't hit the brakes because the tyre would deform and you wouldn't be able to turn in as the steering would be so heavy. So it was a light dab on the brakes and then you'd just be waiting for the twitch. If you got the snap oversteer, you were either off or you lost a massive amount of time. Now, you arrive and slide through the corner and you drift. It's just a very different feeling. It doesn't scare you as much. In 2017, it will be awesome. F1 is doing the right thing with the tyres and aerodynamics. It's where the sport needs to go."

Contrastingly, Lewis Hamilton isn't sure that he agrees with Button, saying: "These days, we slow down as soon as we've done the start. We aren't pushing 100 per cent like we used to. F1 has been about preserving the tyres and batteries, and this isn't what people want to see. The cars will be very heavy in 2017. They will have great grip and still be faster, but they will have the same characteristics as in 2016, so I think we'll still drive the same: save fuel, save tyres, do the same thing."

Time will tell.

TALKING POINT: FATHERS AND SONS

Max Verstappen earned endless plaudits last year when he became the youngest ever grand prix winner at the age of just 18, but he's far from the first second-generation driver to follow a father's footsteps into the grand prix world.

It's often the case that someone with a doctor, banker or architect as a parent might follow that same career choice. To achieve these aims, they need to clear the required academic hurdles, ruling out those not up to the task.

Racing drivers also seem to beget racing drivers. With no academic hurdles to clear, the deciding elements of whether they will succeed are budget and ability. Of course, if you have enough of the former, then you may yet make up for not having enough of the latter, but it remains a hit-and-miss process.

Graham Hill to Damon Hill has been the ultimate passing of the baton, as they're the only father/son combination to have taken world titles, Graham in 1962 and 1968, for BRM then Lotus, and Damon in 1996 for Williams. Damon also did this without his father's input, as Graham died in a plane crash when Damon was 15.

The driver who followed him to the title, Jacques Villeneuve, came from racing stock as well, and he too did it without his father's support, as Gilles was killed at Zolder in 1982 when Jacques was 11.

Unlike Damon and Jacques, Nico Rosberg has had his father – 1982 World Champion Keke – giving advice where needed to guide him towards F1. He came good last year to become the next second-generation champion, despite the very best efforts of his Mercedes team-mate Lewis Hamilton ...

In general, though, very few of them have the levels of ability that made their fathers great. Possibly the missing element is the burning desire to make it. Furthermore, they have the burden of chasing someone else's dreams.

Michael Andretti, son of 1978 World Champion Mario Andretti, is one who springs to mind. He had been Indycar champion in 1991 when it was decided, perhaps for marketing reasons, that he should try F1. He was signed by McLaren for 1993, albeit with the hardest team-mate to match: Ayrton Senna. Then, despite a winter of testing, he was a major disappointment, being dropped after he had achieved his best result, third place, at Monza. It couldn't have been more clear that he'd rather have stayed on the other side of the Atlantic and that he wasn't prepared to apply himself.

He's not alone in being a second-generation driver who fell short. Nelson Piquet Jr was good enough to push Hamilton in the 2006 GP2 title race. Yet, the desire just wasn't there, so his opportunity to match the three F1 titles earned by his father Nelson in the 1980s went away.

Yet, although Max Verstappen doesn't have to land a world title to emulate his father Jos – in fact, by winning a grand prix, he's ahead already – he looks to be the next one good enough to do so. Indeed, he's the leading exemplar of being a step ahead of their parent, but maybe he has an extra advantage, as his mother Sophie Kumpen was a top-level kart racer.

The skills were there for all to see when Max took the world kart title in 2013, something that none of the other second-generation drivers had managed. When Max jumped direct to European Formula Three, usually the second or third rung of the single-seater ladder, he finished as runner-up in that before graduating to F1 in 2015 at the age of just 17. A pair of fourth-place finishes with Toro Rosso suggested great talent, along with the fact that he feared no one. Then, as soon as he was promoted to Red Bull Racing part way through last year, he scored his first win, in Spain. Such is his pure ability, that more will follow and perhaps he'll go on to become the best second-generation racer. After some rough tactics last year, though, they will have been well advised to have words to calm him down.

If it comes down to genetics, there could yet be glory for Carlos Sainz Jr – whose father, Carlos Sainz, Sr, was a two-time World Rally Champion – and there is also Mick Schumacher (son of Michael), who is showing promise in the junior formulae.

TALKING POINT: MERCEDES THEN AND NOW

Mercedes has been comprehensively dominant and all but unstoppable in recent years. However, if it had not been for a crash in the 1955 Le Mans 24 Hours, it could have laid down a similar period of superiority through the late 1950s to change the face of F1.

Mercedes has won 63 grands prix across the past three World Championship campaigns and claimed the drivers' and constructors' titles each year. This is domination of F1 on a scale rarely seen. McLaren was predominant from the late 1980s to the early 1990s, Ferrari controlled all in the early 2000s and Red Bull Racing won four years in a row from 2010. However, domination of F1 is a rarity, as rules change and teams find technical advantages, meaning that the pendulum has almost always swung the other way within a few years. Right now, though, with only a minor set of rule changes for 2017, few expect Mercedes to be dislodged from the top of the pile.

This has been a golden period for Mercedes, but it's worth highlighting that although Mercedes hadn't won a constructors' title until 2014, it was very much the top team in the mid-1950s. This was, of course, before the constructors' title was created, but Mercedes arrived with a bang and set new standards that propelled F1 to a higher level.

Mercedes had been a powerhouse in the 1930s when it and Auto Union – both financed by the German state to emphasise Germany's might – took racing to new heights. After World War Two, it took until 1954 before Mercedes was ready to race

again. Its W196 racer wasn't ready for the start of the season, so Juan Manuel Fangio kept on racing for Maserati's works team for the first two grands prix of the year, winning both of them.

Making its debut at the French GP at Reims, Fangio gave Mercedes a winning start. Next time out, at the British GP, Fangio struggled to place the car through the fast bends because of its wheel-enclosing aerodynamic bodywork, and finished fourth. Thereafter, the bodywork was dropped and the Argentinian won three races in a row at the Nurburgring, Bremgarten and Monza, where the streamlining bodywork was back because of the circuit's high-speed nature, and this was enough for him to wrap up the title with a race in hand.

Mercedes strengthened its attack for 1955 by placing Stirling Moss in its second car. Fangio qualified on the front row for every round and won four of the six races to be champion again. It remains a mystery whether he was beaten or let himself be beaten by Moss in the Englishman's home grand prix on a day when they finished 0.2s apart but more than a minute clear of the driver in third, team-mate Karl Kling. For good measure, Mercedes entered a fourth car in which Piero Taruffi came home fourth for total domination.

Maserati and Ferrari were the best of the rest, but were far behind and didn't seem to have the wherewithal to challenge for 1956. However, a dreadful accident at Le Mans in June 1955 gave them their break, as Pierre Levegh's Mercedes was pitched into the crowd in an incident that claimed 80 lives, forcing Mercedes to elect to withdraw from the sport at the end of the year. Had Mercedes carried on, maybe the situation wouldn't have arisen in which Cooper was able to transform F1 by breaking with the tradition of fitting the engine at the front of the car. Perhaps F1 machinery would have headed off in a different direction.

There is no connection with the team that shone so brightly yet briefly in the 1950s and today's other than name, as the contemporary team's bloodline began in 1999 as BAR, morphed into Honda Racing in 2006 then Brawn GP for 2009 before being renamed and financed by Mercedes from 2010.

Showing how serious the new Mercedes team was, not only did it run its cars in silver again, but it signed seven-time World Champion Michael Schumacher to lead its attack. However, it was Nico Rosberg who proved its sharper tool, taking its first win in 2013 before Lewis Hamilton came along and bagged the first of its titles. The team hasn't stopped winning since.

Top: Back in the 1930s, Mercedes' Silver Arrows and the rival Auto Unions took racing car engineering to new heights.

Middle left: Stirling Moss, left, celebrates with his mentor and team-mate Juan Manuel Fangio after the British GP at Aintree in 1955.

Middle right: Nico Rosberg shows his delight at taking Mercedes' second modern-generation win, at Monaco in 2013.

Bottom: The use of hybrid power has been a key attraction for Mercedes, and it has produced the best of these power plants.

KNOW THE TRACKS 2017

There are only minor tweaks to the World Championship following F1's take-over by Liberty Media, but expect more in the future. For 2017, Germany is dropped, China and Bahrain swap places, with this year's 20-grand-prix schedule a week shorter than 2016's as there's an extra week to help the teams to get race-ready.

The World Championship has had a run of new circuits introduced into its pattern over the past couple of decades as F1's owners have added ever more races to boost its earnings. Many of these have come and gone, lasting as long as their government's money has kept flowing. For 2017, however, there is no novelty on the World Championship calendar, albeit with last year's newcomer in Azerbaijan still very much a discovery.

The changes to this year's calendar come at either end of the 21-race calendar, with the second and third rounds being swapped so that the Chinese GP moves back ahead of the one in Bahrain. Then, instead of the Malaysian and Japanese GPs being paired together in a flyaway bundle, the race at Suzuka will be partnered by the one on the streets of Singapore, with the race at Sepang being brought forward to a mid-September date.

As has been the case predominantly for the past couple of decades, the World Championship season kicks off in March with the Australian GP held at Melbourne's Albert Park. Then, packaged as a pair, that's to say with grands prix on consecutive weekends, come the races in Shanghai and at the Bahrain International Circuit at Sakhir.

A fortnight later, it's off to the Russian GP at Sochi. The races are then held every second weekend, which is just how the teams

like their spacing, with the race in Russia followed by grands prix in Spain, Monaco and Canada. At this point of the season, the calendar avoids pitching the next race as a direct clash with the Le Mans 24 Hours sportscar race that has a huge global following, as it has been moved back a week to 25 June to avoid the teams having the logistical nightmare of getting their equipment from Montreal to Azerbaijan for races just seven days apart.

When Baku, capital city of Azerbaijan, hosted the European GP for the first time last year, it offered a whole new backdrop for the World Championship and a distinctive one at that, for which F1 fans should be grateful, even though its track proved largely too narrow to facilitate overtaking. This year, at least, the drivers will know where the bumps are...

The Austrian and British GPs are also run back-to-back, but are located much closer to each other, so this is manageable. A fortnight later, the Hungaroring hosts the final grand prix of July. Then, sound the fanfare, F1's exhausted personnel will have a chance for a well-earned summer break with their families.

Fully four weeks after the race in Hungary, the F1 circus fires up again for the Belgian GP at Spa-Francorchamps, a circuit that never fails to show F1 in the best light. The Italian GP at Monza the following weekend is also a time-honoured and intrinsic part of the World Championship's fabric.

After that, Europe bids the World Championship farewell and the team transporters are taken back to base and all transport is done via air freight for the remaining seven races of the season. The race at Singapore will test the drivers' endurance with its soaring heat and sapping humidity. At least it is held after nightfall, lowering the temperatures there from what they will experience a week later at Sepang. Then comes the same run-in as last year, with grands prix in Japan, the USA, Mexico, Brazil and Abu Dhabi completing the programme.

What does the future hold? Well, Liberty Media's F1 chairman Chase Carey said that he doesn't want to move F1's traditional centre from Europe, which is what has been happening since the start of the millennium. Against these positive noises, the European circuits continue to baulk at their race-hosting fees, with Silverstone suggesting last October that it might not be able to pay for the race in future as its own ownership was up for negotiation. Yes, Silverstone, which had 139,000 fans through its gates across the British GP's three days last July. If those sort of numbers can't make a grand prix work, something must change. Liberty might be more amenable than F1's previous owner CVC was, and lower its fee to keep the races in the "right" places. Having already lost the French GP and, most recently, Germany's GP, too, questions need to be asked about the long-term future of F1 and how it sees itself. Time will tell.

MELBOURNE

Australia had to wait an age to host a round of the World Championship, until 1985, but Melbourne's race now feels like part of F1's traditions, as home to the opening round of the year.

Some circuits stand out as great places to go racing, as they're circuits with wonderful sections of sweeping corners where the cars look at their best, but also dotted with tight corners at the end of long straights where overtaking is more than a possibility.

Melbourne's Albert Park is not one of these. Its parkland setting constricts it to such an extent that its lap around the lake in the middle of the park is too frequently interrupted by yet another corner, so it cannot achieve the sort of flow offered by the likes of Silverstone, Suzuka or Spa-Francorchamps. Yet, the fact that racing happens at all so close to the centre of Melbourne, drawing wonderful crowds, is more than a balance for this.

In truth, races in Albert Park are remembered more for incident than lights-to-flag racing, but the fact that a new season is underway, giving F1 fanatics a first chance to see how their heroes will perform in the new campaign, more than makes up for this.

The lap has a feel of being in three parts. The first part runs from the right/left esse of Turns 1 and 2 to Turn 7, with trees flanking the ever-present concrete barriers through the sequence of tight turns. Then comes the second section, with trees no longer shading the track, giving it a more expansive feel as drivers get to stretch their legs through the long left-handed sweeper around the far side of the leg. Heavy braking into Turn 13 marks the start of the third part, a series of slower turns between the trees and grandstands, with the final corner far tighter than it appears.

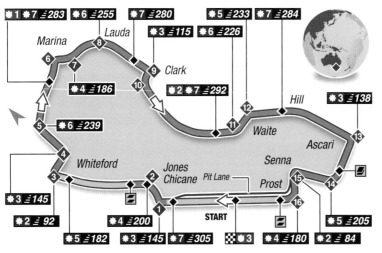

■1 Gear **☰111** Km/h **■1** Timing sector **⧉** DRS detection **⧉** DRS activation

2016 POLE TIME: **HAMILTON (MERCEDES)**, 1M23.837S, 141.494MPH/227.713KPH
2016 WINNER'S AVERAGE SPEED: 104.095MPH/167.525KPH

2016 FASTEST LAP: **RICCIARDO (RED BULL)**, 1M28.997S, 133.290MPH/214.510KPH
LAP RECORD: **M SCHUMACHER (FERRARI)**, 1M24.125S, 141.016MPH/226.944KPH, 2004

INSIDE TRACK
AUSTRALIAN GRAND PRIX

Date:	**26 March**
Circuit name:	**Albert Park**
Circuit length:	**3.295 miles/5.300km**
Number of laps:	**58**
Email:	**enquiries@grandprix.com.au**
Website:	**www.grandprix.com.au**

PREVIOUS WINNERS

2007	**Kimi Raikkonen** FERRARI
2008	**Lewis Hamilton** McLAREN
2009	**Jenson Button** BRAWN
2010	**Jenson Button** McLAREN
2011	**Sebastian Vettel** RED BULL
2012	**Jenson Button** McLAREN
2013	**Kimi Raikkonen** LOTUS
2014	**Nico Rosberg** MERCEDES
2015	**Lewis Hamilton** MERCEDES
2016	**Nico Rosberg** MERCEDES

Location: Albert Park isn't in the city centre, but it's just a short tram ride to the track in the inner suburbs of Melbourne. As a consequence, there are few traffic jams.

How it started: Despite having two World Champions, Jack Brabham and Alan Jones, Australia only landed its first World Championship round at Adelaide in 1986. It was in 1996 that its more celebrated sporting cousin, Melbourne, took over the race.

Most memorable race: The 1999 grand prix was ace, but for spectacle, the race in 1996 stands out. The field got through Turn 1, but Martin Brundle caught all the attention when his Jordan took flight into Turn 3 after David Coulthard's McLaren had been knocked into its path. It ended up a Williams one-two, as Damon Hill finished ahead of Jacques Villeneuve, who had led on his debut until slowed by an oil leak with five laps to go.

Australia's greatest drivers: Jack Brabham won the F1 title in 1959 and 1960 for Cooper, then became champion in a car fielded by his own team in 1966. Alan Jones was World Champion with Williams in 1980.

Rising star: Australia's greatest rising talent is Will Power, but he seems unlikely to make the move from Indycars, in which he was champion in 2014.

SHANGHAI

China took a while to embrace F1 but, with the rise of its middle class and young Chinese drivers ascending racing's ladder, the attitude has changed. Now it just needs to fill the grandstands.

Familiarity can breed contempt, but no arrival at the Shanghai International Circuit can fail to impress, unless the frequent smog is obscuring the view, as the facilities are otherworldly in scale. These aren't pit buildings on a conventional scale, but a supersized version that would fit well into the city's central business district. Everything is huge, even the paddock, which is so large that many use scooters to travel from one end to the other.

The circuit itself is a work of art, one of Hermann Tilke's best, with clever use of the minimal gradient in the first sequence of corners augmented by a sweeping middle section that is broken up by two hairpins and then the epic back straight down to the best overtaking spot at Turn 14.

The first three corners need to be considered as one, as the track turns right and up at Turn 1. It then keeps turning right as it crests at Turn 2 before dipping sharply down into the tight left of Turn 3. Get shoved off the racing line at Turn 1 and the rest is compromise.

Turn 6, a righthand hairpin after a kink, offers excitement, and a bent nose wing or two. Turn 11 then initiates a reversed version of Turns 1 to 3, albeit without much gradient change. However, the circuit's trademark is the 200mph straight down to Turn 14, where most of the passing happens.

All too often, the place used to lack atmosphere, with the giant grandstands at Turns 11 to 13 empty. However, increasingly large crowds are being attracted, adding extra passion to the event.

INSIDE TRACK
CHINESE GRAND PRIX

Date:	**9 April**
Circuit name:	**Shanghai International Circuit**
Circuit length:	**3.390 miles/5.450km**
Number of laps:	**56**
Email:	**f1@china-sss.com**
Website:	**www.f1china.com.cn**

PREVIOUS WINNERS	
2007	**Kimi Raikkonen** FERRARI
2008	**Lewis Hamilton** McLAREN
2009	**Sebastian Vettel** RED BULL
2010	**Jenson Button** McLAREN
2011	**Lewis Hamilton** McLAREN
2012	**Nico Rosberg** MERCEDES
2013	**Fernando Alonso** FERRARI
2014	**Lewis Hamilton** MERCEDES
2015	**Lewis Hamilton** MERCEDES
2016	**Nico Rosberg** MERCEDES

Location: Shanghai International Circuit is far from the city centre, being 20 miles to the north. However, such is the rate of urban spread that it will surely be a suburb soon.
How it started: The World Championship wanted to have a race in China and the government wanted the exposure, so the money was found to ensure it happened, with the circuit rising from a swamp and amazing all who turned up for F1's first visit in 2004 by its sheer size.
Most memorable race: There have been many races in which there have been moments of excitement, yet none can match 2007's grand prix for sheer drama. It was all looking good for Lewis Hamilton to stride towards a rookie F1 title, but the weather was changeable and McLaren tarried too long before calling him in to change tyres. Lacking grip, he slid into a gravel trap and certain victory turned to disaster as Ferrari's Kimi Raikkonen took the points that would help him to the title.
Rising star: Three Chinese drivers have tested F1 cars - Franky Cheng, Ho-Pin Tung and Ma Qing Hua - but all have moved on, leaving European F3 racer Guan Yu Zhou as the nation's greatest hope.

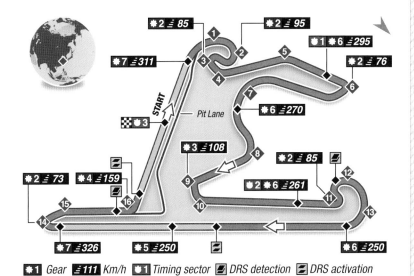

1 *Gear* **111** *Km/h* **1** *Timing sector* *DRS detection* *DRS activation*

2016 POLE TIME: **ROSBERG (MERCEDES), 1M35.402S, 127.811MPH/205.693KPH**
2016 WINNER'S AVERAGE SPEED: **115.002MPH/185.078KPH**

2016 FASTEST LAP: **HULKENBERG (FORCE INDIA), 1M39.824S, 122.150MPH/196.581KPH**
LAP RECORD: **M SCHUMACHER (FERRARI), 1M32.238S 132.202MPH/212.759KPH, 2004**

SAKHIR

In 2004, Bahrain won the race to become the first Middle Eastern country to host a round of the World Championship, but it has since been overshadowed by Abu Dhabi.

When drawing up a World Championship venue to break its traditional bounds of Europe and a few outposts beyond, a circuit in a desert would possibly be on the wish list to provide a different backdrop. That its race would be government-backed would help with the problem of how to raise the funds to bring F1 to town. And so it was that, in 2004, F1's teams were faced with the problem of sand blowing across the track for the first time since they had deserted Zandvoort, home of the Dutch GP, after 1985. Bahrain had joined the show and has remained so every year since, bar 2011 when political unrest led to the World Championship staying away.

Like at Sepang, and also Shanghai, the Sakhir International Circuit's first corner turns sharply right, then immediately doubles back on itself before opening out after Turn 3. Jockeying for position on the dash to the first corner can mean being on the correct line into Turn 1, but not so for Turn 2.

Hermann Tilke designed the circuit so that the area around the pits was an oasis, that's to say with grass verges and the odd palm tree around the elaborate buildings. Out of Turn 3, the track enters the desert sector that covers most of the lap, with a rocky landscape. After the first visit, it was clear that more needed to be done to keep sand from blowing on to the sweeping corners, so the surrounding area is sprayed with glue to prevent drivers finding themselves in a 180mph slide...

The key to a good lap is a clean run through Turns 14 and 15 on to the start/finish straight.

INSIDE TRACK
BAHRAIN GRAND PRIX

Date:	**16 April**
Circuit name:	**Bahrain International Circuit**
Circuit length:	**3.363 miles/5.412km**
Number of laps:	**57**
Email:	**info@bic.com.bh**
Website:	**www.bahraingp.com.bh**

PREVIOUS WINNERS

2006	**Fernando Alonso** RENAULT
2007	**Felipe Massa** FERRARI
2008	**Felipe Massa** FERRARI
2009	**Jenson Button** BRAWN
2010	**Fernando Alonso** FERRARI
2012	**Sebastian Vettel** RED BULL
2013	**Sebastian Vettel** RED BULL
2014	**Lewis Hamilton** MERCEDES
2015	**Lewis Hamilton** MERCEDES
2016	**Nico Rosberg** MERCEDES

Location: The land to the south of capital city Manama is rocky and dusty desert, an inhospitable outback but, as it had no other uses, the circuit was built at Sakhir.

How it started: Through the 1990s, Bahrain began to feel it was in the shadow of one of its neighbours as Dubai made a global name for itself by hosting international sporting events. To regain some glory, Bahrain clinched a round of the F1 World Championship for 2004 with a brand-new, state-funded circuit.

Most memorable race: The 2009 Bahrain GP was made interesting by little-fancied Toyota leading, but the race here in 2015 was intriguing right to the finish. Lewis Hamilton won, but his Mercedes was hampered by brake-by-wire problems, as was team-mate Nico Rosberg's and Kimi Raikkonen closed right in in his Ferrari, passing Rosberg with a lap to go.

Rising star: Bahrain has never had a champion driver, in any category of top-line circuit racing, with Hamad Al Fardan's title in Asian FV6 in 2009 its most meritorious. Of its current young guns, Ali Al Khalifa is the best placed, racing in the BRDC British F3 Championship last year, albeit without success.

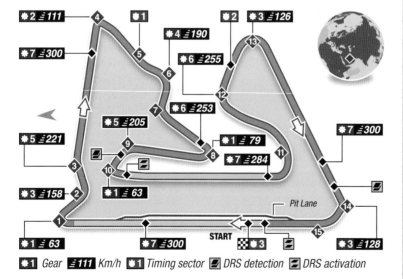

❋1 *Gear* **≡111** *Km/h* **❏1** *Timing sector* **▨** *DRS detection* **▧** *DRS activation*

2016 POLE TIME: **HAMILTON (MERCEDES),**
1M29.493S, 135.276MPH/217.706KPH
2016 WINNER'S AVERAGE SPEED:
122.804MPH/197.634KPH

2016 FASTEST LAP: **ROSBERG (MERCEDES),**
1M34.482S, 128.133MPH/206.210KPH
LAP RECORD: **M SCHUMACHER (FERRARI),**
1M30.252S, 134.262MPH/216.074KPH, 2004

SOCHI

Last year's spring date for the Russian GP made the teams learn Sochi afresh, as cooler conditions changed the track's nature, making it harder to find grip from tyres not up to temperature.

This is a circuit on the coast, of the Black Sea, not that the drivers would know, since at no point can they see it as they drive around the Sochi Autodrom. Instead, they can see the mountains in the background – home of the 2014 Winter Olympic Games – a few buildings, grandstands and concrete walls surrounding every metre of the lap.

Fortunately, there's run-off too, as some notably high speeds can be achieved, especially after the kink on the run to the first real corner, Turn 2, with the fastest drivers touching 200mph before having to hit the brakes hard to be able to negotiate the 90-degree right. On the opening lap, especially, this is the best place for drivers to try to overtake.

What follows is a seemingly never-ending lefthander that turns through about 160 degrees before snapping to the right at Turn 4. Then the next quarter of the lap is a sequence of short straights and fairly tight corners, making it difficult for drivers to find a flow.

Fortunately, it opens out again after Turn 8, with an arcing stretch down to the right/left Turn 11/12 complex, with braking from 190mph required. There is plenty of run-off ahead of them as they turn in, but it's easy to wash wide over the outer kerb, thus compromising the second part of the combination.

From here to the end of the lap it's more of the same, with short straights and tight corners. A tidy entry is required for the final corner, as optimum balance on exiting is crucial for getting the power down as early as possible for the blast past the pits.

INSIDE TRACK
RUSSIAN GRAND PRIX

Date:	**30 April**
Circuit name:	**Sochi Autodrom**
Circuit length:	**3.634 miles/5.848km**
Number of laps:	**53**
Email:	**info@sochiautodrom.ru**
Website:	**www.sochiautodrom.ru/en**

PREVIOUS WINNER

2014	**Lewis Hamilton** MERCEDES
2015	**Lewis Hamilton** MERCEDES
2016	**Nico Rosberg** MERCEDES

Location: Sochi is a year-round resort on Russia's Black Sea coast, with the Caucasus mountains behind for skiing in winter. The Sochi Autodrom is to the edge of the city, making use of some of the buildings erected when the city hosted the Winter Olympics at the start of 2014.

How it started: It took a long flirtation before a Russian GP became part of the World Championship. There had been several plans for circuits to be built near Moscow then one near St Petersburg. However, nothing happened until President Putin gave the go-ahead for the Sochi Autodrom, with the first Russian GP being held in 2014.

Most memorable race: Of the three grands prix held at Sochi Autodrom, the first remains the most exciting, with images still strong of Nico Rosberg locking up and ruining his chances as he dived past Lewis Hamilton into Turn 2 on the opening lap. Because he'd flat-spotted his tyres, Rosberg had to pit and so presented the race to his Mercedes team-mate on a platter. Their dominance was such that Rosberg was able to race back through the field to finish second ahead of Williams' Valtteri Bottas.

Russia's greatest drivers: There has yet to be a Russian F1 winner, but both Vitaly Petrov and Daniil Kvyat have made it to the podium. Petrov did so by finishing third for Renault in Australia in 2011, then Kvyat finished second in Hungary in 2015 and third in China in 2016 for Red Bull Racing, just before being demoted back to Scuderia Toro Rosso.

Circuit map with the following labels:

❄6 ≣265 ❄4 ≣165 10 ❄5 ≣215 ❄2 ❄8 ≣330

❄6 ≣265 · 7 · 8 · 9 · 5 · ❄1 · ❄3 ≣125 · 4 · ❄7 ≣275 · ❄4 ≣165 · 2 · ❄3 ≣125 · ❄8 ≣325 · 3 · 11 · 12 · 13 · 16 · 14 · 15 · ❄2 ≣90 · ❄6 ≣260 · ❄3 ≣115 · 17 · 18 · 1

Pit Lane

❄8 ≣310 · START · ❄3

❄1 *Gear*   ≣111 *Km/h*   ❄1 *Timing sector*   🔲 *DRS detection*   🔲 *DRS activation*

2016 POLE TIME: **ROSBERG (MERCEDES)**, 1M35.417S, 137.098MPH/220.639KPH

2016 WINNER'S AVERAGE SPEED: **124.574MPH/200.482KPH**

2016 FASTEST LAP: **ROSBERG (MERCEDES)**, 1M39.049S, 132.011MPH/212.452KPH

LAP RECORD: **ROSBERG (MERCEDES)**, 1M39.094S, 132.011MPH/212.452KPH, 2016

BARCELONA

When it hosted the Spanish GP for the first time in 1991, Barcelona's Circuit de Catalunya seemed like a brave new world. A quarter of a century later, it feels somewhat outdated.

Back in the 1990s, when F1 testing had no limit, the teams appeared to live at the Circuit de Catalunya. Not only was the weather appreciably warmer for testing than at, say, Silverstone, but also the circuit offered such a broad array of types of corner that it was good for getting an understanding of how their cars would handle at most circuits through the season. Its one letdown was that it had, back then, just one truly fast corner. This was the final one, but even that was neutered in 2007 by the insertion of the chicane just before it that chops its entry speed.

The start/finish straight is a long one, dipping towards its conclusion, and Turn 1 offers a rare chance for a driver to pass the car ahead. Getting alongside on the left, the outside line, tends to compromise a driver's run through Turn 2, from where it's a flat-out blast through long Turn 3, the corner out of which Nico Rosberg and Lewis Hamilton clashed last year.

From here, the circuit uses the gradient of the local hills to twist and dip and then rise through to the midpoint of the lap, with the corner over the crest, Campsa, perhaps the most interesting of the entire lap.

It takes an appreciable speed advantage for a driver to be able to pass into the downhill hairpin, Turn 10, and the tighter Turn 13 and associated insertion of that chicane at Turn 14 have removed the opportunity for drivers to get a great tow on to the start/finish straight and thus to line up a passing move, which is a shame.

The lap is brought to a weak end with the left-then-right chicane before a short blast to the final corner which is taken only in fourth gear and provides little challenge.

INSIDE TRACK
SPANISH GRAND PRIX

Date:	**14 May**
Circuit name:	**Circuit de Catalunya**
Circuit length:	**2.892 miles/4.654km**
Number of laps:	**66**
Email:	**info@circuitcat.com**
Website:	**www.circuitcat.com**

PREVIOUS WINNERS	
2007	**Felipe Massa** FERRARI
2008	**Kimi Raikkonen** FERRARI
2009	**Jenson Button** BRAWN
2010	**Mark Webber** RED BULL
2011	**Sebastian Vettel** RED BULL
2012	**Pastor Maldonado** WILLIAMS
2013	**Fernando Alonso** FERRARI
2014	**Lewis Hamilton** MERCEDES
2015	**Nico Rosberg** MERCEDES
2016	**Max Verstappen** RED BULL

Location: Barcelona has hosted World Championship rounds at two venues within its city bounds but opted in the 1990s to build the Circuit de Catalunya at Montmelo, 15 miles to the north of the city.

How it started: There were Spanish grands prix at Pedralbes, in Barcelona's suburbs, in the 1950s. From 1969 to 1975, Barcelona alternated with Madrid's Jarama on a circuit laid out around its Montjuich Park.

Most memorable race: It's hard not to pick Max Verstappen's maiden win in 2016, but the most memorable race was in 1991, for the moment that Nigel Mansell passed Ayrton Senna, going wheel-to-wheel down the main straight.

Spain's greatest drivers: The list of Spanish racing champions was short before Fernando Alonso came along. There wasn't even a grand prix winner. The Asturian then put that right by claiming the crown in 2005 and 2006 for Renault, then narrowly missing out with McLaren the following year.

Rising star: Jaime Alguersuari came into F1 by 19, and was out of it by 21 to become a DJ. Next in line is clearly Carlos Sainz Jr, but other young Spanish stars are way off F1, with several rungs of junior formulae to negotiate before they go for a seat in F1.

70

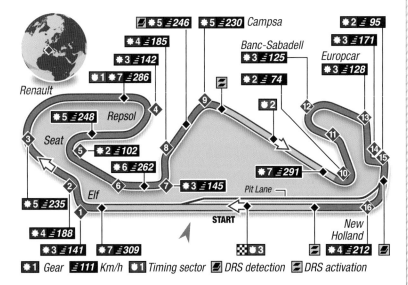

Gear ▮1   Km/h ▰111   Timing sector ◉1   DRS detection ▰   DRS activation ▰

2016 POLE TIME: HAMILTON (MERCEDES),
1M22.000S, 126.986MPH/204.365KPH
2016 WINNER'S AVERAGE SPEED:
112.618MPH/181.241KPH

2016 FASTEST LAP: KVYAT (TORO ROSSO),
1M26.948S, 119.760MPH/192.735KPH
LAP RECORD: RAIKKONEN (FERRARI),
1M21.670S, 127.500MPH/205.192KPH, 2008

MONACO

Monaco is a love it or hate it sort of place for teams and drivers. Facilities are limited and access is awful, but it is, undoubtedly, the jewel in F1's crown, packed with history and rare glamour.

Anyone who tries to tell you that this street circuit in the heart of Monte Carlo hasn't changed since its inception in 1929 is plain wrong. Of course, there have been adaptations over the decades, to make the track safer and flow a little more freely. However, the major changes have come in what lies around it, with villas being replaced by towering blocks of apartments and the yachts moored in the harbour probably trebling in size.

Yet, it is still discernibly the same place, and that's a considerable achievement. It's still the Monaco GP, simply an ancient race in an ancient place made modern.

What is seldom appreciated is that there is very little on the 2.075-mile lap that is either straight or on the level. The start/finish straight is nothing of the sort, curving like a banana. Then it kicks up

an appreciable climb from Ste Devote to Massenet, just before the drivers burst into Casino Square and start dropping again down past Mirabeau to the Grand Hotel hairpin. It falls on from there to Portier where the track turns sharp right as it hits the seafront, arcs right through the tunnel under the Grand Hotel, then slopes down some more to the harbourfront chicane.

The largest grandstands overlook the blast to Tabac and then the sweep through the left/right then right/left esses around Piscine before the tighter left Rascasse hairpin, with just the tricky flick over a brow at Anthony Noghes to complete the lap.

There's precious little space to pass or even to make a mistake, but it's where F1 needs to be as it provides a fabulous backdrop, and the all-important sponsors love it.

INSIDE TRACK
MONACO GRAND PRIX

Date:	**28 May**
Circuit name:	**Monte Carlo Circuit**
Circuit length:	**2.075 miles/3.339km**
Number of laps:	**78**
Email:	**info@acm.mc**
Website:	**www.acm.mc**

PREVIOUS WINNERS	
2007	**Fernando Alonso** McLAREN
2008	**Lewis Hamilton** McLAREN
2009	**Jenson Button** BRAWN
2010	**Mark Webber** RED BULL
2011	**Sebastian Vettel** RED BULL
2012	**Mark Webber** RED BULL
2013	**Nico Rosberg** MERCEDES
2014	**Nico Rosberg** MERCEDES
2015	**Nico Rosberg** MERCEDES
2016	**Lewis Hamilton** MERCEDES

Location: Using both the harbourside and the streets ascending the hills behind, up to a high point at Casino Square, the circuit could not be more centrally located in Monte Carlo.

How it started: This year will be 88 years since a cigarette manufacturer by the name of Anthony Noghes convinced Monaco's royal family that the principality needed a grand prix around its streets, with the first in 1929 being won by William Grover Williams in a Bugatti. Nothing has earned it more fame.

Most memorable race: For pure unadulterated madness, nothing comes close to the 1982 Monaco GP. With three laps to go, Alain Prost crashed his Renault out of the lead. Brabham's Riccardo Patrese led but spun, then stalled. So Didier Pironi took over, but his Ferrari stopped with electrical failure. Andrea de Cesaris should have taken over, only his Alfa Romeo was out of fuel. Derek Daly's Williams, in third, went out with a seized gearbox, allowing Patrese to hit the front again and then take the chequered flag.

Monaco's greatest driver: Many drivers live in Monaco, primarily for tax reasons, but very few actually come from there. Louis Chiron remains the most successful Monegasque racer, thanks to finishing third in his home race in 1950 for the works Maserati team.

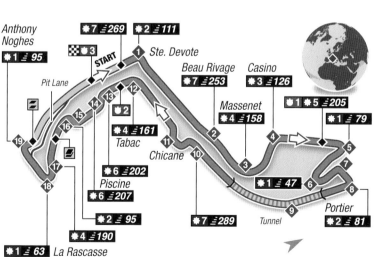

Anthony Noghes				
7 *269*	*2* *111*			
1 *95*	*3* START	*1* Ste. Devote		
Pit Lane		*Beau Rivage* *7* *253*	*Casino* *3* *126*	
	12	*Massenet* *4* *158*		
13	*2* *4* *161*		*1* *5* *205*	
15 *14*	*Tabac*		*1* *79*	
16	*11*		*4*	
19	*Chicane* *10*	*2*	*5*	
17	*6* *202*	*3*	*7*	
18	*Piscine* *6* *207*	*1* *47* *6*	*8*	
	2 *95*	*9*	*Portier* *2* *81*	
	4 *190*	*7* *289* *Tunnel*		
1 *63* *La Rascasse*				

1 Gear   *111* Km/h   *1* Timing sector   DRS detection   DRS activation

2016 POLE TIME: **RICCIARDO (RED BULL),** 1M13.622S, 101.391MPH/163.174KPH
2016 WINNER'S AVERAGE SPEED: 81.215MPH/130.703KPH

2016 FASTEST LAP: **HAMILTON (MERCEDES),** 1M17.939S, 95.755MPH/154.135KPH
LAP RECORD: **M SCHUMACHER (FERRARI),** 1M14.439S, 100.369MPH/161.528KPH, 2004

Most grand prix circuits are situated in the countryside, but Montreal is a short hop from downtown and its metropolitan flavour makes it one of the tracks the F1 teams love the most.

On paper, the Circuit Gilles Villeneuve shouldn't work as a place for great racing, as it's too narrow, many of its corners seeming too tight. Fortunately, cars don't go racing on paper...

Ever since its World Championship bow in 1978, this circuit on a narrow island in the St Lawrence Seaway has provided great racing with way more than its share of incident. It is considered to be the result of the lap's several long straights followed by tight corners, where heavy braking is required.

The layout of the start of the lap doesn't look that promising, however the kink to the right before the first turn leads to the pack resorting on the opening lap with the chance of contact either at the left or the entry to Island Hairpin that follows directly after it.

Once through here, it's hard acceleration in a chasm of concrete as the track turns towards the city on the far side of the river and snakes its way around the back of the circuit. Overtaking is possible, but not always well advised. Get a good run out of Pont de la Concorde, though, and a lunge up the inside into L'Epingle hairpin can yield results, although they're not always as the driver would have wished.

The last chance to make a passing move comes after the long straight past the casino back to the final chicane.It is where drivers have to haul their cars down from close to 200mph and the view through the corner is denied until the driver is almost upon it. The wall on the exit of the corner has been the resting place of many a broken car.

72

INSIDE TRACK
CANADIAN GRAND PRIX

Date:	**11 June**
Circuit name:	**Circuit Gilles Villeneuve**
Circuit length:	**2.710 miles/4.361km**
Number of laps:	**70**
Email:	**info@circuitgillesvilleneuve.ca**
Website:	**www.circuitgillesvilleneuve.ca**

PREVIOUS WINNERS

2006	**Fernando Alonso** RENAULT
2007	**Lewis Hamilton** McLAREN
2008	**Robert Kubica** BMW SAUBER
2010	**Lewis Hamilton** McLAREN
2011	**Jenson Button** McLAREN
2012	**Lewis Hamilton** McLAREN
2013	**Sebastian Vettel** RED BULL
2014	**Daniel Ricciardo** RED BULL
2015	**Lewis Hamilton** MERCEDES
2016	**Lewis Hamilton** MERCEDES

Location: Look across the St Lawrence River from downtown and you can see Ile de Notre Dame, site of the Circuit Gilles Villeneuve and the venue of Expo 67, the World's Fair. The rowing lake was used in the 1976 Olympics.

How it started: Canada had grands prix at Mosport Park, near Toronto, from 1967, and two at Ste Jovite, until 1977. However, it wanted one closer to a metropolitan area and so created this one just as Gilles Villeneuve's career took off. His win, on Montreal's debut in 1978, was a fairytale start.

Most memorable race: Jenson Button's win against the odds for McLaren in 2011 has yet to be beaten. He had a clash with team-mate Lewis Hamilton, took a drivethrough penalty, endured a two-hour stoppage after torrential rain, had a puncture and still passed Sebastian Vettel on the last lap.

Canada's greatest drivers: Gilles Villeneuve, never a World Champion, remains Canada's stand-out driver, but his son Jacques was. Gilles was spectacular, some said taking too many risks, but he won the hearts of F1 fans with his maximum attack style. Sadly he died in qualifying for the 1982 Belgian GP at Zolder.

Rising star: New to F1 in 2017 is 18-year-old Lance Stroll, the son of a billionaire, who owns a stake in the Williams F1 team.

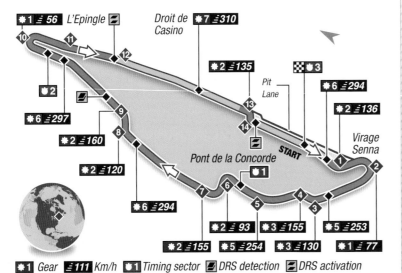

1 Gear · 111 Km/h · 1 Timing sector · DRS detection · DRS activation

2016 POLE TIME: **HAMILTON (MERCEDES),**
1M12.812S, 133.979MPH/215.618KPH
2016 WINNER'S AVERAGE SPEED:
124.946MPH/201.081KPH

2016 FASTEST LAP: **ROSBERG (MERCEDES),**
1M15.599S, 129.039MPH/207.669KPH
LAP RECORD: **BARRICHELLO (FERRARI),**
1M13.622S, 132.511MPH/213.256KPH, 2004

BAKU

With a top speed of 235mph, achieved at the end of a long run from Turn 16 to Turn 1, this new street circuit provided the fast with the tight and slow that left drivers with their hearts in their mouths.

Oil-rich Azerbaijan secured a grand prix for last year and into the future not because the government or country had a love of motor racing, but because it wanted another prestige event to use as a showcase. It was awarded the right to host the Grand Prix of Europe which was a loophole as the country lies beyond its boundaries, but done to use one of the allocated dates allotted to grands prix in Europe. For 2017, though, it will bear its own identity and run as the Azerbaijan GP.

By employing circuit architect Hermann Tilke to shape a layout from its streets, it was always going to include the capital's premier street: Baku Boulevard. Long and wide, with the Caspian Sea to drivers' right, it offered an obvious start/finish straight, being in front of the government buildings

as well as a straight down which speeds seen only the Valencia street circuit have been seen in recent years. As with almost all street circuits, there are 90-degree turns to be negotiated, but this circuit has fewer than many as there are few such corners in the streetscape around the old town. Instead, the drivers had to thread their cars through a hairpin and then an incredibly narrow esse at Turn 8 as they worked their way around Maiden Tower.

From here, the drivers have to keep turning left as they run anti-clockwise around the jagged edge of the old town. Then, if a driver is to make a good exit from just one corner all lap, they pray that it's Turn 16, as this 90-degree left brings the cars on to a kinked but flat-out run all the way to Turn 1.

INSIDE TRACK
AZERBAIJAN GRAND PRIX

Date:	**25 June**
Circuit name:	**Baku Street Circuit**
Circuit length:	**3.753 miles/6.006km**
Number of laps:	**51**
Email:	**info.bakugp.az**
Website:	**www.bakugp.az**

PREVIOUS WINNERS

2016	**Nico Rosberg** MERCEDES

Location: Look for Europe in an atlas and keep going east until you hit Azerbaijan, with the circuit in the centre of capital city Baku on the southern face of the Absheron Peninsula where it protrudes into the Caspian Sea. It is known as the "City of Winds", with the Khazri from the north keeping it cool in summer.

How it started: Bahrain and Abu Dhabi used their oil wealth to build new circuits and buy their entry into the World Championship. Seeing this, and the global image it concocted for each of them, Azerbaijan wanted to use its oil wealth to do the same. Its first step was to host a race for GT cars, something it did three times, with ones in 2013 and 2014 for the prestigious Blancpain Sprint series. Then, after saying that it would build a different street track layout, its debut was put back from 2015, and it held a grand prix for the first time last year.

Most memorable race: The GT races weren't particularly notable, so the best race in Baku so far has to be its maiden grand prix last year, even though Mercedes' Nico Rosberg controlled proceedings from start to finish, helped first by Lewis Hamilton starting 10th after clipping a wall in qualifying, and then having an ERS setting problem, leaving him fifth at the end and Ferrari's Sebastian Vettel in second place, 16s down on Rosberg.

Rising star: There are no Azerbaijani drivers on the international racing scene, and never have been, so the government must be hoping that they can throw some funds around and find one. Building a permanent race circuit will help, or invest considerably in a selection of drivers to race overseas.

73

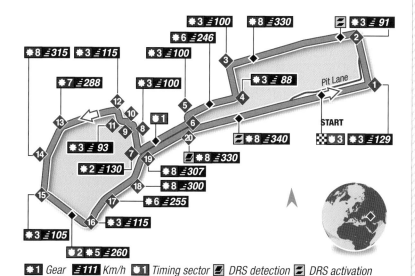

⚙1 *Gear* ⚡111 *Km/h* ⏱1 *Timing sector* 📊 *DRS detection* 📊 *DRS activation*

2016 POLE TIME: **ROSBERG (MERCEDES),**
1M42.758S, 130.678MPH/210.307PH
2016 WINNER'S AVERAGE SPEED:
129.858MPH/197.721KPH

2016 FASTEST LAP: **ROSBERG (MERCEDES),**
1M46.485S, 126.105MPH/202.946KPH
LAP RECORD: **ROSBERG (MERCEDES),**
1M46.485S, 126.105MPH/202.946KPH, 2016

The scenery is breathtaking, but even if the track lacks high-speed corners, Turn 2 can always be relied on to be the scene of action. Just ask Nico Rosberg and Lewis Hamilton...

Any country that can produce Jochen Rindt, Niki Lauda and Gerhard Berger is deserving of a great circuit. For many years it had just that: the Osterreichring. The modern Red Bull Ring is not the Osterreichring, merely a circuit using most of the old layout, albeit with the best bits chopped off. The news that circuit owner Dietrich Mateschitz wants to restore it to something close to the Osterreichring format is wonderful indeed.

The key is the setting. Photographers cannot help but take stunning shots of this circuit, built on a mountainside in the picturesque Styrian region. The pits are set close to the meadows, before the track climbs a slope almost up to the treeline.

The sharp slope away from the start-line is as it was in the Osterreichring days, but the first corner, at its crest, is closer than it was before. Then it's up a gentle slope with a left kink before it kicks up at the end to Turn 2, Remus, the corner where most of the action happens. This tight right feeds the circuit across the face of the hillside before dipping down to Schlossgold, a tightish right.

The middle section is a collection of mid-speed corners as the cars work their way back down to just behind the paddock before rising slightly, running through a band of woods and reaching the final two corners. The first of these is Rindt - named after Austria's first World Champion - a tricky right where the track falls away sharply, and the dipping Red Bull Mobile that returns the drivers to the start/finish straight.

74

INSIDE TRACK
AUSTRIAN GRAND PRIX

Date:	**9 July**
Circuit name:	**Red Bull Ring**
Circuit length:	**2.688 miles/4.326km**
Number of laps:	**71**
Email:	**information@projekt-spielberg.at**
Website:	**www.projekt-spielberg.at**

PREVIOUS WINNERS

1997	**Jacques Villeneuve** WILLIAMS
1998	**Mika Hakkinen** McLAREN
1999	**Eddie Irvine** FERRARI
2000	**Mika Hakkinen** McLAREN
2001	**David Coulthard** McLAREN
2002	**Michael Schumacher** FERRARI
2003	**Michael Schumacher** FERRARI
2014	**Nico Rosberg** MERCEDES
2015	**Nico Rosberg** MERCEDES
2016	**Lewis Hamilton** MERCEDES

Location: No World Championship circuit is as remote from major cities as the Red Bull Ring. Its hillside location, above the village of Zeltweg, is 44 miles north-west of Graz.

How it started: Austria's first taste of racing's big time came on a temporary circuit marked out by hay-bales on Zeltweg's military airfield in 1963. This was upgraded to a World Championship round in 1964, but was too bumpy for F1 cars and a purpose-built circuit, called the Osterreichring, was built just up the valley slope. It hosted World Championship rounds 1970-87, was shortened and revamped as the A-1 Ring, 1997-2003, before further work and rebranding saw the Red Bull Ring return in 2014.

Most memorable race: Only races on the Osterreichring can be considered for this. The 1982 GP provided a super-close finish between Elio de Angelis and Keke Rosberg, Lotus pipping Williams, but the 1975 race is recalled for Vittorio Brambilla crashing in the rain immediately after taking a surprise win and wiping the nose off his March.

Greatest Austrian drivers: Jochen Rindt was Austria's first - and F1's only posthumous - World Champion, in 1970. Niki Lauda was thrice a champion, in 1975, 1997 and 1984. Also Gerhard Berger won 10 Grands Prix.

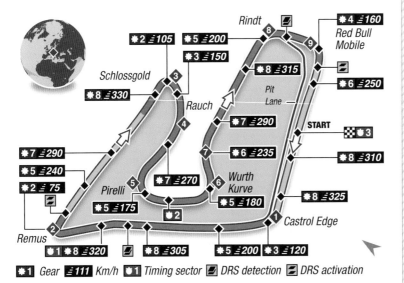

1 Gear **≡111** Km/h **1** Timing sector **⊿** DRS detection **⊿** DRS activation

2016 POLE TIME: **HAMILTON (MERCEDES), 1M07.922S, 142.471MPH/229.286KPH**
2016 WINNER'S AVERAGE SPEED: **130.614MPH/210.203KPH**

2016 FASTEST LAP: **HAMILTON (MERCEDES), 1M08.411S, 141.453MPH/227.647KPH)**
LAP RECORD: **M SCHUMACHER (FERRARI), 1M08.337S, 141.606MPH/227.894KPH, 2003**

SILVERSTONE

There can be no denying that some circuits have a greater standing than others. Silverstone is one such venue, as it hosted the first World Championship round in 1950 and it is going strong today.

Silverstone is one of the circuits that has changed the most over the decades, yet its essence is not that far from that of the circuit layout that got the World Championship off the mark 67 years ago. That's not surprising, though, as a track built on an airfield is always going to feel like a track built on an airfield: it's open, fast and often windswept.

What Silverstone has always had, however, is flow, corners coming in a sequence rather than one at a time, and a good exit from one can be carried through several of the more open stretches.

Since the latest transformation – moving the pits from after Woodcote to after Club on the opposite side of the track – the start of the lap has been changed. Instead of simply the sweep through Copse, drivers now have to turn right, at speed, through

Abbey, then Farm, before standing on the anchors for the hairpin at Village, where contact is no stranger.

The Loop follows before drivers accelerate hard through Aintree on to the Wellington Straight. The next passing point is at Luffield at the conclusion of the sector. Copse remains a challenge, but it's nothing next to the kink at Maggots followed by the wonderful esses at Becketts.

The Hangar Straight down to Stowe isn't a place for slipstreaming any more, with overtaking now more likely to take place at the end of the Vale, where the cars have to brake very hard before turning through long, 180-degree Club to complete the lap.

Get the flow right and anything is possible, with crowds flanking the entire tour lapping up the action.

INSIDE TRACK
BRITISH GRAND PRIX

Date:	**16 July**
Circuit name:	**Silverstone**
Circuit length:	**3.659 miles/5.900km**
Number of laps:	**52**
Email:	**sales@silverstone-circuit.co.uk**
Website:	**www.silverstone-circuit.co.uk**

PREVIOUS WINNERS	
2007	**Kimi Raikkonen** FERRARI
2008	**Lewis Hamilton** McLAREN
2009	**Sebastian Vettel** RED BULL
2010	**Mark Webber** RED BULL
2011	**Fernando Alonso** FERRARI
2012	**Mark Webber** RED BULL
2013	**Nico Rosberg** MERCEDES
2014	**Lewis Hamilton** MERCEDES
2015	**Lewis Hamilton** MERCEDES
2016	**Lewis Hamilton** MERCEDES

Location: Silverstone is in open countryside near Towcester on the Northamptonshire side of the border with Buckinghamshire.

How it started: Many airfields, built around the country during WW2, needed to have new uses in peacetime, so it was decided, in 1948, that the one next to Silverstone might work as a motor racing circuit, using a combination of the perimeter roads and the runways. It held its first British GP that year and the first ever World Championship round two years later.

Most memorable race: The atmosphere was electric when Nigel Mansell powered his way to the front past Williams team-mate Nelson Piquet for victory in 1987. However, the race 21 years later was even more action-packed as Lewis Hamilton produced a master-class of how to race in changing conditions as rivals spun around him at rain-lashed Silverstone, going on to win by more than a minute.

Greatest British drivers: The list is long as Britain has had 10 World Champions, with Jackie Stewart and Lewis Hamilton on three each, Jim Clark and Graham Hill on two, and Jenson Button, Mike Hawthorn, Damon Hill, James Hunt, Nigel Mansell and John Surtees on one title apiece.

Rising star: Oliver Rowland is the pick of a trio in GP2, ahead of Jordan King and Alex Lynn.

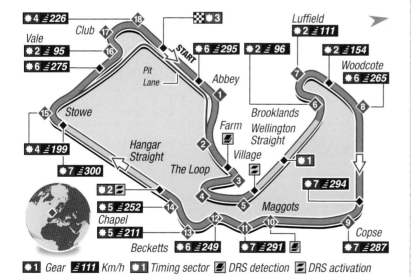

Gear | Km/h | Timing sector | DRS detection | DRS activation

2016 POLE TIME: **HAMILTON (MERCEDES),** 1M29.287S, 147.588MPH/237.521KPH
2016 WINNER'S AVERAGE SPEED: 120.253MPH/193.529KPH

2016 FASTEST LAP: **ROSBERG (MERCEDES),** 1M35.548S, 137.917MPH/221.957KPH
LAP RECORD: **ALONSO (FERRARI),** 1M30.874S, 145.011MPH/233.373KPH, 2011

The narrow streets around Baku's citadel really made the drivers concentrate on F1's first visit to Azerbaijan. This is Sebastian Vettel's Ferrari negotiating Turn 9.

With a little bit of redesigning, to include a few high-speed corners, the Hungaroring could be a great circuit, as its attractive setting deserves more than its mixture of mid-speed turns.

The Hungaroring's greatest ingredient is the topography of its setting. The lap starts on one side of a valley before dropping into the dip, crossing the river at its foot, then rising to the far side before traversing it and making the return journey. Views from either side of the valley are fantastic, not only for the beauty of their spectacle, but also for the sheer amount of the lap that can be taken in.

The drawback is always that the racing has been close, very close, but overtaking moves are few and far between. The advent of DRS has changed that somewhat, for the better, but the thought of how this track could be improved with a few high-speed curves is a tantalising one. The track slopes down to the first corner and it's wide enough

on entry for drivers to at least line up a passing move. However, it then tightens into Turn 2.

On the opening lap, when the field is bunched, places can be made in the melee at Turn 3. Then, falling into the valley, it tends to be line astern, through the blind flick at Turn 5, before its snaking run across the opposite side of the valley offers little.

Any thought that the drivers might be able to line up a passing move are scotched by the tight nature of the remaining corners. Frustratingly, this also includes the uphill, 180-degree final corner, meaning that it's incredibly hard to slipstream and then pass a car of similar performance before having to turn into Turn 1. Thankfully, plenty of drivers still try...

INSIDE TRACK
HUNGARIAN GRAND PRIX

Date:	**30 July**
Circuit name:	**Hungaroring**
Circuit length:	**2.722 miles/4.381km**
Number of laps:	**70**
Email:	**office@hungaroring.hu**
Website:	**www.hungaroring.hu**

PREVIOUS WINNERS

2007	**Lewis Hamilton** McLAREN
2008	**Heikki Kovalainen** McLAREN
2009	**Lewis Hamilton** McLAREN
2010	**Mark Webber** RED BULL
2011	**Jenson Button** McLAREN
2012	**Lewis Hamilton** McLAREN
2013	**Lewis Hamilton** MERCEDES
2014	**Daniel Ricciardo** RED BULL
2015	**Sebastian Vettel** FERRARI
2016	**Lewis Hamilton** MERCEDES

Location: Drive north-east for 12 miles from capital city Budapest, and the Hungaroring can be found just where the river plain kicks up into gentle hills, just above the village of Mogyorod.

How it started: It felt revolutionary when the World Championship changed course to Hungary in 1986, as the country was still behind the Iron Curtain. Yet it was an instant hit and the country's economy then opened up as Communism dwindled a few years later.

Most memorable race: The 2014 encounter, won by Danel Ricciardo for Red Bull, was a great race, but Jenson Button's maiden win in changeable conditions for Honda in 2006 was even more special, as it required immense precision and perfect tactical calls as the circuit dried.

Greatest Hungarian driver: Since only the lacklustre Zsolt Baumgartner has made it to F1, with Jordan - then Minardi - in 2003 and 2004, the greatest driver that this central European country has produced has to be the winner of the first ever grand prix, the French of 1906. This was Ferenc Szisz who triumphed in a works Renault.

Rising star: There are no young Hungarians standing out at present, with Dominik Fekete at the highest level, and that only Auto GP.

78

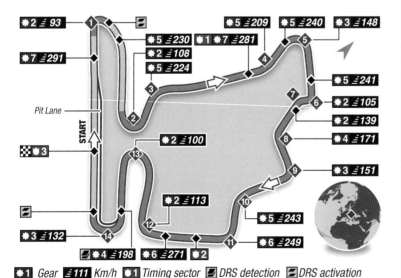

Pit Lane

START

1 *Gear* | **111** *Km/h* | **1** *Timing sector* | **◩** *DRS detection* | **◪** *DRS activation*

2016 POLE TIME: **ROSBERG (MERCEDES)**, 1M19.965S, 122.553MPH/197.231KPH
2016 WINNER'S AVERAGE SPEED: 113.747MPH/183.059KPH

2016 FASTEST LAP: **RAIKKONEN (FERRARI)**, 1M23.086S, 117.950MPH/189.822KPH
LAP RECORD: **M SCHUMACHER (FERRARI)**, 1M19.071S, 123.828MPH/199.282KPH, 2004

The hillside topography provides spectators with wonderful viewing across the valley. This is Valtteri Bottas turning his Williams into Turn 1.

SPA-FRANCORCHAMPS

If the gods designed a circuit, you feel like this would be the result, as it has scenery, high-speed curves, gradient changes and offers fans panoramic views, with rain often spicing up the action.

Not only is the Spa-Francorchamps circuit a magnificent stretch of tarmac, but also it comes with the appreciable bonus of a long and illustrious history that only adds to its mystique. In fact, it celebrates its 93rd birthday in 2017 and early photos show how the downhill/uphill twister of Eau Rouge has always been a challenge. Add to that the history of the great duels here and there is every reason why this Belgian beauty should always host a round of the World Championship.

The uphill dash from the grid to the first bend is the shortest in F1 before the field has to, somehow, feed its way through the tight, righthand hairpin at La Source. Thankfully, there is ample run-off for those who are forced wide.

Then it's downhill to the circuit's landmark corner, Eau Rouge. A kink to the left then sharply right as the circuit bucks upwards is what makes this corner so special, especially as the track then snaps left at its crest at Raidillon, and it's vital for drivers to get hard on the power as soon as possible for the Kemmel Straight that follows.

This uphill straight is long enough to catch a tow, with passing a frequent feature into the esse at the top of the hill, where drivers have to brake hard, jink right then left. From Les Combes, there's a wonderful twisting downhill stretch through the double-apex Pouhon, a lengthy lefthander. The gradient eases off for more twisters down to Campus before a wonderful ascent through Curve Paul Frere and Blanchimont to the Bus Stop. This final corner is a kink left, then a right/left chicane.

»

80

INSIDE TRACK
BELGIAN GRAND PRIX

Date:	**27 August**
Circuit name:	**Spa-Francorchamps**
Circuit length:	**4.352 miles/7.004km**
Number of laps:	**44**
Email: secretariat@spa-francorchamps.be	
Website: www.spa-francorchamps.be	

PREVIOUS WINNERS

2007	**Kimi Raikkonen** FERRARI
2008	**Felipe Massa** FERRARI
2009	**Kimi Raikkonen** FERRARI
2010	**Lewis Hamilton** McLAREN
2011	**Sebastian Vettel** RED BULL
2012	**Jenson Button** McLAREN
2013	**Sebastian Vettel** RED BULL
2014	**Daniel Ricciardo** RED BULL
2015	**Lewis Hamilton** MERCEDES
2016	**Nico Rosberg** MERCEDES

Location: The circuit is inserted into a fold in the hills of the Ardennes, five miles to the south of Spa, just down the slope from the village of Francorchamps, hence the name.

How it started: It is easy to imagine this as a circuit made up of public roads, for that is what it was in 1924. The lap – more triangular in shape and going into the next valley – was nine miles long, but was cut to less than half that length and took on its current shape in 1979.

Most memorable race: Lewis Hamilton was battling against Felipe Massa for the title when F1 visited in 2008. There was a thrilling conclusion as Lewis Hamilton was first to the finish, but he was pushed back to third, behind Ferrari's Massa and BMW Sauber's Nick Heidfeld, as he was hit with a 25s penalty for gaining an advantage by cutting the Bus Stop chicane, even though he gave the position back, albeit accelerating by again before La Source.

Greatest Belgian drivers: Belgium has not produced an F1 champion. Closest was Jacky Ickx, a runner-up for Brabham in 1969 and Ferrari in 1970. Thierry Boutsen won three GPs for Williams in 1989 and 1990.

Rising star: McLaren gave Stoffel Vandoorne his F1 debut in 2016, standing in for Fernando Alonso at the Bahrain GP, finishing 10th.

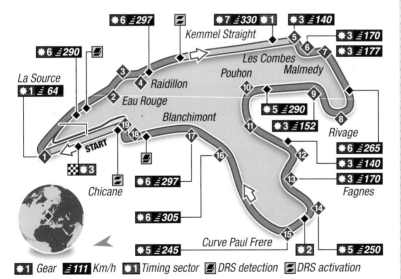

❄1 Gear ≡111 Km/h ▢1 Timing sector ▨ DRS detection ▨ DRS activation

2016 POLE TIME: ROSBERG (MERCEDES), 1M46.744S, 146.774MPH/236.214KPH
2016 WINNER'S AVERAGE SPEED: 109.577MPH/176.351KPH

2016 FASTEST LAP: HAMILTON (MERCEDES), 1M51.583S, 140.700MPH/226.002KPH
LAP RECORD: **VETTEL (RED BULL), 1M47.263S** 146.065MPH/235.069KPH, 2009

MONZA

Negotiations for future races led to stories last year that the Italian GP would be transferred to Imola, but sense has prevailed and this Italian temple to motorsport remains part of the show.

Hosting a round of the World Championship is something desired by countries around the world, many with money to burn but no history of motorsport within their borders. So, when talk is bandied around, usually at contract renewal time, that traditional circuits such as Monza might lose their race, Formula 1 fans throw up their hands in horror. F1 needs places such as these, as they're the backbone of the sport. Imola, albeit with an F1 history of its own, is neither an equivalent nor suitable for the cars.

The essence of Monza can be defined in two elements: the sense of its history, dating back to 1922, and its flow through its parkland setting.

Although the banked oval that was included in its lap until the 1960s is no longer used, the outline of the rest is little changed. The blast to the first chicane is wide, but the right flick is sharp and the left flick even more so. Getting the power down as early as possible for the charge from Variante del Rettifilio through Curva Biassono to the second chicane is vital.

Roggia goes left then right, with a definite overtaking opportunity on the way in. From this second chicane, the track reverts to its pre-1972 format through the pair of righthanded Lesmos and then all the way down the tree-flanked straight back to Ascari.

This is where the third of the chicanes was inserted to break the slipstreaming bunches in 1972 and a slight rise into this left/right combination can unsettle the cars. All that's left of the lap is another straight down to the Curva Parabolica, a long, long righthander on to the start/finish straight.

INSIDE TRACK
ITALIAN GRAND PRIX

Date:	3 September
Circuit name:	Autodromo Monza
Circuit length:	3.600 miles/5.793km
Number of laps:	53
Email:	infoautodromo@monzanet.it
Website:	www.monzanet.it

PREVIOUS WINNERS

2007	**Fernando Alonso** McLAREN
2008	**Sebastian Vettel** TORO ROSSO
2009	**Rubens Barrichello** BRAWN
2010	**Fernando Alonso** FERRARI
2011	**Sebastian Vettel** RED BULL
2012	**Lewis Hamilton** McLAREN
2013	**Sebastian Vettel** RED BULL
2014	**Lewis Hamilton** MERCEDES
2015	**Lewis Hamilton** MERCEDES
2016	**Nico Rosberg** MERCEDES

Location: Milan's suburbs almost spread the 10 miles out to the circuit, but there's a buffer of countryside before the town of Monza and, of course, the royal park in which the circuit is situated.

How it started: This is another circuit dating back to the 1920s. Monza was built in 100 days in 1922 and became famous for having a high-speed bowl that could be included in the lap.

Most memorable race: The 1971 Italian GP was memorable for the first five finishers being covered by just 0.61s. Ten years earlier was memorable, but for all the wrong reasons. Jim Clark's Lotus clashed with Wolfgang von Trips's Ferrari, sending him into a public area before Parabolica, killing him and 13 fans. Von Trips's team-mate Phil Hill won the race and the title.

Greatest Italian drivers: When F1 began in 1950, Italy had the top teams and top drivers. Giuseppe Farina, in 1950, and Alberto Ascari in 1952 and 1953, won titles, but there have been no Italian champions since. The closest were Michele Alboreto, runner-up to Alain Prost in 1985, and Riccardo Patrese, a distant second to Williams team-mate Nigel Mansell in 1992.

Rising star: Raffaele Marciello is most likely to advance to F1 in the near future. A member of the Ferrari Driver Academy since leaving karts in 2011, he was a Sauber F1 test driver in 2015.

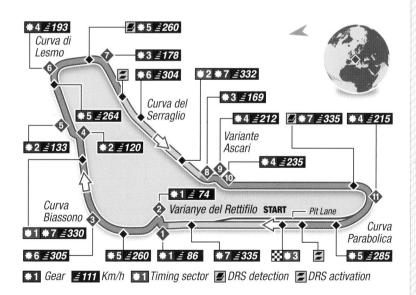

Curva di Lesmo

Curva del Serraglio

Variante Ascari

Curva Biassono

Varianye del Rettifilo START Pit Lane

Curva Parabolica

1 Gear   **111** Km/h   **1** Timing sector   DRS detection   DRS activation

2016 POLE TIME: **HAMILTON (MERCEDES)**, 1M21.135S, 159.734MPH/257.071KPH
2016 WINNER'S AVERAGE SPEED: 147.750MPH/237.798KPH

2016 FASTEST LAP: **ALONSO (McLAREN)**, 1M25.340S, 151.844MPH/244.373KPH
LAP RECORD: **BARRICHELLO (FERRARI)**, 1M21.046S, 159.909MPH/257.349KPH, 2004

MARINA BAY

Nobody can deny that the Singapore skyline is a spectacle, but when the lights go down it can become even more dramatic, especially when the F1 circus comes to town.

A handful of cities host grands prix, but only a few – Monte Carlo, Singapore and now Baku – have their race in their very centre. The others host theirs in the suburbs.

Singapore has long been South-East Asia's predominant trading centre. This commercial success led to a towering central business district and it's there that Singapore chose to host its grand prix, on a circuit at the foot of the buildings that mark its financial pre-eminence. As the race is held after dark, their illuminated forms add extra appeal.

Used since 2008, the Marina Bay Circuit could be described as a series of 90-degree bends with straights in between, but that doesn't do it justice. Indeed, there is way more flow than that, as the straights are long and there are a few open corners to keep speeds high.

Ducking under a flyover – complete with traffic going about its regular duties – the run to the first corner is concluded with a left flick, a swerve to the right and then a left-hand hairpin. A good position into one doesn't necessarily lead to being in the right position into the next part on the opening lap.

Don't expect any passing on the next stretch as the circuit opens out and runs down 185mph Raffles Boulevard to a sharp left at Turn 7. Although the circuit is downtown, the next section winds its way around the Padang playing fields, with the great Turn 11/12 twister.

After crossing the iconic Anderson Bridge, there's a straight up to Turn 14, then a section around and even under grandstands before the long lefthander on to the start/finish straight.

82

INSIDE TRACK
SINGAPORE GRAND PRIX

Date:	**17 September**
Circuit name:	**Marina Bay Circuit**
Circuit length:	**3.152 miles/5.073km**
Number of laps:	**61**
Email:	**info@singaporegp.sg**
Website:	**www.singaporegp.sg**

PREVIOUS WINNERS

2008	**Fernando Alonso** RENAULT
2009	**Lewis Hamilton** McLAREN
2010	**Fernando Alonso** FERRARI
2011	**Sebastian Vettel** RED BULL
2012	**Sebastian Vettel** RED BULL
2013	**Sebastian Vettel** RED BULL
2014	**Lewis Hamilton** MERCEDES
2015	**Sebastian Vettel** FERRARI
2016	**Daniel Ricciardo** RED BULL

Location: The Marina Bay circuit is right in the heart of the city, running along Singapore's main streets and under its flyovers.

How it started: Although expats working in Singapore organised races on a street circuit in the 1960s and early 1970s, it took until 2008 for a circuit good enough for F1 to be created when the nation was welcomed into the World Championship, with its agreement to run the race after dark meaning that it happened at peak European afternoon TV viewing time.

Most memorable race: The race in 2008 is remembered for Nelson Piquet Jr crashing his Renault intentionally to bring out the safety car to help team-mate Fernando Alonso, but 2015's is recalled for more regular mayhem. Mercedes was off form, giving Ferrari and Red Bull the chance of glory. Daniel Ricciardo was left cursing a safety car period, caused by a fan walking on the track; he felt it scuppered his chances and helped Sebastian Vettel to triumph.

Rising star: No Singaporean drivers have yet made it to F1, so one needs to go to the junior single-seater categories to see where the first might come from. Singapore-born Brit Richard Bradley was the most proficient, but he is now in the World Endurance Championship, racing sports-prototypes. So, although he's only 14, look to Danial Nielsen Frost, who was a race winner in South-East Asian F4 last year.

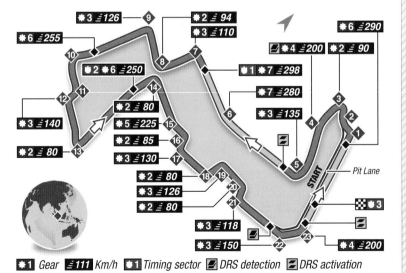

♦1 *Gear* **≡111** *Km/h* **◐1** *Timing sector* **◪** *DRS detection* **◪** *DRS activation*

2016 POLE TIME: **ROSBERG (MERCEDES),**
1M42.584S, 110.614MPH/178.028KPH
2016 WINNER'S AVERAGE SPEED:
99.609MPH/160.316KPH

2016 FASTEST LAP: **RICCIARDO (RED BULL),**
1M47.187S, 105.696.MPH/170.113KPH
LAP RECORD: **RAIKKONEN (FERRARI),**
1M45.599S, 107.358MPH/172.776KPH, 2008

SEPANG

Sepang was once the future. On its debut in 1999, this track, cut from a palm plantation near Kuala Lumpur airport, heralded a series of tailor-made venues. It's still great, but no longer startling.

Hermann Tilke was little known as other than a German club racer until he started designing circuits and Sepang was his first for F1. Offered a virgin plot, he crafted a circuit that was a real breath of fresh -- albeit searing hot and very humid - air when it broke cover at the end of the 1990s.

The Sepang circuit oozed flow, sweeping its way around its compound, with more long turns than straights. What we didn't know at the time was that the first corner sequence would become a Tilke trademark, with its long approach into a tight right that fed almost immediately into a second turn that flicked the cars back the other way. Then, with a third turn to keep the drivers fighting for position, it finally opens out.

Using the available gradient, the track drops a little as it arcs right before a short straight, with a flick up at its end as drivers hit the brakes hard for Turn 4. After this tight right, there starts a snaking sequence through Turns 5 and 6, where balance is everything, then on to Turn 9, a lefthand hairpin that is slightly uphill at its exit.

Cresting the short rise that follows, open reverts to tight at Turn 11 before the track dips downwards again in a wonderful, twisting run down to Turn 14. This righthand hairpin feeds the cars on to the back straight past the reverse side of the main grandstand up to the final corner, a lefthand hairpin. One of the keys to why Sepang enables so much overtaking is the width of the track, and this offers plenty of scope for different lines, as it does into Turn 1.

INSIDE TRACK
MALAYSIAN GRAND PRIX

Date:	**1 October**
Circuit name:	**Sepang Circuit**
Circuit length:	**3.444 miles/5.542km**
Number of laps:	**56**
Email:	**inquiries@sepangcircuit.com.my**
Website:	**www.malaysiangp.com.my**

PREVIOUS WINNERS	
2007	**Fernando Alonso** McLAREN
2008	**Kimi Raikkonen** FERRARI
2009	**Jenson Button** BRAWN
2010	**Sebastian Vettel** RED BULL
2011	**Sebastian Vettel** RED BULL
2012	**Fernando Alonso** FERRARI
2013	**Sebastian Vettel** RED BULL
2014	**Lewis Hamilton** MERCEDES
2015	**Sebastian Vettel** FERRARI
2016	**Daniel Ricciardo** RED BULL

Location: The circuit, 30 miles south of the capital Kuala Lumpur, is handy for the international airport, built in a clearing amid palm plantations.

How it started: Malaysia wanted the prestige that F1 brings, particularly to advertise itself as a tourist destination. F1 wanted a race in South-east Asia and so the deal was done. Hermann Tilke produced a landmark design and it was an instant hit from its debut in 1999.

Most memorable race: Sepang has three extreme weather elements: searing heat, towering humidity and torrential rain, the last striking often. In 2001, it came just after the start, and it led not only to Ferrari's downfall but also to its recovery to victory. On lap 3, Michael Schumacher and Rubens Barrichello were first and second, but flew off the track at Turn 5. Along with almost everyone else, they teetered around to the pits but changed not to rain tyres but to intermediates. No one could resist their charge back to the front.

Greatest Malaysian driver: Alex Yoong is the only Malaysian to make it to F1, driving for Minardi 2001-02. He was seventh at Melbourne in 2002, when only eight cars completed.

Rising star: Jazeman Jaafar gave up his F1 dream when not graduating from GP2 in 2015. Nabil Jeffri is now GP2, but with less success.

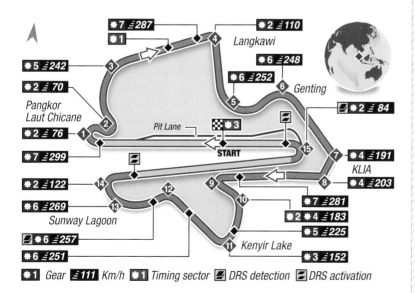

Langkawi

Genting

Pangkor Laut Chicane

Pit Lane

START

KLIA

Sunway Lagoon

Kenyir Lake

1 Gear **111** Km/h **1** Timing sector DRS detection DRS activation

2016 POLE TIME: **HAMILTON (MERCEDES)**, 1M32.850S, 133.508MPH/214.876KPH
2016 WINNER'S AVERAGE SPEED: 119.399MPH/192.167KPH

2016 FASTEST LAP: **ROSBERG (RED BULL)**, 1M36.424S, 128.583MPH/206.948KPH
LAP RECORD: **MONTOYA (WILLIAMS)**, 1M34.223S, 131.991MPH/212.419KPH, 2004

SUZUKA

The weather can be a major factor here, but the principal challenge is the sheer difficulty offered by this old-school circuit's combination of corners. It's very much a drivers' track.

Gradient is one of the key ingredients to the majority of great circuits and, at Suzuka, it's the making of the most challenging corners, from the downhill first corner to the uphill esses.

Apart from the unusual combination of race circuit and fun fair, as they're built on the same site, one thing that strikes first-time visitors to Suzuka is how narrow the circuit is, with a feeling of a lack of space along many of the outer reaches.

The lap starts with a downward-sloping start/finish straight, where First Curve looks benign yet is anything but, because a difficult camber can catch out the unwary. Then the track turns right again and starts its ascent through a wild sequence of esses to Dunlop Curve, a tricky lefthander at the crest of the hill.

A pair of double rights, the second tighter, take the track to one of its most unusual features, where it crosses under itself, under the homeward leg.

The Turn 11 hairpin offers a chance to make a passing move, but space is tight. Then follows a long, long, slightly uphill right that eventually alters course to turn to the left and start a short descent through Spoon Curve on to the back straight. This is lengthy, cars reaching 190mph, and contains seventh-gear 130R, with almost all of that speed needing to be scrubbed off for Casio Triangle, a right/left chicane just before the final right on to the start/finish straight.

Severe weather has struck Suzuka several times over the past decade, with cyclones almost curtailing all action in 2014. When the rain does fall, it offers the chance for the very best to stand out.

INSIDE TRACK
JAPANESE GRAND PRIX

Date:	8 October
Circuit name:	Suzuka Circuit
Circuit length:	3.608 miles/5.806km
Number of laps:	53
Email:	info@suzukacircuit.com.jp
Website:	www.suzukacircuit.co.jp

PREVIOUS WINNERS

2005	**Kimi Raikkonen** McLAREN
2006	**Fernando Alonso** RENAULT
2009	**Sebastian Vettel** RED BULL
2010	**Sebastian Vettel** RED BULL
2011	**Jenson Button** McLAREN
2012	**Sebastian Vettel** RED BULL
2013	**Sebastian Vettel** RED BULL
2014	**Lewis Hamilton** MERCEDES
2015	**Lewis Hamilton** MERCEDES
2016	**Nico Rosberg** MERCEDES

Location: It's not the most obvious place for a circuit to be built, as it's not particularly close to any of Japan's major conurbations. Yet this circuit on a hillside, 30 miles to the south-west of Nagoya, was built principally as a test circuit by Honda.

How it started: National racing was all that was on Suzuka's diet when the circuit opened in 1962 and that was how it stayed for decades. Apart from two grands prix at Fuji in 1976 and 1977, Japan stayed on F1's sidelines until 1987, when Suzuka was given the nod to have a round of the World Championship. Gerhard Berger and Ferrari were the inaugural winners.

Most memorable race: The Japanese GP hosted many title deciders, including Mika Hakkinen and Michael Schumacher's 1998 shoot-out. Michael stalled on pole, so started from the back. His great drive ended with a blow-out, giving Mika the win and the title.

Greatest Japanese drivers: Japan's strong effort to push its best young drivers into F1 has fared poorly. Satoru Nakajima was its first F1 regular, and Aguri Suzuki, Takuma Sato and Kamui Kobayashi all had third-place finishes, but all were shock results in extraordinary races.

Rising star: Nobuharu Matsushita is a driver Honda is pushing towards F1. He raced for ART Grand Prix in GP2 last year and won at Monaco.

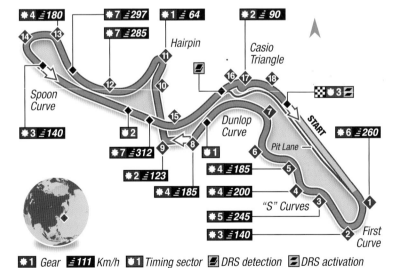

1 Gear **111** Km/h **1** Timing sector ⬛ DRS detection ⬛ DRS activation

2016 POLE TIME: **ROSBERG (MERCEDES), 1M30.647S, 143.267MPH/230.582KPH**
2016 WINNER'S AVERAGE SPEED: **132.280MPH/212.899KPH**

2016 FASTEST LAP: **VETTEL (FERRARI), 1M35.118S, 136.556MPH/219.781KPH**
LAP RECORD: **RAIKKONEN (McLAREN), 1M31.540S, 141.904MPH/228.373KPH, 2005**

84

CIRCUIT OF THE AMERICAS

Financial woes never seem far from the surface at this Texan circuit, but F1 fans undoubtedly hope that they can be sorted out, because it's a great place to go racing and for the USA to watch F1.

The United States of America and Formula 1 have not been easy bedfellows over the decades, since the World Championship made its continental bow at Sebring in the late 1950s – notwithstanding the Indianapolis 500's inclusion in the first 10 World Championships – as the nation has tried to decide how much it likes F1 and whether to support it fully. However, in the Circuit of the Americas, it finally has its first circuit since Watkins Glen in the 1970s that is worthy of the name.

Built from scratch outside the Texas state capital, Austin, COTA was designed by Hermann Tilke to a brief to make a circuit that included curves mimicking the greatest corners from the best circuits around the world.

The steep ascent to Turn 1 is like that at the Red Bull Ring, except that the corner bends left rather than right. Then the track drops down to a righthander, after which a really tricky run of esses follows, most notably from Turns 5 to 9. Any deviation from the ideal line costs momentum.

Descending once more, the track goes out to its most distant point, Turn 11. The return run from this lefthand hairpin is appreciable, affording drivers the chance to catch a slipstream and line up a passing move as they brake from more than 200mph.

Turn 12 is a sharp left and, with the remainder of the lap – eight turns in all – the track weaves its way around its iconic observation tower being tight in formation, it's usually the final chance for drivers to overtake until they reach the end of the start/finish straight on the following lap.

INSIDE TRACK
UNITED STATES GRAND PRIX

Date:	**22 October**
Circuit name:	**Circuit of the Americas**
Circuit length:	**3.400 miles/5.472km**
Number of laps:	**56**
Email:	**info@circuitoftheamericas.com**
Website:	**www.circuitoftheamericas.com**

PREVIOUS WINNERS	
2012	**Lewis Hamilton** McLAREN
2013	**Sebastian Vettel** RED BULL
2014	**Lewis Hamilton** MERCEDES
2015	**Lewis Hamilton** MERCEDES
2016	**Lewis Hamilton** MERCEDES

Location: The circuit is situated on rolling hills around 10 miles to the south-east of the Texan state capital Austin.

How it started: The size of the United States had worked against it building an F1 venue and sticking to it. This is why the USA had nine F1 venues – Sebring, Riverside, Watkins Glen, Long Beach, Caesars Palace, Detroit, Dallas, Phoenix and Indianapolis – before the Circuit of the Americas in Texas was built for F1 in 2012.

Most memorable race: With three wins in the first four visits, Lewis Hamilton has an affinity for the place and his 2012 win remains the pick of these. Sebastian Vettel led from pole, with Mark Webber making it a Red Bull one-two, ahead of Hamilton's McLaren. Hamilton got past the Australian, closed in on Vettel and seized the moment when they came up to lap Narain Karthikeyan's HRT to dive past both at Turn 12 before going on to win.

Greatest American drivers: Phil Hill was America's first World Champion in 1961, and he has three Le Mans 24 Hours wins to his name, but he was outranked by Mario Andretti who won the title in 1978 for Lotus and is armed with four Indycar titles and victory in the 1969 Indianapolis 500 as well.

Rising star: Alexander Rossi was that man, but he left after a handful of outings for Marussia. Forced to try Indycars in 2016, he snapped up its biggest prize: the Indianapolis 500. Gustavo Menezes looked promising, but he has veered from F3 to sportscars, leaving GP3 racer Santino Ferrucci as the next in line.

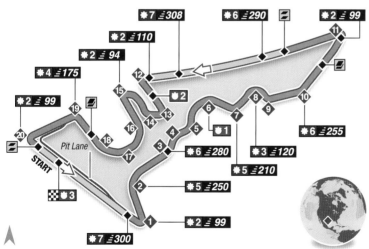

1 Gear   **111** Km/h   **1** Timing sector   DRS detection   DRS activation

2016 POLE TIME: HAMILTON (MERCEDES),
1M34.999S, 128.841MPH/207.362KPH
2016 WINNER'S AVERAGE SPEED:
129.506MPH/208.433KPH

2016 FASTEST LAP: VETTEL (FERRARI),
1M39.877S, 123.465MPH/198.712KPH
LAP RECORD: **VETTEL (RED BULL), 1M39.347S**
124.132MPH/199.772KPH, 2012

MEXICO CITY

One of the most popular sporting returns in recent years has been the World Championship's to Mexico, with huge crowds coming back to the capital city's circuit to cheer on their heroes.

Venturing to pastures new, to countries with money to burn but with little popular love for the sport, hasn't given F1 the best of images. This is why the World Championship's return to Mexico in 2015, after a 23-year hiatus, has given F1 such a welcome boost. The fans, to put it mildly, are chock full of enthusiasm and not afraid to show it.

The Autodromo Hermanos Rodriguez – named after 1960s heroes Ricardo and Pedro (*hermanos* is Spanish for brothers) – is built in a park on the outskirts of the sprawling metropolis and its modern iteration differs only at its conclusion from how it was when these sporting brothers took on the world.

The blast to the first corner along a broad, tree-lined straight, with cars touching 190mph before heavy braking into a 90-degree right and then, almost immediately, the left/right Ese Moises Solana, named after another Mexican racing hero. Another esse, this one left then right, follows at Ese del Lago, before a short straight to the Horquilla hairpin.

Then starts the return journey from this furthest point, with a fabulous run of interconnected sweepers between Turns 9 and 13, all with shade from the park's trees not far away.

The end of the lap is the part where circuit modernisation has led to the greatest transformation. Instead of simply running through one, long, lightly banked righthander back on to the start/finish straight, the lap has been transformed by a sharp right turn some distance before that to thread the circuit into a loop through the grandstands surrounding a baseball stadium and then back out for the second half of the original Peraltada.

INSIDE TRACK
MEXICAN GRAND PRIX

Date:	29 October
Circuit name:	Autodromo Hermanos Rodriguez
Circuit length:	2.747 miles/4.421km
Number of laps:	70
Email:	rosario@cie.com.mx
Website:	
www.autodromohermanosrodriguez.com.mx	

PREVIOUS WINNERS	
1970	**Jacky Ickx** FERRARI
1986	**Gerhard Berger** BENETTON
1987	**Nigel Mansell** WILLIAMS
1988	**Alain Prost** McLAREN
1989	**Ayrton Senna** McLAREN
1990	**Alain Prost** FERRARI
1991	**Riccardo Patrese** WILLIAMS
1992	**Nigel Mansell** WILLIAMS
2015	**Nico Rosberg** MERCEDES
2016	**Lewis Hamilton** MERCEDES

Location: Mexico City sprawls across a huge area in its 6,000-foot-high plateau, with the Autodromo Hermanos Rodriguez being situated in the eastern suburbs.

How it started: The form of the Rodriguez brothers encouraged Mexico to build a home circuit where they could shine, but its maiden F1 event in 1962, a non-championship trial, had a tragic outcome as Ricardo died in practice. The circuit wasn't to blame, so it got a World Championship round from 1963.

Most memorable race: F1 returned to Mexico in 1986 for the penultimate round. Championship challengers Nigel Mansell, Alain Prost and Nelson Piquet all fought hard. But the Pirelli rubber on Gerhard Berger's Benetton lasted best, so the Austrian came through to score both his and the team's first victories.

Greatest Mexican drivers: The Rodriguez brothers remain the best, but both died racing. Ricardo was the quicker, but perished aged 20 in 1962. Pedro won two grands prix, for Cooper in 1967 and for BRM in 1970, but died in a sportscar event at Germany's Norisring in 1971.

Rising stars: Mexico has Esteban Guttierez and Sergio Perez in F1, but their closest challengers from Mexico are not shining in junior formulae.

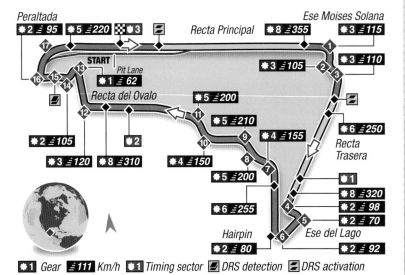

Peraltada
Recta Principal
Ese Moises Solana
START
Pit Lane
Recta del Ovalo
Recta Trasera
Ese del Lago
Hairpin

🔧1 Gear 🏁111 Km/h ⏱1 Timing sector 🔲 DRS detection 🔲 DRS activation

2016 POLE TIME: **HAMILTON (MERCEDES),** 1M18.704S, 125.646MPH/202.221KPH
2016 WINNER'S AVERAGE SPEED: **114.769MPH/184.715KPH**

2016 FASTEST LAP: **RICCIARDO (RED BULL),** 1M21.134S, 118.656MPH/190.972KPH
LAP RECORD: **ROSBERG (MERCEDES),** 1M20.521S, 119.568MPH/192.426KPH, 2015

INTERLAGOS

If Mexico is voluble about F1, then Brazil takes it on to its highest level of excitement, with its fans lapping up every moment of on-track action around this aged but charismatic circuit.

Circuits come and go, with some being dropped because they are no longer suitable for Formula 1, others because they can no longer afford the fee to host a round of the World Championship. Somehow, with Brazil's economy really struggling, Interlagos is still with us, and this is how it should be, because this is a country with exceptional passion for racing.

The circuit is not only steeped in the history of local heroes Emerson Fittipaldi and Ayrton Senna, but it's a great if somewhat faded place to go racing, with gradient changes aplenty to make the lap interesting.

The lap starts with one of its toughest corners, a dive into the Senna S, followed, immediately, by the sweep left on to the downhill straight to Descida do Lago.

From here, via two quickish lefthanders, the track starts to climb back up the hillside into a bowl cut into the slope beneath the back of the paddock. Two fast rights here are followed by the need to brake harder for Laranjinha, a second gear righthander.

The next stretch down to Pinehirinho, up to Cotovelo and down again to Mergulho is a switchback, but it opens out for the run to the most critical corner of the lap: Juncao, a tight left. Its importance stems from the fact that its exit feeds on to the start of the lengthy blast through two kinks on to the start/finish straight. With the track submerged between high walls on either side, it has a claustrophobic feel as drivers keep their heads down and start imagining the blind entry to the first corner all over again.

INSIDE TRACK
BRAZILIAN GRAND PRIX

Date:	12 November
Circuit name:	Autodromo Jose Carlos Pace Interlagos
Circuit length:	2.667 miles/4.292km
Number of laps:	71
Email:	info@gpbrazil.com
Website:	www.gpbrazil.com

PREVIOUS WINNERS

2007	**Kimi Raikkonen** FERRARI
2008	**Felipe Massa** FERRARI
2009	**Mark Webber** RED BULL
2010	**Sebastian Vettel** RED BULL
2011	**Mark Webber** RED BULL
2012	**Jenson Button** McLAREN
2013	**Sebastian Vettel** RED BULL
2014	**Nico Rosberg** MERCEDES
2015	**Nico Rosberg** MERCEDES
2016	**Lewis Hamilton** MERCEDES

Location: Just as Mexico City has spread to surround the Autodromo Hermanos Rodriguez, so Sao Paulo now envelops Interlagos, even though the hillside on which it is built is nine miles from the city centre.

How it started: A circuit was finally built here in 1940. After a diet of national racing, it held a non-championship F1 race in 1972, and a World Championship round from 1973, alternating with Rio de Janeiro's Jacarepagua 1978-89.

Most memorable race: In the 1994 season-opener, Benetton's Michael Schumacher held off Ayrton Senna's challenge. Behind them, Martin Brundle was limping back to the pits when Eric Bernard swerved past him, only to be collected by Eddie Irvine's Ferrari and debutant Jos Verstappen piled in trying to pass them all.

Greatest Brazilian drivers: Emerson Fittipaldi was Brazil's first World Champion, in 1972 and 1974 and Nelson Piquet bagged a trio. However, Ayrton Senna, who died on three titles in 1994, is acknowledged as Brazil's greatest racer of all. Indeed, to many, he was the greatest racer, full stop. The circuit is named in memory of former F1 star, Carlos Pace, who won here in 1975.

Rising star: Brazilian fans may have to wait on for a new generation of Fittipaldis and Piquets; they are still only in the junior ranks.

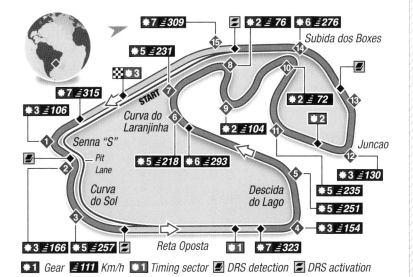

Subida dos Boxes · *Curva do Laranjinha* · START · *Senna "S"* · Pit Lane · *Curva do Sol* · *Descida do Lago* · *Juncao* · *Reta Oposta*

1 Gear **111** Km/h **1** Timing sector ▧ DRS detection ▧ DRS activation

2016 POLE TIME: **HAMILTON (MERCEDES)**, 1M10.736S, 135.720MPH/218.434KPH
2016 WINNER'S AVERAGE SPEED: 64.816MPH/104.318KPH

2016 FASTEST LAP: **VERSTAPPEN (RED BULL)**, 1M25.735S, 111.976MPH/180.220KPH
LAP RECORD: **MONTOYA (WILLIAMS)**, 1M11.473S, 134.837MPH/217.000KPH, 2004

YAS MARINA

It's sleek, modern, surrounded by a marina and futuristic architecture in the contrived setting of a leisure complex, but the Yas Marina Circuit is beginning to develop a character of its own.

It's undeniable that hosting the final round of the World Championship adds excitement to a venue. The stakes are so much higher, every lunge or parry carrying greater importance as a year's work can be rewarded or lost on the smallest of decisions.

Yas Marina is thus blessed, after just eight grands prix, with more history than a mid-season venue could dream of. Add the fact that the race has an evening slot, to miss the worst of the desert area's daytime heat, the action looks extra dramatic under the spotlights, with the extravagant buildings surrounding the track also lending a sense of occasion.

A tight left as the first corner is unusual, but it's the start of a rare anti-clockwise lap. Not too much happens here on the opening lap as the run to it from the grid is so short. Then comes the wide esse from Turn 2 to Turn 4, followed by a short straight before a left/right chicane into the Turn 7 hairpin.

The Yas Marina circuit has two trademark straights, down to Turn 8 and then down to Turn 11. Both require drivers to scrub off next to 140mph, with 50mph left/right/left chicanes at their conclusions. Both, therefore, offer chances to pass.

The nature of the lap changes from here, as it abuts the marina and the yachts moored there, full of well-heeled fans, as it becomes a sequence of minimal straights and frequent, tight corners. Every track needs to have a trademark, and Yas Marina's is the bizarre element of running under a wing of a hotel between Turns 18 and 19, and this is most spectacular when it is illuminated as day turns to night.

INSIDE TRACK

ABU DHABI GRAND PRIX

Date:	**26 November**
Circuit name:	**Yas Marina Circuit**
Circuit length:	**3.451 miles/5.554km**
Number of laps:	**56**
Email:	
customerservice@yasmarinacircuit.com	
Website:	**www.yasmarinacircuit.com**

PREVIOUS WINNERS		
2009	**Sebastian Vettel**	RED BULL
2010	**Sebastian Vettel**	RED BULL
2011	**Lewis Hamilton**	McLAREN
2012	**Kimi Raikkonen**	LOTUS
2013	**Sebastian Vettel**	RED BULL
2014	**Lewis Hamilton**	MERCEDES
2015	**Nico Rosberg**	MERCEDES
2016	**Lewis Hamilton**	MERCEDES

Location: The Yas Marina Circuit is located on the Yas island to the east of Abu Dhabi's main island, included as the principal part of a marina and sports complex.

How it started: Abu Dhabi is the lead emirate in the United Arab Emirates and so it decided after Dubai had built a circuit and was pitching without success for a grand prix that it would show its junior partner how it should be done. The circuit set new standards when it was unveiled in 2009.

Most memorable race: Mercedes' domination since 2014 has led to less than exciting two-horse races here. So, 2010's four-way battle still stands out as Abu Dhabi's best. It was billed as a title shoot-out between Ferrari's Fernando Alonso and Red Bull's Mark Webber, with Sebastian Vettel and Lewis Hamilton as long shots. Both Alonso and Webber were disappointed as poor race strategies brought them out in traffic, while Vettel stole through to win the race and the title.

Rising star: Abu Dhabi is rich in oil wealth but short on promising drivers of its own. Khaled Al Qubaisi continues to develop his craft in the GTE Am ranks of the World Endurance Championship, but the country has no hotshot single-seater driver yet, although the introduction of the UAE's own Formula 4 championship in late 2016 was a positive step.

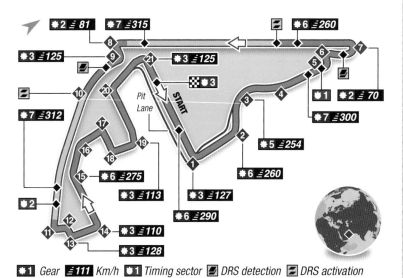

Gear ⚙1 Km/h ☰111 Timing sector ◼1 DRS detection ▨ DRS activation

2016 POLE TIME: **HAMILTON (MERCEDES),**
1m38.755s, 125.805MPH/202.464KPH
2016 WINNER'S AVERAGE SPEED:
116.087MPH/186.824KPH

2016 FASTEST LAP: **VETTEL (FERRARI),**
1M43.729S, 119.773MPH/192.756KPH
LAP RECORD: **VETTEL (FERRARI), 1M43.729S,**
119.773MPH/192.756KPH, 2016

This spectacular display before the start of the 2016 Abu Dhabi GP was typical of the emirate's efforts and "no expense spared" approach to hosting the race.

The entry to the first corner at Sepang is unusually wide, but that doesn't stop cars from tangling further around the bend, with Vettel and Rosberg getting personal in 2016.

SEASON REVIEW 2016

The question before the 2016 World Championship kicked off was whether any team could rise to the challenge of taking on Mercedes. The answer was soon revealed. They couldn't, with their only two successes coming when Mercedes' drivers either took each other out or hit mechanical trouble. So, all the battling for Championship honours was between the Mercedes drivers, with Nico Rosberg coming out on top, then immediately deciding to retire.

Their rivals knew that Mercedes was likely to be as strong in 2016 as before. Indeed, the silver Mercedes took pole at all but one of the 21 grands prix (Daniel Ricciardo put his Red Bull on pole at Monaco). Worse still, the Mercedes F1 W07s had race-long pace as well. Yet, at the opening race in Melbourne, there was a chance of Ferrari taking victory, only to make a mess of its tyre strategy. Any encouragement that the Italian team might have taken from this was soon extinguished as Mercedes seemed to shift up a gear and were pretty much untouchable thereafter. In fact, the final Constructors' Cup standings show Mercedes finishing 297 points clear of Red Bull, having achieved 19 wins and eight second-place finishes in 21 races.

Ferrari then went into one of its periods of self-inflicted harm and got rid of technical director James Allison, with further management turmoil making matters worse. Sebastian Vettel became more and more fractious through the year, as exemplified by his on-air expletives in Mexico, and only Kimi Raikkonen seemed capable of getting on with things unruffled. In truth, they had fair pace but no answers to Mercedes' supremacy.

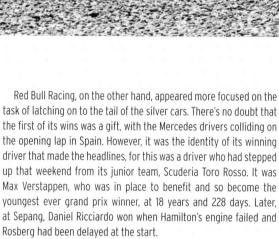

Red Bull Racing, on the other hand, appeared more focused on the task of latching on to the tail of the silver cars. There's no doubt that the first of its wins was a gift, with the Mercedes drivers colliding on the opening lap in Spain. However, it was the identity of its winning driver that made the headlines, for this was a driver who had stepped up that weekend from its junior team, Scuderia Toro Rosso. It was Max Verstappen, who was in place to benefit and so become the youngest ever grand prix winner, at 18 years and 228 days. Later, at Sepang, Daniel Ricciardo won when Hamilton's engine failed and Rosberg had been delayed at the start.

No other team was ever in with a shout of victory and, apart from the top three teams, only Force India and Williams got to celebrate a podium finish. Force India's Sergio Perez managed third-place finishes on the streets of Monaco and Baku, with team-mate Nico Hulkenberg often threatening, but often being denied.

Williams's form fluctuated, then tailed away, leaving Valtteri Bottas with no opportunity to add to his third place in Canada, and Felipe Massa no chance to end his F1 career on a high, his spin-off and walk back to the pits at Interlagos being particularly emotional.

McLaren and Honda remained a work in progress, as even the talents of former World Champions Fernando Alonso and Jenson Button couldn't get higher than the Spaniard's pair of fifth places and Button's sixth. Then, in November, Ron Dennis, the man who dragged the team to the top in the 1980s, was ousted.

Scuderia Toro Rosso dipped in and out of the points all year, with Carlos Sainz Jr becoming the team's lead driver following Verstappen's departure to Red Bull Racing after the first four races. He was able to match the Dutchman's best 2016 result for STR of sixth place, doing so three times and outperforming the dispirited Daniil Kvyat who had been demoted from Red Bull.

Haas was the surprise package. Scoring a point was seen as highly unlikely for the all-new team. Yet, to everybody's surprise, Romain Grosjean raced to sixth place at the opening race, then went one better for fifth next time out. Top-10 finishes were then harder to come by, but the team made a good first impression.

Renault was a team in disarray, offering Kevin Magnussen and rookie Jolyon Palmer little chance of scoring, although both managed it. With investment from Renault, this once great team should advance.

Sauber was given a boost when it was taken over, with proper investment promised for the future. Yet, until the penultimate race, it was last overall, behind Manor, so looking at losing a share of travel money from FOM. Then Brazilian Felipe Nasr grabbed its first points, for ninth, on home soil, triggering celebrations. The team knows it is likely to have to run drivers equipped primarily by large budgets as their main asset or those placed with them by manufacturers to bring them on.

Manor was also a team low in money, so it was delighted when Pascal Wehrlein raced to 10th at Monaco. However, Esteban Ocon joined midway through the season and outraced him.

AUSTRALIAN GP

It was always expected that Mercedes would lead the way in the opening round, and so it proved in Melbourne, but it took a helping hand from Ferrari, who made the wrong tyre choice, to achieve maximum points.

Nico Rosberg had won the final three rounds of the 2015 World Championship and he started his 2016 campaign in the same vein. However, the German Mercedes driver's run wasn't in that same dominant fashion. Indeed, victory could certainly have gone to Ferrari's Sebastian Vettel.

He powered past both Mercedes on the run to the first corner. Rosberg then pushed pole-sitter Lewis Hamilton wide and Kimi Raikkonen took the second Ferrari past them too. As Hamilton fought to pull his Mercedes back into line, Max Verstappen's Toro Rosso and Felipe Massa's Williams further demoted him. Although Hamilton soon passed Massa, Verstappen proved a harder nut to crack.

The Ferrari duo remained ahead until Vettel pitted on lap 13 and changed to super soft tyres. Even though he returned to the lead within three laps as his team-mate pitted, it was to prove to be a pivotal moment after what happened on lap 17.

Fernando Alonso clashed with Esteban Gutierrez attempting to pass the Haas F1 for 11th place at Turn 3. His MP4-31 rolled before ending up inverted against the wall on the outside of the corner, bringing out the red flags. The teams had the chance to bring their cars in for a further tyre change. Inexplicably, Ferrari fitted Vettel with another set of super softs, as all the other teams changed to mediums, so they could go all the way to the finish on those rims. Vettel, thus, had to come in once more so that he completed his mandatory stint on mediums. It allowed Hamilton to take second, with Vettel third, ruing Ferrari's choice.

Impressively, Haas F1 came away with points on its debut. Romain Grosjean used a one-stop strategy and exceeded all expectations by taking eight points for sixth.

One downside was the ridiculous new qualifying format, in which the slowest driver at each 90s point in Q3 was eliminated. It led to all the drivers rushing out to set a quick time and then parking up, and it meant the track silent for the final four minutes. Some climax.

Sebastian Vettel made a great start at Melbourne but was undone by Ferrari's tyre strategy.

MELBOURNE ROUND 1
DATE: **20 MARCH 2016**

Laps: **57** • Distance: **187.822 miles/302.271km** • Weather: **Warm & sunny**

Pos	Driver	Team	Result	Stops	Qualifying Time	Grid
1	**Nico Rosberg**	Mercedes	1h48m15.565s	2	1m24.197s	2
2	**Lewis Hamilton**	Mercedes	1h48m23.625s	2	1m23.837s	1
3	**Sebastian Vettel**	Ferrari	1h48m25.208s	2	1m24.675s	3
4	**Daniel Ricciardo**	Red Bull	1h48m39.895s	3	1m25.589s	8
5	**Felipe Massa**	Williams	1h49m14.544s	2	1m25.458s	6
6	**Romain Grosjean**	Haas	1h49m27.646s	1	1m28.322s	19
7	**Nico Hulkenberg**	Force India	1h49m29.764s	2	1m25.865s	10
8	**Valtteri Bottas**	Williams	1h49m30.718s	2	1m25.961s	11
9	**Carlos Sainz Jr**	Toro Rosso	1h49m31.245s	3	1m25.582s	7
10	**Max Verstappen**	Toro Rosso	1h49m32.398s	3	1m25.434s	5
11	**Jolyon Palmer**	Renault	1h49m38.964s	2	1m27.601s	14
12	**Kevin Magnussen**	Renault	1h49m41.171s	3	1m27.742s	15
13	**Sergio Perez**	Force India	1h49m47.264s	2	1m25.753s	9
14	**Jenson Button**	McLaren	56 laps	3	1m26.304s	13
15	**Felipe Nasr**	Sauber	56 laps	2	1m27.958s	17
16	**Pascal Wehrlein**	Manor	56 laps	3	1m29.642s	22
R	**Marcus Ericsson**	Sauber	38 laps/tyre	2	1m27.435s	16
R	**Kimi Raikkonen**	Ferrari	21 laps/fire	2	1m25.033s	4
R	**Rio Haryanto**	Manor	17 laps/gearbox	1	1m29.627s	21
R	**Esteban Gutierrez**	Haas	16 laps/collision	0	1m29.606s	20
R	**Fernando Alonso**	McLaren	16 laps/collision	1	1m26.125s	12
NS	**Daniil Kvyat**	Red Bull	0 laps/electrics	0	1m28.006s	18

FASTEST LAP: RICCIARDO, 1M28.997S, 133.290MPH/214.510KPH ON LAP 49 • RACE LEADERS: VETTEL 1-12 & 16-34, RAIKKONEN 13-15, ROSBERG 35-57
* 5-PLACE GRID PENALTY FOR GEARBOX CHANGE; ‡ 3-PLACE GRID PENALTY FOR PULLING OUT OF GARAGE WITHOUT DUE ATTENTION.

BAHRAIN GP

A slow start and then a first corner clash with Valtteri Bottas's Williams at Sakhir left Lewis Hamilton to set off on another recovery drive. These combined to put Nico Rosberg on course, again, for a victory in Bahrain that gave him a 17-point lead just two races into the season.

Normal service was resumed in qualifying with the disastrous Q3 elimination system eliminated. Hamilton didn't need any tricks to take the premier position on the grid, edging out Rosberg in traditional manner. However, Hamilton made a poor getaway at the start and his Mercedes team-mate Nico Rosberg was first into and first out of the three-corner sequence that starts the lap.

Bottas had made a strong start but his attempt to get past Hamilton didn't come off and the contact earned him a drivethrough penalty that would delay him enough to drop him to ninth place. The sort-out elevated his Williams team-mate Felipe Massa to second and dropped Hamilton, with a damaged floor, to seventh, making a run to third no easy feat.

Ferrari was already down to one car as Sebastian Vettel had qualified third fastest but failed to take the start after engine failure. Kimi Raikkonen, jumped by Red Bull's Daniel Ricciardo, ran fifth, but drove well to advance to second, a place he held to the end, equalling his best finish since returning to Ferrari. Rosberg, though, was 10s clear, with everything under control. Hamilton finished 20s further back in third.

Red Bull still wasn't on the pace, and Ricciardo was more than a minute down in fourth. Amazingly, Grosjean improved on his surprise sixth place in Australia by finishing fifth, just ahead of the fast-closing Max Verstappen's Toro Rosso. All other finishers were lapped, including Massa, irked by the team deciding he should stop only twice, for mediums, while others ran three-stop strategies and used the softs.

With Alonso absent injured, McLaren gave test driver Stoffel Vandoorne a late call-up and he took one point for 10th place. Team-mate Jenson Button suffered early engine failure.

Notable was the impressive form of rookie Pascal Wehrlein, who gave Manor its best ever qualifying position – 16th – and then raced hard against the two Saubers and Kevin Magnussen's Renault to finish in 13th place.

SAKHIR ROUND 2
DATE: **3 APRIL 2016**

Laps: **57** • Distance: **191.530 miles/308.238km** • Weather: **Warm & sunny**

Pos	Driver	Team	Result	Stops	Qualifying Time	Grid
1	**Nico Rosberg**	Mercedes	1h33m34.696s	3	1m29.570s	2
2	**Kimi Raikkonen**	Ferrari	1h33m44.978s	3	1m30.244s	4
3	**Lewis Hamilton**	Mercedes	1h34m04.844s	3	1m29.493s	1
4	**Daniel Ricciardo**	Red Bull	1h34m37.190s	3	1m30.854s	5
5	**Romain Grosjean**	Haas	1h34m52.995s	3	1m31.756s	9
6	**Max Verstappen**	Toro Rosso	1h34m55.625s	3	1m31.772s	10
7	**Daniil Kvyat**	Red Bull	56 laps	3	1m32.241s	15
8	**Felipe Massa**	Williams	56 laps	2	1m31155s	7
9	**Valtteri Bottas**	Williams	56 laps	3	1m31.153s	6
10	**Stoffel Vandoorne**	McLaren	56 laps	3	1m31.934s	12
11	**Kevin Magnussen**	Renault	56 laps	3	1m33.181s	22*
12	**Marcus Ericsson**	Sauber	56 laps	2	1m32.840s	17
13	**Pascal Wehrlein**	Manor	56 laps	2	1m32.806s	16
14	**Felipe Nasr**	Sauber	56 laps	3	1m34.388s	21
15	**Nico Hulkenberg**	Force India	56 laps	4	1m31.620s	8
16	**Sergio Perez**	Force India	56 laps	3	1m32.911s	18
17	**Rio Haryanto**	Manor	56 laps	3	1m34.190s	20
R	**Carlos Sainz Jr**	Toro Rosso	29 laps/collision	2	1m331.816s	11
R	**Esteban Gutierrez**	Sauber	9 laps/brakes	1	1m31.945s	13
R	**Jenson Button**	McLaren	6 laps/power unit	0	1m31.998s	14
NS	**Sebastian Vettel**	Ferrari	0 laps/engine	0	1m30.012s	3
NS	**Jolyon Palmer**	Renault	0 laps/hydraulics	0	1m33.438s	19

FASTEST LAP: ROSBERG, 1M34.482S, 128.133MPH/206.210KPH ON LAP 41 • RACE LEADERS: ROSBERG 1-39 & 41-57, HAMILTON 40.
* STARTED FROM PITLANE FOR FAILING TO HAVE CAR WEIGHED IN P2.

Nico Rosberg took the first corner ahead of polesetter Lewis Hamilton and drove off to victory.

Nico Rosberg made it three wins in a row after Mercedes team-mate Lewis Hamilton had to start from the rear of the grid, clashed with Felipe Nasr on lap 1 and could recover only to seventh by the end of the race.

Hamilton had problems before qualifying. His car had a gearbox change – a five-place grid penalty – and he didn't even get a qualifying run in as it suffered an MGU-H problem.

Daniel Ricciardo powered past Rosberg at the start, and stayed there for two laps. Behind them, the Ferraris came together at the first corner, Sebastian Vettel hitting Kimi Raikkonen after his options became limited when jinking for position under braking as Daniil Kvyat dived up his inside. Raikkonen had to pit for repairs. That wasn't the end of the Turn 1 contact, though, as those behind were caught out by the concertina effect from the Ferrari clash and Hamilton damaged his Mercedes' nose on Felipe Nasr's Sauber.

These dramas were nothing next to what followed, as Ricciardo's lead ended spectacularly when the Red Bull's left rear tyre shredded itself racing down the back straight on lap 3. This brought out the safety car, but Rosberg elected not to pit, saving his two planned stops until later. From there, he simply controlled proceedings. Vettel, who did pit, was slowed by some car damage, but still had enough speed to take second, albeit 37s behind Rosberg. Third on the podium was Kvyat, who was roasted by Vettel as they went there, the latter certain the Turn 1 clash had been Kvyat's fault. Others weren't so sure.

Ricciardo and Raikkonen did well to make it back to fourth and fifth, while Hamilton recovered to seventh place, not far behind Massa's Williams, and he would have gained more places had he not pitted five times against the three stops made by the majority of his rivals.

Haas F1's dream start to its maiden F1 season came to a halt as neither Romain Grosjean nor Esteban Gutierrez got close to scoring points, with Grosjean ending up 19th after colliding with Marcus Ericsson.

So, after just three rounds, Hamilton found himself 36 points down on his team-mate and increasingly aware that he was going to have to make his fortune change, and soon.

SHANGHAI ROUND 3

DATE: **17 APRIL 2016**

Laps: **56** • Distance: **189.840 miles/305.518km** • Weather: **Warm & sunny**

Pos	Driver	Team	Result	Stops	Qualifying Time	Grid
1	Nico Rosberg	Mercedes	1h38m53.891s	2	1m35.402s	1
2	Sebastian Vettel	Ferrari	1h39m31.667s	3	1m36.246s	4
3	Daniil Kvyat	Red Bull	1h39m39.827s	3	1m36.399s	6
4	Daniel Ricciardo	Red Bull	1h39m46.579s	3	1m35.917s	2
5	Kimi Raikkonen	Ferrari	1h39m59.763s	3	1m35.972s	3
6	Felipe Massa	Williams	1h40m09.402s	2	1m37.347s	10
7	Lewis Hamilton	Mercedes	1h40m12.121s	5	-	22
8	Max Verstappen	Toro Rosso	1h40m13.159s	3	1m37.194s	9
9	Carlos Sainz Jr	Toro Rosso	1h40m18.018s	3	1m36.881s	8
10	Valtteri Bottas	Williams	1h40m20.083s	3	1m36.296s	5
11	Sergio Perez	Force India	1h40m28.174s	3	1m36.865s	7
12	Fernando Alonso	McLaren	1h40m31.144s	2	1m38.826s	11
13	Jenson Button	McLaren	1h40m35.881s	3	1m39.093s	12
14	Esteban Gutierrez	Haas	55 laps	3	1m38.770s	18
15	Nico Hulkenberg	Force India	55 laps	4	-	13*
16	Marcus Ericsson	Sauber	55 laps	2	1m40.742s	15
17	Kevin Magnussen	Renault	55 laps	3	1m38.673s	17
18	Pascal Wehrlein	Manor	55 laps	3	-	21
19	Romain Grosjean	Haas	55 laps	4	1m39.830s	14
20	Felipe Nasr	Sauber	55 laps	3	1m42.430s	16
21	Rio Haryanto	Manor	55 laps	3	1m40.264s	20
22	Jolyon Palmer	Renault	55 laps	3	-	

FASTEST LAP: HULKENBERG, 1M39.824S, 122.150MPH/196.581KPH ON LAP 48 • RACE LEADERS: RICCIARDO 1-2, ROSBERG 3-56.
* 3-PLACE GRID PENALTY FOR UNSAFE RELEASE IN QUALIFYING.

In splendid isolation – 37s clear of the field – Nico Rosberg takes his third win of the season.

RUSSIAN GP

Further problems in qualifying forced Lewis Hamilton to start from 10th on the grid, and this made it easy for Nico Rosberg to escape for his fourth win from four as Hamilton had to pick his way through the field to claim second.

Hamilton's Mercedes suffered the same MGU-H problem as before qualifying in China. This time, he had made it to Q3, so started 10th rather than the back of the grid. But Sochi isn't great for passing.

Rosberg got away well from pole, but there was drama behind him at the first corner. Daniil Kyvat ran into Sebastian Vettel for the second race in succession and this time it was clearly the Russian's fault. His Red Bull team-mate Daniel Ricciardo also suffered damage, slowing him for the rest of the race. Little wonder, then, that Red Bull Racing's management decided to relegate Kvyat to Scuderia Toro Rosso.

With the rush to the pits for repairs, Rosberg led from Kimi Raikkonen and Williams duo Valtteri Bottas and Felipe Massa, all of whom had kept clear of the trouble. Others weren't so lucky as Nico Hulkenberg and Rio Haryanto were both eliminated at Turn 2 when the German's Force India was pitched into a spin by Esteban Gutierrez's Haas. The Mexican was hit with a drivethrough penalty.

Such was the Mercedes' performance advantage that Hamilton was up to second place by lap 32, and then closed in on Rosberg. The World Champion's charge was aided by Rosberg's car being slowed by an MGU-K problem. Yet, just when it looked as though Rosberg would lose out, Mercedes noticed that Hamilton's water pressure was dropping and he was instructed to slow. They were still far enough clear to finish first and second ahead of Ferrari's Kimi Raikkonen, but the team said it showed just how hard the team was pushing the technical boundaries to keep at the front.

Williams claimed fourth and fifth finishes for Bottas and Massa, respectively. McLaren ought to have been pleased with Fernando Alonso's sixth place, Jenson Button was 10th, as the team continued to make up ground. However, Alonso being lapped shows just how far there is to go for this once great team.

Renault claimed its first points of the year as Kevin Magnussen finished in seventh place.

Kvyat ran into the back of Vettel at the first corner and damaged team-mate Ricciardo's car too.

SOCHI ROUND 4
DATE: **1 MAY 2016**

Laps: **53** • Distance: **192.466 miles/309.745km** • Weather: **Warm & sunny**

Pos	Driver	Team	Result	Stops	Qualifying Time	Grid
1	**Nico Rosberg**	Mercedes	1h32m41.997s	1	1m35.417s	1
2	**Lewis Hamilton**	Mercedes	1h33m07.019s	1	-	10
3	**Kimi Raikkonen**	Ferrari	1h33m13.995s	1	1m36.663s	4
4	**Valtteri Bottas**	Williams	1h33m32.214s	1	1m36.536s	3
5	**Felipe Massa**	Williams	1h33m56.424s	1	1m37.016	5
6	**Fernando Alonso**	McLaren	52 laps	1	1m37.807s	14
7	**Kevin Magnussen**	Renault	52 laps	1	1m38.914s	17
8	**Romain Grosjean**	Haas	52 laps	1	1m38.055s	15
9	**Sergio Perez**	Force India	52 laps	1	1m37.212s	7
10	**Jenson Button**	McLaren	52 laps	1	1m37.701s	12
11	**Daniel Ricciardo**	Red Bull	52 laps	2	1m37.125s	6
12	**Carlos Sainz Jr**	Toro Rosso	52 laps	1	1m37.652s	11
13	**Jolyon Palmer**	Renault	52 laps	1	1m39.009s	18
14	**Marcus Ericsson**	Sauber	52 laps	1	1m39.519s	22
15	**Daniil Kvyat**	Red Bull	52 laps	1	1m37.459s	8
16	**Felipe Nasr**	Sauber	52 laps	1	1m39.018s	19
17	**Esteban Gutierrez**	Haas	52 laps	1	1m38.115s	16
18	**Pascal Wehrlein**	Manor	51 laps	2	1m39.399s	20
R	**Max Verstappen**	Toro Rosso	33 laps/power unit	1	1m37.583s	9
R	**Sebastian Vettel**	Ferrari	0 laps/collision	0	1m36.123s	2
R	**Nico Hulkenberg**	Force India	0 laps/collision	0	1m37.771s	13
R	**Rio Haryanto**	Manor	0 laps/collision	0	1m39.463s	21

FASTEST LAP: **ROSBERG, 1M39.094S, 132.011MPH/212.452KPH ON LAP 52** • RACE LEADERS: **ROSBERG 1-53.**
* 5-PLACE GRID PENALTY FOR GEARBOX CHANGE.

Promotion to Red Bull Racing was a boost for Max Verstappen, but he then sent the Dutch nation wild as he exceeded even their expectations to become F1's youngest ever winner on a day when the Mercedes drivers collided.

Two incredibly powerful images were taken away from the Spanish GP. First was an opening lap clash between Nico Rosberg and Lewis Hamilton which ended both their races. Recriminations were rife in the Mercedes camp. Second, and more treasured by F1 fans, was the one of Max Verstappen taking the chequered flag, arm aloft, to become an F1 winner at just 18 years and 227 days.

Mercedes dominated qualifying, with Red Bull Racing's third-placed Daniel Ricciardo 0.4s slower. So Hamilton and Rosberg had only themselves to play with as they negotiated the often-troublesome first two corners. Slipstreaming polesitter Hamilton, Rosberg ducked to the outside at Turn 1 and went ahead. Running out of Turn 3, Hamilton was closing fast, but Rosberg had a problem with his engine power, reduced by being put into the wrong mode. Hamilton went for the inside, but Rosberg blocked him, sending Hamilton on to the grass, where the car lost traction and hit Rosberg as they reached Turn 4. Exit both.

This left Daniel Ricciardo in the lead, with new team-mate Verstappen second and Toro Rosso's Carlos Sainz Jr third, ahead of Sebastian Vettel's Ferrari to give Red Bull a huge thrill. Red Bull Racing then made a strategic call that cost Ricciardo the win. Looking to counter the Ferrari challenge, it decided to switch the Australian to a three-stop strategy but kept him out too long on soft tyres. It allowed Verstappen and both Ferraris to move ahead. Although faster on fresher tyres, Ricciardo could not rise from fourth.

The final 20 laps were agonising for Dutch fans, as Kimi Raikkonen put him under huge pressure, but the teenager had saved his tyres in the early laps of his final stint. He stayed calm, soaked up the pressure like a veteran, and was 0.6s in front at the end. Vettel took third, 38s clear of Ricciardo, with Valtteri Bottas not much further back. Toro Rosso continued to exceed expectations as Sainz Jr led Bottas early on, but although passed by the Finn, was more than happy to claim the points for sixth.

Max Verstappen, left of board, celebrates becoming Formula One's youngest ever race winner.

BARCELONA ROUND 5

DATE: **15 MAY 2016**

Laps: **66** • Distance: **190.904 miles/307.231km** • Weather: **Warm & sunny**

Pos	Driver	Team	Result	Stops	Qualifying Time	Grid
1	Max Verstappen	Red Bull	1h41m40.017s	2	1m23.087s	4
2	Kimi Raikkonen	Ferrari	1h41m40.0633s	2	1m23.113s	5
3	Sebastian Vettel	Ferrari	1h41m45.598s	3	1m23.334s	6
4	Daniel Ricciardo	Red Bull	1h42m23.967s	4	1m22.680s	3
5	Valtteri Bottas	Williams	1h42m25.288s	2	1m23.522s	5
6	Carlos Sainz Jr	Toro Rosso	1h42m41.412s	2	1m23.643s	8
7	Sergio Perez	Force India	1h42m59.555s	2	1m23.782s	9
8	Felipe Massa	Williams	1h43m00.724s	3	1m24.941s	18
9	Jenson Button	McLaren	65 laps	2	1m24.348s	12
10	Daniil Kvyat	Toro Rosso	65 laps	3	1m24.445s	13
11	Esteban Gutierrez	Haas	65 laps	2	1m24.778s	16
12	Marcus Ericsson	Sauber	65 laps	3	1m25.202s	19
13	Jolyon Palmer	Renault	65 laps	2	1m24.903s	17
14	Felipe Nasr	Sauber	65 laps	2	1m25.579s	20
15	Kevin Magnussen	Renault	65 laps*	3	1m24.625s	15
16	Pascal Wehrlein	Manor	65 laps	2	1m25.745s	21
17	Rio Haryanto	Manor	65 laps	2	1m25.939s	22
R	Romain Grosjean	Haas	56 laps/brakes	3	1m24.480s	14
R	Fernando Alonso	McLaren	45 laps/power unit	2	1m23.981s	10
R	Nico Hulkenberg	Force India	20 laps/oil leak	1	1m24.230s	11
R	Lewis Hamilton	Mercedes	0 laps/collision	0	1m22.000s	1
R	Nico Rosberg	Mercedes	0 laps/collision	0	1m222.80s	2

FASTEST LAP: **KVYAT, 1M26.948S, 119.76OMPH/192.735KPH ON LAP 53** • RACE LEADERS: **RICCIARDO 1-10, 16-27 & 36-43, VERSTAPPEN 11, 28-33 & 44-66, VETTEL 12-15, RAIKKONEN 34-35.**
* 10 SECOND PENALTY FOR CAUSING A COLLISION, DROPPING HIM ONE PLACE.

MONACO GP

Lewis Hamilton got back on to the winner's trail in Monaco, but it was a race that may well have gone to Red Bull Racing's Daniel Ricciardo, but his run was ruined by the team not having his tyres ready at his second pitstop.

Imagine the scene: you're the team leader and you've been taking the battle to Mercedes and Ferrari. Then you get a new team-mate, an 18-year-old, and he wins first time out. Sure, Max Verstappen had luck in Spain, but he grasped the opportunity with both hands. In Monaco, then, Ricciardo was primed to reassert his authority.

Verstappen showed well in the principality, but pressed too hard and clipped the barriers at Piscine in Q1, leaving him 21st on the grid. Ricciardo released some of the pressure by claiming his first F1 pole as both Mercedes had fuel pressure problems and, helped by wet conditions and a safety car start, he led away. The Australian was controlling proceedings ahead of Lewis Hamilton – who had taken second as Nico Rosberg struggled to get heat into his first set of tyres. Ricciardo looked on course for the win he so desperately wanted, but it all went wrong as the track began to dry.

He was given a set of intermediates, but Hamilton stayed on full wets for a further eight laps and then changed to ultra soft slicks. Red Bull responded on the following lap, bringing in Ricciardo for a change to slicks. Unfortunately, the pit-crew took ten seconds to find the correct tyres, blowing all chance of victory. He did finish in front of the impressive Sergio Perez, who finished third for Force India.

Other race incidents included a heavy shunt for Jolyon Palmer, who lost control of his Renault on the start/finish straight just as the safety car withdrew at the end of lap 7. Ferrari's Kimi Raikkonen was out three laps later; he locked up and hit the barriers at the Grand Hotel hairpin. Kevin Magnussen, in the other Renault, was tipped into the barriers at Piscine by Daniil Kvyat, who was out instantly. The Dane returned, but he, too, went out after an accident of his own making on lap 32.

Worst of all, the two Saubers took each other out. Felipe Nasr didn't let Marcus Ericsson by and they met at Rascasse. The Swede recklessly attempted to pass and was punished with a three-place grid penalty next time out.

MONACO ROUND 6

DATE: 29 MAY 2016

Laps: **78** • Distance: **161.887 miles/260.532km** • Weather: **Wet then drying**

Pos	Driver	Team	Result	Stops	Qualifying Time	Grid
1	**Lewis Hamilton**	Mercedes	1h59m29.133s	1	1m13.942s	3
2	**Daniel Ricciardo**	Red Bull	1h59m36.385s	2	1m13.622s	1
3	**Sergio Perez**	Force India	1h59m42.948s	2	1m14.902s	7
4	**Sebastian Vettel**	Ferrari	1h59m44.979s	2	1m14.552s	4
5	**Fernando Alonso**	McLaren	2h00m54.209s	2	1m15.262s	9
6	**Nico Hulkenberg**	Force India	2h01m02.132s	2	1m14.726s	5
7	**Nico Rosberg**	Mercedes	2h01m02.423s	2	1m13.791s	2
8	**Carlos Sainz Jr**	Toro Rosso	77 laps	2	1m14.749s	6
9	**Jenson Button**	McLaren	77 laps	2	1m15.352s	13
10	**Felipe Massa**	Williams	77 laps	2	1m15.385s	14
11	**Esteban Gutierrez**	Haas	77 laps	2	1m15.293s	12
12	**Valtteri Bottas**	Williams	77 laps	3	1m15.273s	10
13	**Romain Grosjean**	Haas	76 laps	2	1m15.571s	15
14	**Pascal Wehrlein**	Manor	76 laps	1	1m17.452s	20
15	**Rio Haryanto**	Manor	74 laps	3	1m17.295s	19
R	**Marcus Ericsson**	Sauber	51 laps/collision	3	1m16.299s	17
R	**Felipe Nasr**	Sauber	48 laps/collision	3	no time	22!
R	**Max Verstappen**	Red Bull	34 laps/spun off	2	1m22.467s	21!
R	**Kevin Magnussen**	Renault	32 laps/spun off	4	1m16.058s	16
R	**Daniil Kvyat**	Toro Rosso	18 laps/collision	3	1m15.273s	8
R	**Kimi Raikkonen**	Ferrari	10 laps/spun off	0	1m14.732s	11*
R	**Jolyon Palmer**	Renault	7 laps/spun off	0	1m16.856s	18

FASTEST LAP: HAMILTON, 1M17.939S, 95.775MPH/154.135KPH ON LAP 71 • RACE LEADERS: RICCIARDO 1-22 & 31-32, HAMILTON 23-30 & 33-78.
* 5-PLACE GRID PENALTY FOR GEARBOX CHANGE; ! STARTED FROM PIT LANE.

Lewis Hamilton's win was overdue, but the big story was Sergio Perez taking third for Force India.

CANADIAN GP

This could have been Ferrari's redemption, its first win of 2016, after Sebastian Vettel leapt into the lead at the start, but the team made a bad call, so Lewis Hamilton collected the 25 points while Nico Rosberg could finish only fifth.

For all of the attributes of Mercedes' pace-setting performance, its starts continued to be a weak point. It happened again in Montreal as Hamilton bogged down at the start, allowing Rosberg to pull alongside. Quicker off the mark than both of them, Vettel was already in front as they approached the first corner. Then, in an attempt to enter Turn 1 on the outside line, Rosberg found that Hamilton wasn't prepared to give him any room, they touched and the German was forced up the escape road.

Although Hamilton continued without real issue, in second behind Vettel, Rosberg rejoined the track behind both Red Bulls and was demoted further by the two Wiliams before they reached the first chicane. When Fernando Alonso and Nico Hulkenberg both passed him by the second chicane, instead of challenging for second or leading, Rosberg was 10th at the end of lap 1.

Presented with a chance to make the first of two planned pitstops during a virtual safety car period as Jenson Button's broken McLaren was recovered, Ferrari brought in both Vettel and Kimi Raikkonen for sets of super soft tyres. Vettel was soon back, and in to second place, but Hamilton stayed out considerably longer before finally pitting on lap 24.

By putting him on to softs, Mercedes felt he could run to the finish. They were right; Hamilton resisted everything Vettel threw at him, even when he was on fresher rubber. Vettel was left frustrated behind Romain Grosjean's Haas as he came up to lap it, then twice locked up and missed the final chicane. These slips allowed Hamilton to back off the power and win by 5s. Vettel just rued the fact Ferrari had not thought of stopping only once.

Valtteri Bottas took third place, 41s down on Vettel, but 6.5s clear of Max Verstappen. Rosberg, in fifth, ceded 15 points to Hamilton which cut his championship lead down to nine.

Romain Grosjean said in Spain that he was unhappy with front wing failures on his Haas, and he suffered the same fate during the race, his fourth of 2016, which dropped him to 14th.

MONTREAL ROUND 7   DATE: **12 JUNE 2016**

Laps: **70** • Distance: **189.686 miles/305.271km** • Weather: **Cool & overcast**

Pos	Driver	Team	Result	Stops	Qualifying Time	Grid
1	**Lewis Hamilton**	Mercedes	1h31m05.296s	1	1m12.812s	1
2	**Sebastian Vettel**	Ferrari	1h31m10.307s	2	1m12.990S	3
3	**Valtteri Bottas**	Williams	1h31m51.718s	1	1m13.670S	7
4	**Max Verstappen**	Red Bull	1h31m58.316s	2	1m13.414s	5
5	**Nico Rosberg**	Mercedes	1h32m07.389s	2	1m12.874s	2
6	**Kimi Raikkonen**	Ferrari	1h32m08.313s	2	1m13.579s	6
7	**Daniel Ricciardo**	Red Bull	1h32m08.930s	2	1m13.166s	4
8	**Nico Hulkenberg**	Force India	69 laps	2	1m13.952s	9
9	**Carlos Sainz Jr**	Toro Rosso	69 laps	2	1m21.956s	20!
10	**Sergio Perez**	Force India	69 laps	2	1m14.317s	11
11	**Fernando Alonso**	McLaren	69 laps	1	1m14.338s	10
12	**Daniil Kvyat**	Toro Rosso	69 laps	2	1m14.457s	15*
13	**Esteban Gutierrez**	Haas	68 laps	2	1m14.571s	13
14	**Romain Grosjean**	Haas	68 laps	3	1m14.803s	14
15	**Marcus Ericsson**	Sauber	68 laps	2	1m15.635s	21*
16	**Kevin Magnussen**	Renault	68 laps	1	No time	22!
17	**Pascal Wehrlein**	Manor	68 laps	2	1m15.599s	17
18	**Felipe Nasr**	Sauber	68 laps	2	1m16.663s	18
19	**Rio Haryanto**	Manor	68 laps	2	1m17.052s	19
R	**Felipe Massa**	Williams	35 laps/overheating	1	1m13.769s	8
R	**Jolyon Palmer**	Renault	16 laps/water leak	0	1m15.459s	16
R	**Jenson Button**	McLaren	9 laps/gearbox	0	1m14.437s	12

FASTEST LAP: ROSBERG, 1M15.599S, 129.039MPH/207.669KPH ON LAP 60 • RACE LEADERS: VETTEL 1-10 & 24-36, HAMILTON 11-23 & 37-70.
* 3-PLACE GRID PENALTY FOR CAUSING A COLLISION IN MONACO; ! 5-PLACE PENALTY FOR GEARBOX CHANGE.

Lewis Hamilton celebrates his second win as Sebastian Vettel (left) rues what might have been.

GP OF EUROPE

Formula 1's first visit to Azerbaijan was eye-opening. Not just for the new, urban backdrop, but also for the way that Lewis Hamilton lost it in qualifying, making it easy for team-mate Nico Rosberg to start winning again.

The teams didn't enjoy the logistical nightmare of getting from the Canadian GP to set up their equipment in Baku – around 9,000km away – just four days later. It was far from the best piece of scheduling. That they were coming to a venue new to them made every element of the operation more of a struggle than usual.

That said, the circuit created on the streets of Azerbaijan's capital earned much praise and awe at the flat-out blast from Turn 16 to the distant Turn 1. Valtteri Bottas's Williams hit 234.9mph before it slowed for the 90-degree left... It had echoes of Valencia, but tempered by the narrowest esse in F1. One bad mark on the track, though, was a drain cover that was more like a grille. It damaged Bottas's Williams and he had to miss the third practice session.

Hamilton appeared to take to the track best, being fastest in all three practice sessions, but then Rosberg moved ahead of him in Q1 and Q2. And when it really mattered, Hamilton clipped the wall at Turn 12, and was 10th on the grid. Rosberg took pole by 0.75s over Force India's Sergio Perez, but he fell to seventh as he had a five-place grid penalty for a gearbox change. This put Daniel Ricciardo on the front row.

Rosberg led away from Ricciardo and Vettel, but the Red Bull driver struggled on his first set of tyres and was an early pit-caller, on lap 6 for the soft compound, having already been passed by Vettel. At the front, Rosberg was able to drop the Ferraris by almost 1s per lap. Hamilton was also on the move, reaching fourth by lap 11, but he knew from lap 1 that he had a problem. It was an ERS setting problem, leaving him short of the electrical boost he should have received under acceleration, and it cost him any chance of a podium shot.

So, Rosberg ran, untroubled, to victory, 16s ahead of Vettel, with Perez taking third from a tyre-exhausted Raikkonen on the final lap. The Finn was disgruntled, as he reckoned that the 5s penalty he collected for crossing the white line at pit entry despite not then calling at the pits, cost him the chance of staying ahead of Perez for the final podium position.

Nico Rosberg almost has enough time to enjoy the Baku scenery on his way to an easy win.

BAKU ROUND 8
DATE: **19 JUNE 2016**
Laps: **51** • Distance: **190.170 miles/306.049km** • Weather: **Hot & sunny**

Pos	Driver	Team	Result	Stops	Qualifying Time	Grid
1	**Nico Rosberg**	Mercedes	1h32m52.366s	1	1m42.758s	1
2	**Sebastian Vettel**	Ferrari	1h33m09.062s	1	1m43.966s	3
3	**Sergio Perez**	Force India	1h33m17.607s	1	1m43.515s	7*
4	**Kimi Raikkonen**	Ferrari	1h33m25.468s!	1	1m44.269s	4!
5	**Lewis Hamilton**	Mercedes	1h33m48.701s	1	2m01.954s	10
6	**Valtteri Bottas**	Williams	1h33m53.252s	1	1m45.246s	8
7	**Daniel Ricciardo**	Red Bull	1h34m01.595s	2	1m43.966s	2
8	**Max Verstappen**	Red Bull	1h34m03.062s	2	1m45.570s	9
9	**Nico Hulkenberg**	Force India	1h34m10.074s	1	1m44.824s	12
10	**Felipe Massa**	Williams	1h34m17.741s	2	1m44.483s	5
11	**Jenson Button**	McLaren	1h34m37.183s	2	1m45.804s	19
12	**Felipe Nasr**	Sauber	50 laps	2	1m46.048s	15
13	**Romain Grosjean**	Haas	50 laps	2	1m44.755s	11
14	**Kevin Magnussen**	Renault	50 laps	1	1m46.348s	22*
15	**Jolyon Palmer**	Renault	50 laps	2	1m46.394s	21
16	**Esteban Gutierrez**	Haas	50 laps	2	1m45.349s	14
17	**Marcus Ericsson**	Sauber	50 laps	2	1m46.231s	20
18	**Rio Haryanto**	Manor	49 laps	1	1m45.665s	16
R	**Fernando Alonso**	McLaren	42 laps/gearbox	2	1m45.270s	13
R	**Pascal Wehrlein**	Manor	39 laps/brakes	1	1m45.750s	17
R	**Carlos Sainz Jr**	Toro Rosso	31 laps/suspension	2	1m45.000s	18*
R	**Daniil Kvyat**	Toro Rosso	6 laps/suspension	1	1m44.717s	6

FASTEST LAP: ROSBERG, 1M46.485S, 126.105MPH/202.946KPH ON LAP 48 • RACE LEADERS: ROSBERG 1-51.
* 5-PLACE GRID PENALTY FOR GEARBOX CHANGE; ! 5S PENALTY FOR CROSSING PIT ENTRY WHITE LINE & NOT ENTERING THE PITS.

It was back to war between the Mercedes drivers as Nico Rosberg and Lewis Hamilton came into contact again, this time on the final lap, after the German had displayed poor judgement while trying to defend his lead.

Left to his own devices, Nico Rosberg can be as fast as Lewis Hamilton. Put them in a racing scenario, though, and Hamilton is the better bet to finish first. Sadly for Rosberg, the reason why was shown again in Austria.

The race had been a strong one for him up to that final lap. He had worked his way to the front of the field after his second place in qualifying had been made worse by a five-place grid penalty for a gearbox change. Rosberg's late lead came after the team had changed its mind over Hamilton completing the race on a one-stop strategy. Mercedes reversed its decision and brought him in for a second stop on lap 54. So, instead of simply taking the lead back and keeping it when Rosberg called in for his second stop on lap 55, Hamilton found himself behind after a slow pitstop and a slight mistake on his out lap.

Hamilton knew he had to pass his team-mate and, after a few more laps, realised that Rosberg was nursing a braking problem. For the final three laps, he was right on Rosberg's tail. Then, on the last lap, Rosberg made an error at the first corner. Hamilton carried more momentum up the hill to Turn 2 and went for the outside line. Rosberg, on the inside, turned in very late and tipped Hamilton over the kerb and grass beyond. Rosberg still led, but his damaged nose folded under the car and Hamilton flashed by for victory.

Max Verstappen made only one stop and what had seemed likely to be an excellent third-place finish became second after the two Mercedes clashed. Indeed, Kimi Raikkonen nipped past too, leaving Rosberg to end up in fourth. Hamilton and Rosberg would leave the Red Bull Ring with the threat of team orders being imposed in future ringing in their ears.

Jenson Button put in a fine performance; he qualified fifth, closed to second early on, and finished sixth for McLaren. His team-mate, Fernando Alonso retired with battery failure, and Nico Hulkenberg, who started his Force India from the front row, suffered tyre woes and then retired with a brake problem.

Nico Rosberg led Lewis Hamilton for all but one of the last 11 laps, but that lap was the final one.

RED BULL RING ROUND 9

DATE: **3 JULY 2016**

Laps: **71** • Distance: **190.773 miles/307.020km** • Weather: **Warm & bright**

Pos	Driver	Team	Result	Stops	Qualifying Time	Grid
1	**Lewis Hamilton**	Mercedes	1h27m38.107s	2	1m07.922s	1
2	**Max Verstappen**	Red Bull	1h27m43.826s	1	1m11.153s	8
3	**Kimi Raikkonen**	Ferrari	1h27m44.131s	1	1m09.901s	4
4	**Nico Rosberg**	Mercedes	1h28m04.817s*	2	1m08.465s	6!!
5	**Daniel Ricciardo**	Red Bull	1h28m09.088s	2	1m09.980s	5
6	**Jenson Button**	McLaren	1h28m15.813s	2	1m09.900s	3
7	**Romain Grosjean**	Haas	1h28m22.775s**	1	1m07.850s	13
8	**Carlos Sainz Jr**	Toro Rosso	1h28m25.507s	2	no time	15
9	**Valtteri Bottas**	Williams	70 laps	2	1m10.440s	7
10	**Pascal Wehrlein**	Manor	70 laps	2	1m07.700s	12
11	**Esteban Gutierrez**	Haas	70 laps	2	1m07.758s	11
12	**Jolyon Palmer**	Renault	70 laps	2	1m07.965s	19!
13	**Felipe Nasr**	Sauber	70 laps	1	1m08.446s	21!
14	**Kevin Magnussen**	Renault	70 laps	2	1m07.941s	17
15	**Marcus Ericsson**	Sauber	70 laps	2	1m08.418s	18
16	**Rio Haryanto**	Manor	70 laps	2	1m08.026s	20!
17	**Sergio Perez**	Force India	69 laps/brakes	2	no time	16
18	**Fernando Alonso**	McLaren	64 laps/power unit	2	1m08.154s	14
19	**Nico Hulkenberg**	Force India	64 laps/brakes	3	1m09.285s	2
20	**Felipe Massa**	Williams	63 laps/brakes	2	1m11.977s	10
R	**Sebastian Vettel**	Ferrari	26 laps/xxx	0	1m09.781s	9!!
R	**Daniil Kvyat**	Toro Rosso	2 laps/xxx	0	1m08.409s	22

FASTEST LAP: HAMILTON, 1M08.411S, 141.453MPH/227.647KPH ON LAP 67 • RACE LEADERS: HAMILTON 1–21 & 71, RAIKKONEN 22, VETTEL 23–26, ROSBERG 27–55 & 61–70, VERSTAPPEN 56–60.

* 10S PENALTY FOR CAUSING A COLLISION; ** 5S PENALTY FOR SPEEDING IN THE PIT LANE; ! 3-PLACE GRID PENALTY FOR FAILING TO SLOW FOR YELLOW FLAGS; !! 5-PLACE GRID PENALTY FOR GEARBOX CHANGE.

BRITISH GP

It felt like 1992 all over again, as Lewis Hamilton's home win triggered scenes like those in the days of Mansellmania, with Union Flags flying everywhere in celebration of him topping every session, then winning with ease.

A look at the championship table revealed just what a season of two parts the first half of the 2016 campaign had been for Lewis Hamilton. No wins in the first five rounds were followed by this result that made it four wins from the next five. This was more than just a win to thrill the fans. This was a win in the sort of dominant style to dispirit Nico Rosberg.

The track was wet before the start and the decision to start the race behind the safety car was slammed by many fans, and a few drivers who felt that since they are the best in the world, they ought to be able to cope. Other drivers thought it was right to start behind the safety car, but it should have pulled off a couple of laps earlier. Either way, Hamilton's lead wasn't challenged at the start, and he dropped Rosberg at an impressive rate once the safety car had withdrawn after five laps.

Rosberg then had another problem: the pace of Max Verstappen. The Dutch ace wasn't hanging around, pulling off a pass for second place at the final part of Becketts on lap 16. Only the brave pass there. When Verstappen had a moment at Abbey, however, Rosberg closed in and duly returned the favour, passing the Red Bull at Stowe on lap 38. But Verstappen ended the day in second, 8.25s down on Hamilton, because Rosberg was hit with a 10s penalty for the team using radio messages to help their driver. It meant he still left Silverstone the championship leader, but by only one point. The team did not appeal Rosberg's penalty.

Daniel Ricciardo brought the other Red Bull home fourth, but he would have been anxious at having been outperformed by his junior team-mate. The Australian didn't have to worry about any challenge from behind, though, as Ferrari's Kimi Raikkonen was fully 43s further back, albeit four places ahead of his team-mate Sebastian Vettel who had a poor race. Sergio Perez kept his run of good results going with sixth place for Force India, and he was shadowed across the line by team-mate Nico Hulkenberg, whom he had passed with six laps to go.

SILVERSTONE ROUND 10 — DATE: 10 JULY 2016

Laps: 52 • Distance: **190.262 miles/306.198km** • Weather: **Mild, with showers**

Pos	Driver	Team	Result	Stops	Qualifying Time	Grid
1	**Lewis Hamilton**	Mercedes	1h34m55.831s	2	1m29.287s	1
2	**Max Verstappen**	Red Bull	1h35m04.081s	2	1m30.313s	3
3	**Nico Rosberg**	Mercedes	1h35m12.742s**	2	1m29.606s	2
4	**Daniel Ricciardo**	Red Bull	1h35m22.042s	2	1m30.618s	4
5	**Kimi Raikkonen**	Ferrari	1h36m05.574s	2	1m30.881s	5
6	**Sergio Perez**	Force India	1h36m12.772s	2	1m31.875s	10
7	**Nico Hulkenberg**	Force India	1h36m13.543s	2	1m32.172s	8
8	**Carlos Sainz Jr**	Toro Rosso	1h36m21.689s	2	1m31.989s	7
9	**Sebastian Vettel**	Ferrari	1h36m27.485s*	2	1m31.490s	11!
10	**Daniil Kvyat**	Toro Rosso	1h36m28.431s	2	1m32.306s	15
11	**Felipe Massa**	Williams	51 laps	2	1m32.002s	12
12	**Jenson Button**	McLaren	51 laps	2	1m32.788s	17
13	**Fernando Alonso**	McLaren	51 laps	3	1m32.343s	9
14	**Valtteri Bottas**	Williams	51 laps	2	1m31.557s	6
15	**Felipe Nasr**	Sauber	51 laps	2	1m33.544s	21
16	**Esteban Gutierrez**	Haas	51 laps	2	1m32.241s	14
17	**Kevin Magnussen**	Renault	49 laps/gearbox	3	1m37.060s	16
R	**Jolyon Palmer**	Renault	37 laps/gearbox	3	1m32.905s	18
R	**Rio Haryanto**	Manor	24 laps/spun off	2	1m33.098s	19
R	**Romain Grosjean**	Haas	17 laps/transmission	2	1m32.050s	13
R	**Marcus Ericsson**	Sauber	11 laps/electrical	2	No time	22!!
R	**Pascal Wehrlein**	Manor	6 laps/spun off	1	1m33.151s	20

FASTEST LAP: **ROSBERG, 1M35.548S, 137.917MPH/221.957KPH ON LAP 44** • RACE LEADERS: **HAMILTON 1–17 & 19–52, VERSTAPPEN 18.**
* 5-SECOND PENALTY FOR FORCING MASSA OFF TRACK; ** 10-SECOND PENALTY FOR USING RADIO TEAM MESSAGES; ! 5-PLACE GRID PENALTY FOR CHANGING GEARBOX; !! HAD TO START FROM PITLANE FOR CHANGING SURVIVAL CELL.

Controversy raged at Silverstone when the safety car led the drivers away at the start of the race.

Lewis Hamilton finally got into the championship lead after outracing Nico Rosberg with their rivals far behind at a circuit on which Mercedes was thought to enjoy its smallest performance advantage.

The Hungaroring has a history of producing surprise results. Frustratingly for Red Bull, it didn't happen in 2016. The theory is the circuit's twisting nature doesn't play to the Mercedes W07s' strengths, but the team depressed their rivals by annexing the front row, as usual. With overtaking so hard, most could pray only for changeable conditions.

At the start, Hamilton beat Rosberg to Turn 1, and he then thwarted Daniel Ricciardo's attempted move around the outside. Ricciardo briefly was second but Rosberg repassed him at Turn 2. From there, it was all Mercedes. Ricciardo closed back in, but his soft tyres went first, indicating how hard he'd been pushing. Mercedes kept its drivers out eight and nine laps longer, respectively, and so their third set of tyres were fresher for the run to the flag. By the end Ricciardo was 25s and more behind.

The Australian did finish third, holding off the charging Ferrari of Sebastian Vettel. There was another Red Bull/Ferrari tussle some 20s behind them, and Max Verstappen headed Kimi Raikkonen, though the Finn criticised the teenager's defensive driving. McLaren's form continued to improve and Fernando Alonso picked up the six points for finishing seventh, having started seventh too. However, he was lapped, suggesting there is still much work to be done by the McLaren/Honda partnership.

Team-mate Jenson Button had a less happy time in Hungary, as he picked up a drive-through penalty for receiving radio instruction after his MP4-31 suffered a brake problem early in the race, even though he then pitted. He was livid. Late in the race, he retired with an oil leak. Carlos Sainz Jr took eighth after another strong run for Scuderia Toro Rosso, while team-mate Daniil Kvyat's downward-spiralling career continued; he lost eight places after a terrible start, and couldn't make them back.

Just as disappointed, though, was Jolyon Palmer, who had advanced to 10th place, and was all set for his first point, when he spun his Renault at Turn 4 and lost three places.

HUNGARORING ROUND 11

DATE: 24 JULY 2016

Laps: 70 • Distance: **190.531 miles/306.630km** • Weather: **Hot & sunny**

Pos	Driver	Team	Result	Stops	Qualifying Time	Grid
1	**Lewis Hamilton**	Mercedes	1h40m30.115s	2	1m20.108s	2
2	**Nico Rosberg**	Mercedes	1h40m32.092s	2	1m19.965s	1
3	**Daniel Ricciardo**	Red Bull	1h40m57.654s	2	1m20.280s	3
4	**Sebastian Vettel**	Ferrari	1h40m58.328s	2	1m20.874s	5
5	**Max Verstappen**	Red Bull	1h41m18.774s	2	1m20.557s	4
6	**Kimi Raikkonen**	Ferrari	1h41m19.159s	2	1m25.435s	14
7	**Fernando Alonso**	McLaren	69 laps	2	1m21.211s	7
8	**Carlos Sainz Jr**	Toro Rosso	69 laps	2	1m21.131s	6
9	**Valtteri Bottas**	Williams	69 laps	2	1m22.182s	10
10	**Nico Hulkenberg**	Force India	69 laps	2	1m21.823s	9
11	**Sergio Perez**	Force India	69 laps	2	1m25.416s	13
12	**Jolyon Palmer**	Renault	69 laps	2	1m43.965s	17
13	**Esteban Gutierrez**	Haas	69 laps!	2	1m26.189s	15
14	**Romain Grosjean**	Haas	69 laps	2	1m24.941s	11
15	**Kevin Magnussen**	Renault	69 laps	2	1m44.543s	19
16	**Daniil Kvyat**	Toro Rosso	69 laps	2	1m25.301s	12
17	**Felipe Nasr**	Sauber	69 laps	2	1m27.063s	16
18	**Felipe Massa**	Williams	68 laps	2	1m43.999s	18
19	**Pascal Wehrlein**	Manor	68 laps	1	1m47.343s	20
20	**Marcus Ericsson**	Sauber	68 laps	3	1m46.984s	22**
21	**Rio Haryanto**	Manor	68 laps	2	1m50.189s	21*
R	**Jenson Button**	McLaren	60 laps/oil leak	3	1m21.597s	8

FASTEST LAP: RAIKKONEN, 1M23.086S, 117.950MPH/189.822KPH ON LAP 52 • RACE LEADERS: HAMILTON 1-15, 18-40 & 43-70, ROSBERG 16-17 & 41-42.

* 5-PLACE GRID PENALTY; ** HAD TO START FROM PITLANE FOR CHANGE OF SURVIVAL CELL; ! 5S PENALTY FOR IGNORING BLUE FLAG.

Lewis Hamilton sprays fans surrounding his Mercedes in parc ferme after his win in Hungary.

GERMAN GP

Nico Rosberg wanted glory at home. He wanted the 25 points to go with it, but fluffed his start, trailed home fourth and victory went instead to title rival Lewis Hamilton, who reached the summer break with a 19-point lead.

One-tenth of a second isn't a lot of time, but it's plenty if it puts you on pole. Rosberg started from the premier position, but blew it with an awful getaway letting Hamilton and the Red Bull duo Max Verstappen and Daniel Ricciardo all pass him. And with Red Bull's form rising, Rosberg couldn't pass them on the circuit. And his hopes of passing them with a sleek first pitstop failed as it was a slow one, so fourth Rosberg remained.

He did get, briefly, into third, diving up the inside of Verstappen at the Spitzkehre hairpin, on the lap that the Red Bull driver emerged from his second pitstop. However, Verstappen had to take to the run-off area to avoid him and so the stewards adjudged Rosberg's move to have endangered another driver and hit him with a 5s penalty. Ricciardo had already asserted himself in second as he ran a longer second stint on the soft compound tyres than Verstappen had run on super softs, and this gave him the advantage that he needed. There was nothing that he could do about Hamilton, though, ending the race 7s down.

Ferrari had to settle for Sebastian Vettel and Kimi Raikkonen being fifth and sixth, respectively, with the Finn chastened after electing to override the team's call for him to come in for his final pitstop. He later admitted he had been wrong to think Ferrari was being too conservative. The only other driver not to be lapped was Force India's Nico Hulkenberg, who finished seventh. Williams got its strategy wrong and made Valtteri Bottas run a two-stop strategy, instead of those ahead of him making three. Bottas fell from seventh place to ninth, being passed by Jenson Button. Felipe Massa struggled even more, after being rear-ended by Jolyon Palmer's Renault on the opening lap. The Brazilian fell from the pace, insisting there was a problem, which Williams couldn't find, but the team eventually retired the car.

Mercedes and Sauber have had drivers making contact this season, and Manor joined them at Hockenheim when Rio Haryanto ran into Pascal Wehrlein at the Spitzkehre hairpin.

Daniel Ricciardo, winner Lewis Hamilton and Max Verstappen meant no podium for Nico Rosberg.

HOCKENHEIM ROUND 12

DATE: **31 JULY 2016**

Laps: **67** • Distance: **187.666 miles/306.458km** • Weather: **Warm & overcast**

Pos	Driver	Team	Result	Stops	Qualifying Time	Grid
1	**Lewis Hamilton**	Mercedes	1h30m44.200s	3	1m14.470s	2
2	**Daniel Ricciardo**	Red Bull	1h30m51.196s	3	1m14.726s	3
3	**Max Verstappen**	Red Bull	1h30m57.613s	3	1m14.834s	4
4	**Nico Rosberg**	Mercedes	1h31m00.045s	3	1m14.363s	1
5	**Sebastian Vettel**	Ferrari	1h31m16.770s	3	1m15.315s	6
6	**Kimi Raikkonen**	Ferrari	1h31m21.223s	3	1m15.142s	5
7	**Nico Hulkenberg**	Force India	1h31m54.249s	3	1m15.510s	8*
8	**Jenson Button**	McLaren	66 laps	3	1m15.909s	12
9	**Valtteri Bottas**	Williams	66 laps	2	1m15.530s	7
10	**Sergio Perez**	Force India	66 laps	3	1m15.537s	9
11	**Esteban Gutierrez**	Haas	66 laps	2	1m15.883s	11
12	**Fernando Alonso**	McLaren	66 laps	3	1m16.041s	13
13	**Romain Grosjean**	Haas	66 laps	2	1m16.086s	20!
14	**Carlos Sainz Jr**	Toro Rosso	66 laps	3	1m15.989s	15**
15	**Daniil Kvyat**	Toro Rosso	66 laps	3	1m16.876s	18
16	**Kevin Magnussen**	Renault	66 laps	2	1m16.716s	16
17	**Pascal Wehrlein**	Manor	65 laps	3	1m16.717s	17
18	**Marcus Ericsson**	Sauber	65 laps	2	1m17.238s	22
19	**Jolyon Palmer**	Renault	65 laps	3	1m16.665s	14
20	**Rio Haryanto**	Manor	65 laps	3	1m16.977s	19
R	**Felipe Nasr**	Sauber	57 laps/power unit	3	1m17.123s	21
R	**Felipe Massa**	Williams	36 laps/collision	2	1m15.615s	10

FASTEST LAP: RICCIARDO, 1M18.442S, 130.437MPH/209.918KPH ON LAP 48 • RACE LEADERS: HAMILTON 1-67
* 1-PLACE GRID PENALTY FOR USING TYRES WITHOUT IDENTIFICATION; ** 3-PLACE GRID PENALTY FOR IMPEDING ANOTHER DRIVER;
! 5-PLACE GRID PENALTY FOR CHANGING GEARBOX.

BELGIAN GP

Nico Rosberg had it easy as team-mate Lewis Hamilton had to battle from the back of the grid after the Mercedes team used replacement power units and came though to third. The talk post-race, though, was of how upset Ferrari's drivers were with Max Verstappen.

Grid penalties have become the bane of modern F1, being handed out for changing a gearbox or, worse, changing to an additional power unit beyond the season's allocation. These rules were created to prevent teams from unlimited spending, but take the sting out of many a race.

Take Lewis Hamilton's plight on F1's return from its summer break: he was hit with both a five-place grid penalty for the former and a 55-place penalty for the latter. At a time when Mercedes continued to have a performance advantage over the opposition, albeit with Red Bull Racing and Ferrari getting closer, it only took Hamilton out of the winning equation. All he could do was see how close to the front of the field he could get after 44 laps.

The answer was third place, ending a run of four consecutive wins, as team-mate Rosberg cruised to his sixth win of the year.

Rosberg led from pole, helped by Max Verstappen being slow away from the outside of the front row and then finding himself fighting for the same piece of track as the Ferraris at La Source. This spun Sebastian Vettel around and Kimi Raikkonen picked up a cut tyre that deflated as he ran through Eau Rouge. By the end of the lap, Hulkenberg had passed Verstappen for second, with Fernando Alonso, who'd started from the back row, up to 12th, and Hamilton up to 15th.

Rosberg led with ease, especially when Hulkenberg pitted early to get rid of his supersoft tyres. Hulkenberg then benefited when the red flag was shown three laps later, allowing debris from Kevin Magnussen's sizeable accident at Eau Rouge to be cleared. The Renault driver was fortunate to limp away unaided with just a cut on his ankle.

Hamilton rose to fifth when the green flags flew, then passed Alonso and Hulkenberg. That left just Rosberg and Red Bull's Daniel Ricciardo ahead, but they proved to be too much of a challenge.

SPA-FRANCHORCHAMPS ROUND 13 DATE: 28 AUGUST 2016

Laps: 44 • Distance: **191.414 miles/308.052km** • Weather: **Hot & sunny**

Pos	Driver	Team	Result	Stops	Qualifying Time	Grid
1	**Nico Rosberg**	Mercedes	1h44m51.058s	2	1m46.744s	1
2	**Daniel Ricciardo**	Red Bull	1h45m05.171s	2	1m47.216s	5
3	**Lewis Hamilton**	Mercedes	1h45m18.692s	3	1m50.033s	21!
4	**Nico Hulkenberg**	Force India	1h45m26.965s	3	1m47.543s	7
5	**Sergio Perez**	Force India	1h45m31.718s	3	1m47.407s	6
6	**Sebastian Vettel**	Ferrari	1h45m36.452s	3	1m47.108s	4
7	**Fernando Alonso**	McLaren	1h45m50.503s	2	no time	22!!
8	**Valtteri Bottas**	Williams	1h45m51.209s	3	1m47.612s	8
9	**Kimi Raikkonen**	Ferrari	1h45m52.167s	4	1m46.910s	3
10	**Felipe Massa**	Williams	1h45m56.931s	3	1m48.263s	10
11	**Max Verstappen**	Red Bull	1h46m02.196s	4	1m46.893s	2
12	**Esteban Gutierrez**	Haas	1h46m04.935s	3	1m48.598s	18*
13	**Romain Grosjean**	Haas	1h46m07.532s	3	1m48.316s	11
14	**Daniil Kvyat**	Toro Rosso	1h46m18.155s	3	1m49.058s	19
15	**Jolyon Palmer**	Renault	1h46m24.223s	4	1m48.888s	13
16	**Esteban Ocon**	Manor	43 laps	3	1m49.050s	17
17	**Felipe Nasr**	Sauber	43 laps	3	1m48.949s	16
R	**Kevin Magnussen**	Renault	5 laps/accident	0	1m48.485s	12
R	**Marcus Ericsson**	Sauber	3 laps/gearbox	0	1m49.071s	20**
R	**Carlos Sainz Jr**	Toro Rosso	1 lap/tyre	0	1m49.038s	14
R	**Jenson Button**	McLaren	1 lap/collision	0	1m48.1114s	9
R	**Pascal Wehrlein**	Manor	0 laps/collision	0	1m49.320s	15

FASTEST LAP: HAMILTON, 1M51.583S, 140.410MPH/225.969KPH ON LAP 40. • RACE LEADERS: ROSBERG 1-44.
* 5-PLACE GRID FOR IMPEDING ANOTHER DRIVER; ** 10-PLACE GRID PENALTY FOR USING ADDITIONAL POWER UNIT ELEMENTS;
! 55-PLACE GRID PENALTY FOR USING ADDITIONAL POWER UNIT ELEMENTS; + 5-PLACE GRID PENALTY FOR GEARBOX CHANGE,
!! 60-PLACE GRID PENALTY FOR USING ADDITIONAL POWER UNIT ELEMENTS.

Rosberg leads into Eau Rouge, with Raikkonen's Ferrari (third) about to suffer tyre deflation.

ITALIAN GP

It was back to regular service for Mercedes as the team clocked up yet another one-two finish at Monza. Having qualified on pole position, Lewis Hamilton might have expected to take victory, but he made a poor start, falling to sixth, and Nico Rosberg seized the day.

Hamilton produced an outstanding lap to take pole by almost half a second over Rosberg. With Sebastian Vettel third, 0.3s further back, things looked very promising for Hamilton as he lined up for the race.

Then he suffered from wheelspin at the start as Rosberg grabbed the lead, with Vettel, Kimi Raikkonen, Valtteri Bottas and Daniel Ricciardo all passing him before the first chicane. Hamilton pointed out that a similar problem had caught out Rosberg in Hungary. Considering how Mercedes had got pretty much everything right on the F1 W07, this seemed an all too obvious failing.

Hamilton picked off Ricciardo and Bottas easily. As he and Rosberg were on one-stop runs, Hamilton assumed second when the Ferrari drivers pitted for a second time.

Emerging from his stop 11.5s behind Rosberg, Hamilton clawed back a few seconds, but then lost time by going up the escape road at the first chicane on lap 41.

Vettel was benefiting from the extra life in his third set of tyres, but he wasn't close enough to benefit from this slip-up and would finish 6s behind Hamilton. Vettel and Raikkonen took the points for third and fourth, but it was seen as a failure by the tifosi in front of whom many an upswing in form has materialised over the decades.

Of the rest, Ricciardo got his Red Bull past Bottas's Williams with a bold dive into the first chicane with seven laps to go to finish in fifth place.

With points a rarity for some teams, a shot at the tail of the top 10 remains their target, and this was the case for points-light Renault, which is why Jolyon Palmer – a driver fighting for his F1 future as Renault considered its driver selection for 2017 – was furious after contact with Sauber's Felipe Nasr at the first chicane ended his race. Kevin Magnussen avoided the clash ahead of him, but showed how far Renault had fallen away in 2016 by coming home 17th, ahead only of Manor's Esteban Ocon.

Rosberg celebrates with the team after his second win in a row put him just two points down.

MONZA ROUND 14

DATE: **4 SEPTEMBER 2016**

Laps: **53** • Distance: **190.587 miles/306.720km** • Weather: **Hot & sunny**

Pos	Driver	Team	Result	Stops	Qualifying Time	Grid
1	Nico Rosberg	Mercedes	1h17m28.089s	1	1m21.613s	2
2	Lewis Hamilton	Mercedes	1h17m43.159s	1	1m21.135s	1
3	Sebastian Vettel	Ferrari	1h17m49.079s	2	1m21.972s	3
4	Kimi Raikkonen	Ferrari	1h17m55.650s	2	1m22.065s	4
5	Daniel Ricciardo	Red Bull	1h18m13.384s	2	1m22.389s	6
6	Valtteri Bottas	Williams	1h18m22.325s	2	1m22.388s	5
7	Max Verstappen	Red Bull	1h18m19.104s	2	1m22.411s	7
8	Sergio Perez	Force India	1h18m22.325s	2	1m22.814s	8
9	Felipe Massa	Williams	1h18m33.706s	2	1m22.967s	11
10	Nico Hulkenberg	Force India	1h18m46.745s	2	1m22.836s	9
11	Romain Grosjean	Haas	52 laps	1	1m23.092s	17*
12	Jenson Button	McLaren	52 laps	2	1m23.399s	14
13	Esteban Gutierrez	Haas	52 laps	2	1m23.184s	10
14	Fernando Alonso	McLaren	52 laps	3	1m23.273s	12
15	Carlos Sainz Jr	Toro Rosso	52 laps	2	1m23.496s	15
16	Marcus Ericsson	Sauber	52 laps	1	1m24.087s	19
17	Kevin Magnussen	Renault	52 laps	2	1m21.436s	21
18	Esteban Ocon	Manor	51 laps	1	no time	22*
R	Daniil Kvyat	Toro Rosso	36 laps/battery	2	1m23.825s	16
R	Pascal Wehrlein	Manor	26 laps/oil pressure	1	1m23.315s	13
R	Jolyon Palmer	Renault	7 laps/collision	1	1m24.230s	20
R	Felipe Nasr	Sauber	6 laps/collision	3	1m23.956s	18

FASTEST LAP: **ALONSO, 1M25.340S, 151.844MPH/244.373KPH ON LAP 51.** • RACE LEADERS: **ROSBERG 1–24 & 26–53, HAMILTON 25.**
* 5-PLACE GRID PENALTY FOR CHANGING GEARBOX.

This was the race in which Nico Rosberg laid down his marker and showed Lewis Hamilton that he was also serious about becoming the 2016 World Champion as he took the points lead. Daniel Ricciardo came within an ace, though, of wrecking his result.

Pole by more than half a second to Rosberg was the first sign that this might be a good meeting for the German. Better still, from his point of view, was that the driver who qualified second wasn't team-mate Hamilton but Red Bull Racing's Ricciardo.

The start was a clean one for Rosberg. Behind him, Kimi Raikkonen demoted Max Verstappen from fourth before they reached Turn 1, this after the Dutch teenager spun his wheels, and it led to trouble behind. Nico Hulkenberg made a great start and dived between the Toro Rossos, only for Carlos Sainz Jr to swerve to avoid Verstappen and pitch Hulkenberg into the wall.

This brought out the safety car and Rosberg was able to stay in front when it withdrew. Ricciardo stayed in contact through this next stint, although it wasn't all smooth running for Rosberg as he was aware that his brakes were overheating.

When the pair made their first call to the pits, Raikkonen assumed the lead, only to fall back to fourth, behind Rosberg, Ricciardo and Hamilton, once he'd made his visit.

Likewise, Hamilton led for a lap when they all came in for a second time, but this masked the fact that he'd ceded third place to Raikkonen earlier that lap when he ran too deep into Turn 9.

Aware that it might have to change its tactics to get Hamilton back ahead, Mercedes elected to bring Hamilton in for a third stop on lap 45. This caused Ferrari to change its tactics, too, and bring in Raikkonen next time around. Unfortunately for Ferrari, Raikkonen re-emerged in fourth, and that was how it stayed to the finish.

Ricciardo, 3s behind Rosberg, pitted on lap 47. Felipe Massa got in Rosberg's way on the next lap, meaning Mercedes didn't dare bring him in as he might have come out behind Ricciardo. So, the run to the flag would be between Rosberg and Ricciardo on fresh rubber. Fully 25s down on his return, Ricciardo got to within 0.488s.

108

Hulkenberg's ace start ended up with his car in the wall after being squeezed by the Toro Rossos.

MARINA BAY ROUND 15

DATE: **18 SEPTEMBER 2016**

Laps: **61** • Distance: **191.896 miles/308.828km** • Weather: **Hot & humid**

Pos	Driver	Team	Result	Stops	Qualifying Time	Grid
1	**Nico Rosberg**	Mercedes	1h55m48.950s	2	1m42.584s	1
2	**Daniel Ricciardo**	Red Bull	1h55m49.438s	3	1m43.115s	2
3	**Lewis Hamilton**	Mercedes	1h55m56.988s	3	1m43.288s	3
4	**Kimi Raikkonen**	Ferrari	1h55m59.169s	3	1m43.540s	5
5	**Sebastian Vettel**	Ferrari	1h56m14.644s	2	1m49.116s	22*!!
6	**Max Verstappen**	Red Bull	1h57m00.147s	3	1m43.328s	4
7	**Fernando Alonso**	McLaren	1h57m18.148s	2	1m44.553s	9
8	**Sergio Perez**	Force India	1h57m40.012s	2	1m44.582s	17^!
9	**Daniil Kvyat**	Toro Rosso	1h57m40.507s	2	1m44.469s	7
10	**Kevin Magnussen**	Renault	1h57m48.902s	2	1m46.825s	15
11	**Esteban Gutierrez**	Haas	60 laps	2	1m45.593s	13
12	**Felipe Massa**	Williams	60 laps	3	1m44.991s	11
13	**Felipe Nasr**	Sauber	60 laps	2	1m46.860s	16
14	**Carlos Sainz Jr**	Toro Rosso	60 laps	3	1m44.197s	6
15	**Jolyon Palmer**	Renault	60 laps	2	1m46.960s	18
16	**Pascal Wehrlein**	Manor	60 laps	2	1m47.667s	19
17	**Marcus Ericsson**	Sauber	60 laps	3	1m47.827s	14
18	**Esteban Ocon**	Manor	59 laps	3	1m48.296s	21
R	**Jenson Button**	McLaren	43 laps/collision	3	1m45.144s	12
R	**Valtteri Bottas**	Williams	35 laps/collision	4	1m44.740s	10
R	**Nico Hulkenberg**	Force India	0 laps/accident	0	1m44.479s	8
NS	**Romain Grosjean**	Haas	0 laps/brakes	0	1m45.723s	20*

FASTEST LAP: RICCIARDO, 1M47.187S, 105.703MPH/170.113KPH ON LAP 49 • RACE LEADERS: ROSBERG 1-16, 18-33, 35-61, RAIKKONEN 17; HAMILTON 34; ! 3-PLACE GRID PENALTY FOR OVERTAKING UNDER YELLOW FLAGS, ^ 5-PLACE GRID PENALTY FOR IGNORING WAVED YELLOW FLAGS, * 5-PLACE GRID PENALTY FOR CHANGING GEARBOX, !! 20-PLACE GRID PENALTY FOR USING ADDITIONAL POWER UNIT ELEMENTS.

Sepang provided the pivotal moment in the 2016 World Championship when Lewis Hamilton's engine blew, while leading. It didn't hand victory to team-mate Nico Rosberg, though, but a one-two for Red Bull Racing, led by Daniel Ricciardo.

Hamilton knew he had to start racking up wins to regain the championship lead. Pole position, by fully 0.414s over Rosberg, was a good start. Both Red Bull Racing drivers looked on form as they filled row two, ahead of the Ferraris.

For once no one troubled Hamilton at the start as he got the power down well enough to lead at the first corner. It proved to be the best place to be, as mayhem broke out as Sebastian Vettel, going up the inside of Max Verstappen, missed his braking point for Turn 1, clipped the kerb on the inside and slammed into Rosberg, spinning the German around. Vettel, with broken suspension, was out instantly, while Rosberg completed the lap in 17th.

This wasn't a complete gift to Hamilton, because the Red Bull duo were able to stick to his tail. Verstappen, running third, was convinced he was faster than Daniel Ricciardo and got on to the radio to his team, requesting the chance to be let by to chase Hamilton. No such move was approved.

A virtual safety car period, after Romain Grosjean put his Haas into the gravel at Turn 15, gave Verstappen the chance to change his tactics, and he pitted. This dropped him behind Kimi Raikkonen's Ferrari, and almost behind Valtteri Bottas's Williams, but it proved to be a gamble that didn't work. Hamilton had the pace to win, but his engine failed on lap 41, two laps after Verstappen all but passed Ricciardo. So, their battle was no longer over second but the lead, and Ricciardo prevailed.

Hamilton tweeted later that "something didn't feel quite right about the number of engine failures that he'd been having" and that "someone didn't want him to win this title". The team pointed out that his new engine was one pulled from a pool used by both drivers and non-executive chairman Niki Lauda angrily refuted Hamilton's comments about sabotage as "ridiculous and stupid".

If there was a small consolation for Hamilton, it was that his team-mate left Sepang with only the 15 points for third place to which he recovered after his first lap spin.

SEPANG ROUND 16

DATE: **1 OCTOBER 2016**

Laps: **56** • Distance: **192.879 miles/310.408km** • Weather: **Hot & bright**

Pos	Driver	Team	Result	Stops	Qualifying Time	Grid
1	Daniel Ricciardo	Red Bull	1h37m12.776s	2	1m33.467s	4
2	Max Verstappen	Red Bull	1h37m15.219s	3	1m33.420s	3
3	Nico Rosberg	Mercedes	1h37m38.292s!!	3	1m33.264s	2
4	Kimi Raikkonen	Ferrari	1h37m41.561s	3	1m33.632s	6
5	Valtteri Bottas	Williams	1h38m14.358s	1	1m34.577s	11
6	Sergio Perez	Force India	1h38m16.570s	2	1m34.319s	7
7	Fernando Alonso	McLaren	1h38m17.981s	3	1m37.155s	22*
8	Nico Hulkenberg	Force India	1h38m26.838s	3	1m34.489s	8
9	Jenson Button	McLaren	1h38m34.592s	2	1m34.518s	9
10	Jolyon Palmer	Renault	1h38m48.242s	1	1m35.999s	19
11	Carlos Sainz Jr	Toro Rosso	1h38m51.654s	2	1m35.374s	16
12	Marcus Ericsson	Sauber	55 laps	2	1m35.816s	17!
13	Felipe Massa	Williams	55 laps	3	1m34.671s	10
14	Daniil Kvyat	Toro Rosso	55 laps	3	1m35.369s	14
15	Pascal Wehrlein	Manor	55 laps	3	1m36.587s	21
16	Esteban Ocon	Manor	55 laps	2	1m36.451s	20
R	Felipe Nasr	Sauber	46 laps/brakes	1	1m35.949s	18
R	Lewis Hamilton	Mercedes	40 laps/engine	1	1m32.850s	1
R	Esteban Gutierrez	Haas	39 laps/lost wheel	2	1m35.097s	13
R	Kevin Magnussen	Renault	17 laps/brakes	1	1m35.277s	14
R	Romain Grosjean	Haas	7 laps/brakes	0	1m345.001s	12
R	Sebastian Vettel	Ferrari	0 laps/collision	0	1m33.584s	5

FASTEST LAP: ROSBERG, 1M36.424S, 128.591MPH/206.948KPH ON LAP 44. • RACE LEADERS: HAMILTON 1-20 & 28-40; RICCIARDO 21 & 41-56; VERSTAPPEN 22-27.
* 15-PLACE GRID PENALTY FOR USING ADDITIONAL POWER UNIT ELEMENTS;
! STARTED FROM THE PITLANE; !! 10S PENALTY FOR CAUSING A COLLISION.

The 25 points for victory were heading Lewis Hamilton's way until engine failure left him with none.

JAPANESE GP

Nico Rosberg was able to put one hand on the 2016 World Champion's trophy when Lewis Hamilton was slow away at the start at Suzuka and then had to spend the rest of the race fighting his way back up to third place.

Two races in two weekends seemed to be too much for Lewis Hamilton as his mid-race blow-up in Malaysia was followed by some peculiar behaviour in Japan. From declining to speak to journalists to spending a press conference posting doctored photos of himself and his rivals on social media, he fell short of what F1 expects. Then, when he was slow off the line at the start and fell from second behind Nico Rosberg to eighth, he presented the 25 points for victory to his team-mate on a plate. Not surprisingly, Rosberg gleefully accepted the gift and controlled proceedings from there, thus taking a 33-point lead away from Suzuka with just four rounds remaining, easily enough for second place in each of these races to be sufficient to land his first F1 title.

It was very tight between the Mercedes duo in qualifying, and Rosberg took pole, by 0.013s. It should have been the two Mercedes first and second into the first corner, with the only question being which driver would lead. Hamilton, however, got wheelspin and could only watch as Rosberg ran untroubled down to Turn 1. By the time that Hamilton had got traction, he was back in ninth.

It meant another recovery drive for Hamilton, who did well to finish third. Rosberg, meanwhile, edged clear of Max Verstappen and Sergio Perez, with the latter soon passed by Sebastian Vettel. Hamilton ran a longer first stint than most drivers and was fourth after the first round of stops. That became third after the second round, demoting Vettel, but he could get no closer than 1s behind the impressive Verstappen, with Rosberg 5s further ahead for his ninth win of the year.

Force India was delighted with the points from Perez and Nico Hulkenberg's seventh and eighth places. It stretched their slim advantage over Williams to 10 points in the battle to end the year fourth overall – and the prize money that comes from a good Constructors' Cup finish. Less happy was McLaren, off the pace at the home race for its engine supplier Honda, with both of its drivers far from the points.

SUZUKA ROUND 17   DATE: **9 OCTOBER 2016**

Laps: **53** • Distance: **: 191.053 miles/307.471km** • Weather: **Mild and cloudy**

Pos	Driver	Team	Result	Stops	Qualifying Time	Grid
1	**Nico Rosberg**	Mercedes	1h26m43.333s	2	1m30.647s	1
2	**Max Verstappen**	Red Bull	1h26m48.311s	2	1m31.178s	3
3	**Lewis Hamilton**	Mercedes	1h26m49.109s	2	1m30.660s	2
4	**Sebastian Vettel**	Ferrari	1h27m03.602s	2	1m31.028s	6*
5	**Kimi Raikkonen**	Ferrari	1h27m11.703s	2	1m30.949s	8!
6	**Daniel Ricciardo**	Red Bull	1h27m17.274s	2	1m31.240s	4
7	**Sergio Perez**	Force India	1h27m40.828s	2	1m31.961s	5
8	**Nico Hulkenberg**	Force India	1h27m42.510s	2	1m32.142s	9
9	**Felipe Massa**	Williams	1h28m21.096s	1	1m32.380s	12
10	**Valtteri Bottas**	Williams	1h28m21.656s	1	1m32.315s	11
11	**Romain Grosjean**	Haas	1h28m22.587s	2	1m31.961s	7
12	**Jolyon Palmer**	Renault	52 laps	1	1m32.807s	16
13	**Daniil Kvyat**	Toro Rosso	52 laps	2	1m32.623s	13
14	**Kevin Magnussen**	Renault	52 laps	1	1m33.023s	17
15	**Marcus Ericsson**	Sauber	52 laps	1	1m33.222s	18
16	**Fernando Alonso**	McLaren	52 laps	2	1m32.689s	15
17	**Carlos Sainz Jr**	Toro Rosso	52 laps	2	1m32.685s	14
18	**Jenson Button**	McLaren	52 laps	2	1m32.851s	22!!
19	**Felipe Nasr**	Sauber	52 laps	1	1m33.332s	19
20	**Esteban Gutierrez**	Haas	52 laps	2	1m32.547s	10
21	**Esteban Ocon**	Manor	52 laps	2	1m33.353s	20
22	**Pascal Wehrlein**	Manor	52 laps	2	1m33.561s	21!

FASTEST LAP: VETTEL, 1M35.118S, 136.565MPH/219.781KPH ON LAP 36. • RACE LEADERS: ROSBERG 1–29 & 35–53, VETTEL 30–34.
* 3-PLACE GRID PENALTY FOR CAUSING A COLLISION; ! 5-PLACE GRID PENALTY FOR CHANGING GEARBOX;
!! 35-PLACE GRID PENALTY FOR USING ADDITIONAL POWER UNIT ELEMENTS.

Max Verstappen, Nico Rosberg and Lewis Hamilton all had very different races to reach the podium.

🇺🇸 UNITED STATES GP

Lewis Hamilton knew that there could be no more slip-ups. He had to win in Texas and so he did. That Nico Rosberg had no challengers on his drive to second place meant Hamilton's victory only brought the points difference between the Mercedes drivers down by seven.

Lewis Hamilton, having won three of the four grands prix held at the Circuit of the Americas, knew he went well there, and continued in that vein, dominating first practice at the Texan venue and, in qualifying, took pole from Rosberg by 0.216s. Once again the Red Bulls came next, then the Ferraris.

Daniel Ricciardo doesn't play mind games, but he will have sensed that Rosberg would back out of a challenge, knowing that he no longer needed to win races to secure the crown. The Australian dived up Rosberg's inside into Turn 1 and was proved right as Rosberg didn't resist him.

Red Bull then hit a poor patch. Verstappen, having passed Kimi Raikkonen, was closing in on Rosberg when he misheard a radio message and made his second pitstop, but the pit crew weren't expecting him... That blew his hope of taking third. Soon afterwards, his gearbox failed. This enabled Rosberg to make his second stop during the ensuing virtual safety car period, so Ricciardo fell to third and Rosberg got the 18 points for second.

Hamilton was comfortably clear and should have enjoyed a serene run to the finish. But he was petrified that his engine would fail, as it had so expensively in Malaysia. He backed off and cruised in, happy only when he accelerated out of the final corner for the last time. At least he got there, unlike Raikkonen, whose run was wrecked when a wheel wasn't attached properly.

Only six cars finished on the lead lap, with Fernando Alonso claiming fifth and Carlos Sainz Jr taking sixth. The McLaren driver had gained position by pitting during the virtual safety car period and caught Sainz Jr and Felipe Massa's Williams in the closing laps. A clash at Turn 16 left Massa with a puncture and Sainz, with tyres that were past their best, could not resist him. Thus Alonso equalled his fifth place at Monaco and was especially delighted because it came on a circuit at which the McLaren-Honda was at far more of a disadvantage.

Hamilton leads the way approaching Turn 1 as Ricciardo shapes up to make a move to pass Rosberg.

CIRCUIT OF THE AMERICAS ROUND 18

DATE: 23 OCTOBER 2016

Laps: **56** • Distance: **191.643 miles/308.420km** • Weather: **Hot & sunny**

Pos	Driver	Team	Result	Stops	Qualifying Time	Grid
1	**Lewis Hamilton**	Mercedes	1h38m12.618s	2	1m34.999s	1
2	**Nico Rosberg**	Mercedes	1h38m17.138s	2	1m35.215s	2
3	**Daniel Ricciardo**	Red Bull	1h38m32.310s	2	1m35.509s	3
4	**Sebastian Vettel**	Ferrari	1h38m55.752s	3	1m36.358s	6
5	**Fernando Alonso**	McLaren	1h39m46.571s	2	1m37.417s	12
6	**Carlos Sainz Jr**	Toro Rosso	1h39m48.742s	2	1m37.326s	10
7	**Felipe Massa**	Williams	55 laps	3	1m37.269s	9
8	**Sergio Perez**	Force India	55 laps	2	1m37.353s	11
9	**Jenson Button**	McLaren	55 laps	2	1m38.327s	19
10	**Romain Grosjean**	Haas	55 laps	2	1m38.308s	17
11	**Daniil Kvyat**	Toro Rosso	55 laps	1	1m37.480s	13
12	**Kevin Magnussen**	Renault	55 laps	3	1m38.317s	18
13	**Jolyon Palmer**	Renault	55 laps	2	1m37.935s	15
14	**Marcus Ericsson**	Sauber	55 laps	1	1m39.356s	16
15	**Felipe Nasr**	Sauber	55 laps	1	1m38.583s	21
16	**Valtteri Bottas**	Williams	55 laps	2	1m37.116s	8
17	**Pascal Wehrlein**	Manor	55 laps	2	1m38.548s	20
18	**Esteban Ocon**	Manor	54 laps	3	1m38.806s	22
R	**Kimi Raikkonen**	Ferrari	38 laps/loose wheel	3	1m36.131s	5
R	**Max Verstappen**	Red Bull	28 laps/gearbox	2	1m35.747s	4
R	**Esteban Gutierrez**	Haas	16 laps/brakes	1	1m37.773s	14
R	**Nico Hulkenberg**	Force India	1 lap/steering arm	0	1m36.628s	7

FASTEST LAP: : **VETTEL, 1M39.877S, 123.474MPH/198.713KPH ON LAP 55.**
RACE LEADERS: **HAMILTON 1-11 & 15-56, VETTEL 12-14.**

Lewis Hamilton did what he had to do: he won. Yet Nico Rosberg did what he had to do too: he came second, to leave him 19 points clear. Behind them, Sebastian Vettel was penalised after a feisty battle over third place, leaving the position to be awarded to Daniel Ricciardo.

Arriving in Mexico City 26 points behind Rosberg, Hamilton knew he had to win, and hope his team-mate was forced down, or off, the podium by at least one of Ricciardo and Max Verstappen, the Ferrari duo or someone else raising their game.

Although they hadn't kept Rosberg from the front row of the grid, the Red Bull drivers were determined to get in front by the opening corner. Hamilton made a fair start to lead as they approached the 90-degree right, with Rosberg finding Verstappen lining up the inside line for a pass. Just as the move commenced, Hamilton locked up his right front brake and skated off track. He might have been penalised for an advantage gained by bypassing Turn 2 and rejoining at Turn 3, but none came. Rosberg, who survived side-on contact with Verstappen, had to accept that. Verstappen realised his best shot of passing Rosberg had gone and was the first frontrunner to pit. This briefly elevated Nico Hulkenberg to fourth, but he knew it would take a miracle to keep the Ferraris behind him.

Once the first stops had passed, Sebastian Vettel led, because he hadn't yet come in... He stayed out until lap 32 of 71, then changed to medium compound tyres that were far fresher than his rivals'. This allowed Vettel to attack, and attack he did, working his way into a battle for third with the Red Bulls. By pitting twice, Ricciardo had the freshest tyres, but Verstappen had track position and was defending his position robustly from Vettel. However, Verstappen ran off at Turn 1 and was given a 5s penalty for gaining an advantage. Vettel lost his third place, hit with a 10s penalty after the podium ceremony, as he had moved across at Turn 4 on Ricciardo.

Hulkenberg lost sixth to Raikkonen with a late-race spin, but still came home three places clear of team-mate Sergio Perez, desperate for a strong result in front of his home crowd. The other Mexican driver, Esteban Gutierrez, also was disappointed, pitching Pascal Wehrlein out at the first corner and ending up 19th.

Hamilton is about to run off the track as Verstappen and Rosberg prepare to meet each other.

MEXICO CITY ROUND 19

DATE: **30 OCTOBER 2016**

Laps: **71** • Distance: **189.738 miles/305.354km** • Weather: **Warm & sunny**

Pos	Driver	Team	Result	Stops	Qualifying Time	Grid
1	**Lewis Hamilton**	Mercedes	1h40m31.402s	1	1m18.704s	1
2	**Nico Rosberg**	Mercedes	1h40m39.756s	1	1m18.958s	2
3	**Daniel Ricciardo**	Red Bull	1h40m52.260s	2	1m19.133s	4
4	**Max Verstappen**	Red Bull	1h40m52.725s*	1	1m19.054s	3
5	**Sebastian Vettel**	Ferrari	1h40m58.715s**	1	1m19.381s	7
6	**Kimi Raikkonen**	Ferrari	1h41m20.778s	2	1m19.376s	6
7	**Nico Hulkenberg**	Force India	1h41m30.293s	1	1m19.330s	5
8	**Valtteri Bottas**	Williams	1h41m37.014s	1	1m19.551s	8
9	**Felipe Massa**	Williams	1h41m47.608s	1	1m20.032s	9
10	**Sergio Perez**	Force Inia	1h41m48.200s	1	1m20.287s	12
11	**Marcus Ericsson**	Sauber	70 laps	1	1m21.536s	15
12	**Jenson Button**	McLaren	70 laps	1	1m20.673s	13
13	**Fernando Alonso**	McLaren	70 laps	2	1m20.282s	11
14	**Jolyon Palmer**	Renault	70 laps	1	No time	21
15	**Felipe Nasr**	Sauber	70 laps	1	1m21.692s	19
16	**Carlos Sainz Jr**	Toro Rosso	70 laps*	1	1m20.378s	10
17	**Kevin Magnussen**	Renault	70 laps	2	1m21.131s	14
18	**Daniil Kvyat**	Toro Rosso	70 laps*	2	1m21.454s	18
19	**Esteban Gutierrez**	Haas	70 laps	2	1m21.401s	17
20	**Romain Grosjean**	Haas	70 laps	2	1m21.916s	22!
21	**Esteban Ocon**	Manor	69 laps	1	1m21.881s	20
R	**Pascal Wehrlein**	Manor	0 laps/collision	0	1m21.785s	16

FASTEST LAP: RICCIARDO, 1M21.134S, 118.664MPH/190.972KPH ON LAP 53. • RACE LEADERS: HAMILTON 1-17 & 33-71, ROSBERG 18-20, VETTEL 21-32;
* 5S TIME PENALTY; ** 10S TIME PENALTY; ! STARTED FROM PITLANE AS CAR MODIFIED IN PARC FERME.

BRAZILIAN GP

Lewis Hamilton won in slippery conditions to keep his title hopes alive, but it was Max Verstappen's drive to third that had people enthusing as he passed car after car and ought to have beaten Nico Rosberg too but for the small matter of three extra pitstops.

Some races stay on in fans' memories long after others have been forgotten, and 2016's penultimate grand prix is one such race. Hamilton will remember it for landing his first win in Brazil. Rosberg will recall it because he could carry a 12-point advantage to the final round. For everyone else, though, it will be Verstappen's astonishing drive in streaming wet conditions, passing car after car. His drive was mesmeric.

It was deemed the conditions were too wet for flat-out racing. The pace car led them away and, of course, every driver had to run in grid order. The cars finally were released to race after seven laps behind pole-starter Hamilton, but Kimi Raikkonen lost third when Verstappen simply dived inside him at Turn 1.

A second safety car period came after Marcus Ericsson's crash on the climb to the start straight left debris on the circuit. This was cleared and, on the first lap after the race got going again, Raikkonen spun into the pitwall and was very nearly collected. This incident caused an instant red flag stoppage.

After a half-hour delay, the race restarted but the rain fell harder, requiring a second restart and the safety car stayed out until lap 32. Verstappen was ready to pounce when it withdrew, taking second from Rosberg by going past him around the outside through the Senna S. On lap 43, Verstappen was called in for intermediates and dropped to fifth.

Five laps later, Felipe Massa's crash brought out the safety car, at which time Red Bull brought Verstappen in for a fifth time. This time, he emerged on rain tyres in 14th and his fight back from there was extraordinary, especially his pass of Sebastian Vettel, up the inside at the final corner, as he made it back all the way for third, demoting Sergio Perez with a few laps to go.

INTERLAGOS ROUND 20 — DATE: 13 NOVEMBER 2016

Laps: **71** • Distance: **190.083 miles/305.909km** • Weather: **Warm & wet**

Pos	Driver	Team	Result	Stops	Qualifying Time	Grid
1	Lewis Hamilton	Mercedes	3h01m01.335s	2	1m10.736s	1
2	Nico Rosberg	Mercedes	3h01m12.790s	2	1m10.838s	2
3	Max Verstappen	Red Bull	3h01m22.816s	5	1m11.485s	4
4	Sergio Perez	Force India	3h01m26.681s	2	1m12.165s	9
5	Sebastian Vettel	Ferrari	3h01m27.669s	3	1m11.495s	5
6	Carlos Sainz Jr	Toro Rosso	3h01m30.495s	2	1m12.920s	15
7	Nico Hulkenberg	Force India	3h01m31.162s	3	1m12.104s	8
8	Daniel Ricciardo	Red Bull	3h01m31.821s	5	1m11.540s	6
9	Felipe Nasr	Sauber	3h01m43.955s	2	1m13.681s	21
10	Fernando Alonso	McLaren	3h01m45.767s	3	1m12.266s	10
11	Valtteri Bottas	Williams	3h01m46.627s	4	1m12.420s	11
12	Esteban Ocon	Manor	3h01m47.144s	2	1m13.432s	22*
13	Daniil Kvyat	Toro Rosso	3h01m52.527s	4	1m12.726s	14
14	Kevin Magnussen	Renault	3h01m52.890s	4	1m13.410s	18
15	Pascal Wehrlein	Manor	3h02m01.833s	3	1m13.427s	19
16	Jenson Button	McLaren	3h02m23.329s	5	1m13.276s	17
R	Esteban Gutierrez	Haas	60 laps/electrical	4	1m12.431s	12
R	Felipe Massa	Williams	46 laps/spun off	4	1m12.521s	13
R	Jolyon Palmer	Renault	20 laps/crash damage	2	1m13.258s	16
R	Kimi Raikkonen	Ferrari	19 laps/accident	0	1m11.404s	3
R	Marcus Ericsson	Sauber	11 laps/accident	1	1m13.623s	20
NS	Romain Grosjean	Haas	0 laps/accident	0	1m11.937s	7

FASTEST LAP: **VERSTAPPEN, 1M25.305S, 112.994MPH/181.846KPH ON LAP 6** • RACE LEADERS: **HAMILTON 1-71**
* 3-PLACE GRID PENALTY FOR IMPEDING ANOTHER DRIVER.

Massa walks back to the pits after retiring from what he thought would be his last home race.

Lewis Hamilton did all he could by winning the last race of the year but, with Nico Rosberg safe in second, he knew that wouldn't be enough, so he backed Rosberg into the path of two challengers, yet the German held on to become World Champion.

Hamilton knew that a victory on its own wasn't going to land him his fourth title. Trailing team-mate Rosberg by 12 points, he knew that second or third place would be enough for the German to be champion. So, he started to slow. This allowed Rosberg to close on to his tail, but he was never in a position to attempt a pass for the lead. Instead, he had to defend like crazy through the final few laps as the reduced pace let Ferrari's Sebastian Vettel catch up too. Then there was Max Verstappen, who had made up ground to charge from the rear of the field after a first-lap spin.

Mercedes management was ever more upset on the pitwall when their urging for Hamilton to speed up was ignored. Though the Red Bulls offered the biggest threat to Rosberg for much of the race, it was Vettel on the move in the closing stages, on super soft tyres, and he worked his way through to third.

With Vettel close enough to strike, the pressure on Rosberg was intense, but he did just enough to resist the Ferrari and so, with an understandable release of emotion, he became the second second-generation World Champion. Bizarrely, the gap between Keke Rosberg winning his title in 1982 and Nico landing this one was 34 years, matching the gap between Graham Hill being crowned for the first time in 1962 and his son Damon becoming champion.

Afterwards, there was talk of the team hitting Hamilton with sanctions for ignoring their commands, but Rosberg would later say that Hamilton's tactics had been done well.

Daniel Ricciardo finished fifth and could not match Verstappen's pace. He said he wished that he had also run a one-stop race. Kimi Raikkonen rounded out his season in sixth, to match his end-of-year ranking, ahead of the two Force Indias, with Nico Hulkenberg getting the better of Sergio Perez.

This race marked the final F1 outings for Jenson Button and Felipe Massa, with the British driver's McLaren pulling off with broken suspension to deny him a final finish.

Hamilton and Vettel on the podium, as Rosberg leads the celebrations as the new number one.

YAS MARINA ROUND 21

DATE: **26 NOVEMBER 2016**

Laps: **55** • Distance: **189.805 miles/305.462km** • Weather: **Warm & bright**

Pos	Driver	Team	Result	Stops	Qualifying Time	Grid
1	**Lewis Hamilton**	Mercedes	1h38m04.013s	2	1m38.755s	1
2	**Nico Rosberg**	Mercedes	1h38m04.452s	2	1m39.058s	2
3	**Sebastian Vettel**	Ferrari	1h38m04.856s	2	1m39.661s	5
4	**Max Verstappen**	Red Bull	1h38m05.698s	1	1m39.818s	6
5	**Daniel Ricciardo**	Red Bull	1h38m09.328s	2	1m39.589s	3
6	**Kimi Raikkonen**	Ferrari	1h38m22.829s	2	1m39.604s	4
7	**Nico Hulkenberg**	Force India	1h38m54.127s	2	1m40.501s	7
8	**Sergio Perez**	Force India	1h39m02.789s	2	1m40.519s	8
9	**Felipe Massa**	Williams	1h39m03.449s	2	1m41.213s	10
10	**Fernando Alonso**	McLaren	1h39m03.909s	2	1m41.106s	9
11	**Romain Grosjean**	Haas	1h39m20.790s	2	1m41.564s	14
12	**Esteban Gutierrez**	Haas	1h39m39.126s	2	1m41.480s	13
13	**Esteban Ocon**	Manor	54 laps	2	1m42.286s	20
14	**Pascal Wehrlein**	Manor	54 laps	2	1m41.995s	16
15	**Marcus Ericsson**	Sauber	54 laps	1	1m42.637s	22
16	**Felipe Nasr**	Sauber	54 laps	2	1m42.247s	19
17	**Jolyon Palmer**	Renault	54 laps	2	1m41.820s	15
R	**Carlos Sainz Jr**	Toro Rosso	41 laps/collision	2	1m42.393s	21
R	**Daniil Kvyat**	Toro Rosso	14 laps/gearbox	1	1m42.003s	17
R	**Jenson Button**	McLaren	12 laps/suspension	0	1m41.272s	12
R	**Valtteri Bottas**	Williams	6 laps/suspension	0	1m41.084s	11
R	**Kevin Magnussen**	Renault	5 laps/collision	1	1m42.142s	18

FASTEST LAP: VETTEL, 1M43.729S, 119.773MPH/192.756KPH ON LAP 43. RACE LEADERS: HAMILTON 1-6, 10-28, 38-55; ROSBERG 7-8, 29; RICCIARDO 9; VETTEL 30-37.

Hamilton did all he could in Abu Dhabi, but second place was enough for Rosberg to be champion.

POS	DRIVER	NAT		CAR-ENGINE	R1	R2	R3	R4	R5
1	NICO ROSBERG	GER		MERCEDES F1 W07	1	1F	1P	1PF	R
2	LEWIS HAMILTON	GBR		MERCEDES F1 W07	2P	3P	7	2	RP
3	DANIEL RICCIARDO	AUS		RED BULL-TAG HEUER RB12	4F	4	4	11	4
4	SEBASTIAN VETTEL	GER		FERRARI SF16-H	3	NS	2	R	3
5	MAX VERSTAPPEN	NED		TORO ROSSO-RENAULT STR11	10	6	8	R	-
				RED BULL-TAG HEUER RB12	-	-	-	-	1
6	KIMI RAIKKONEN	FIN		FERRARI SF16-H	R	2	5	3	2
7	SERGIO PEREZ	MEX		FORCE INDIA-MERCEDES VJM09	13	16	11	9	7
8	VALTTERI BOTTAS	FIN		WILLIAMS-MERCEDES FW38	8	9	10	4	5
9	NICO HULKENBERG	GER		FORCE INDIA-MERCEDES VJM09	7	15	15F	R	R
10	FERNANDO ALONSO	SPA		McLAREN-HONDA MP4-31	R	-	12	6	R
11	FELIPE MASSA	BRA		WILLIAMS-MERCEDES FW38	5	8	6	5	8
12	CARLOS SAINZ JR	SPA		TORO ROSSO-FERRARI STR11	9	R	9	12	6
13	ROMAIN GROSJEAN	FRA		HAAS-FERRARI VF-16	6	5	19	8	R
14	DANIIL KVYAT	RUS		RED BULL-TAG HEUER RB12	NS	7	3	15	-
				TORO ROSSO-FERRARI STR11	-	-	-	-	10F
15	JENSON BUTTON	GBR		McLAREN-HONDA MP4-31	14	R	13	10	9
16	KEVIN MAGNUSSEN	DEN		RENAULT RS16	12	11	17	7	15
17	FELIPE NASR	BRA		SAUBER-FERRARI C35	15	14	20	16	14
18	JOLYON PALMER	GBR		RENAULT RS16	11	NS	22	13	13
19	PASCAL WEHRLEIN	GER		MANOR-MERCEDES MRT05	16	13	18	18	16
20	STOFFEL VANDOORNE	BEL		McLAREN-HONDA MP4-31	-	10	-	-	-
21	ESTEBAN GUTIERREZ	MEX		HAAS-FERRARI VF-16	R	R	14	17	11
22	MARCUS ERICSSON	SWE		SAUBER-FERRARI C35	R	12	16	14	12
23	ESTEBAN OCON	FRA		MANOR-MERCEDES MRT05	-	-	-	-	-
24	RIO HARYANTO	INA		MANOR-MERCEDES MRT05	R	17	21	R	17

SCORING

1st	25 points
2nd	18 points
3rd	15 points
4th	12 points
5th	10 points
6th	8 points
7th	6 points
8th	4 points
9th	2 points
10th	1 point

POS	TEAM-ENGINE	R1	R2	R3	R4	R5
1	MERCEDES	1/2	1/3	1/7	1/2	R/R
2	RED BULL-TAG HEUER	4/NS	4/7	3/4	11/15	1/4
3	FERRARI	3/R	2/NS	2/5	3/R	2/3
4	FORCE INDIA-MERCEDES	7/13	15/16	11/15	9/R	7/R
5	WILLIAMS-MERCEDES	5/8	8/9	6/10	4/5	5/8
6	McLAREN-HONDA	14/R	10/R	12/13	6/10	9/R
7	TORO ROSSO-FERRARI	9/10	6/R	8/9	12/R	6/10
8	HAAS-FERRARI	6/R	5/R	14/19	8/17	11/R
9	RENAULT	11/12	11/NS	17/22	7/13	13/15
10	SAUBER-FERRARI	15/R	12/14	16/20	14/16	12/14
11	MANOR-MERCEDES	16/R	13/17	18/21	18/R	16/17

R6	R7	R8	R9	R10	R11	R12	R13	R14	R15	R16	R17	R18	R19	R20	R21	TOTAL
7	5F	1PF	4	3F	2P	4P	1P	1	1P	3F	1P	2	2	2	2	385
1F	1P	5	1PF	1P	1	1	3F	2P	3	RP	3	1P	1P	1P	1P	380
2P	7	7	5	4	3	2F	2	5	2F	1	6	3	3F	8	5	256
4	2	2	R	9	4	5	6	3	5	R	4F	4F	5	5	3F	212
-	-	-	-	-	-	-	-	-	-	-	-	-	-	-	-	-
R	4	8	2	2	5	3	11	7	6	2	2	R	4	3F	4	204
R	6	4	3	5	6F	6	9	4	4	4	5	R	6	R	6	186
3	10	3	R	6	11	10	5	8	8	6	7	8	10	4	8	101
12	3	6	9	14	9	9	8	6	R	5	10	16	8	11	R	85
6	8	9	R	7	10	7	4	10	R	8	8	R	7	7	7	72
5	11	R	R	13	7	12	7	14F	7	7	16	5	13	10	10	54
10	R	10	R	11	18	R	10	9	12	13	9	7	9	R	9	53
8	9	R	8	8	8	14	R	15	14	11	17	6	16	6	R	46
13	14	13	7	R	14	13	13	11	NS	R	11	10	20	NS	11	29
-	-	-	-	-	-	-	-	-	-	-	-	-	-	-	-	-
R	12	R	R	10	16	15	14	R	9	14	13	11	18	13	R	25
9	R	11	6	12	R	8	R	12	R	9	18	9	12	16	R	21
R	16	14	14	17	15	16	R	17	10	R	14	12	17	14	R	7
R	18	12	13	15	17	R	17	R	13	R	19	15	15	9	16	2
R	R	15	12	R	12	19	15	R	15	10	12	13	14	R	17	1
14	17	R	10	R	19	17	R	R	16	15	22	17	R	15	14	1
-	-	-	-	-	-	-	-	-	-	-	-	-	-	-	-	1
11	13	16	11	16	13	11	12	13	11	R	20	R	19	R	12	0
R	15	17	15	R	20	18	R	16	17	12	15	14	11	R	15	0
-	-	-	-	-	-	16	18	18	16	21	18	21	12	13	-	0
15	19	18	16	R	21	20	-	-	-	-	-	-	-	-	-	0

R6	R7	R8	R9	R10	R11	R12	R13	R14	R15	R16	R17	R18	R19	R20	R21	TOTAL
1/7	1/5	1/5	1/4	1/3	1/2	1/4	1/3	1/2	1/3	3/R	1/3	1/2	1/2	1/2	1/2	765
2/R	4/7	7/8	2/5	2/4	3/5	2/3	2/11	5/7	2/6	1/2	2/6	3/R	3/4	3/8	4/5	468
4/R	2/6	2/4	3/R	5/9	4/6	5/6	6/9	3/4	4/5	4/R	4/5	4/R	5/6	5/R	3/6	398
3/6	8/10	3/9	R/R	6/7	10/11	7/10	4/5	8/10	8/R	6/8	7/8	8/R	7/10	4/7	7/8	173
10/12	3/R	6/10	9/R	11/14	9/18	9/R	8/10	6/9	12/R	5/13	9/10	7/16	8/9	11/R	9/R	138
5/9	11/R	11/R	6/R	12/13	7/R	8/12	8/R	12/14	7/R	7/9	16/18	5/9	12/13	10/16	10/R	76
8/R	9/12	R/R	8/R	8/10	8/16	14/15	14/R	15/R	9/14	11/14	13/17	6/11	16/18	6/13	R/R	63
11/13	13/14	13/16	7/11	16/R	13/14	11/13	12/13	11/13	11/NS	R/R	11/20	10/R	19/20	R/NS	11/12	29
R/R	16/R	14/15	12/14	17/R	12/15	16/19	15/R	17/R	10/15	10/R	12/14	12/13	14/17	14/R	17/R	8
R/R	15/18	12/17	13/15	15/R	17/20	18/R	17/R	16/R	13/17	12/R	15/19	14/15	11/R	9/R	15/16	2
14/15	17/19	18/R	10/16	R/R	19/21	17/20	16/R	18/R	16/18	15/16	21/22	17/18	21/R	12/15	13/14	1

FORMULA ONE RECORDS

Jenson Button became the third driver to contest more than 300 grands prix before he bowed out at the end of 2016, ending an F1 career that started with Williams back in 2000.

MOST STARTS

DRIVERS

325	Rubens Barrichello	(BRA)
308	Michael Schumacher	(GER)
306	Jenson Button	(GBR)
274	Fernando Alonso	(SPA)
256	Riccardo Patrese	(ITA)
	Jarno Trulli	(ITA)
253	Kimi Raikkonen	(FIN)
251	Felipe Massa	(BRA)
247	David Coulthard	(GBR)
230	Giancarlo Fisichella	(ITA)
216	Mark Webber	(AUS)
210	Gerhard Berger	(AUT)
208	Andrea de Cesaris	(ITA)
206	Nico Rosberg	(GER)
204	Nelson Piquet	(BRA)
201	Jean Alesi	(FRA)
199	Alain Prost	(FRA)
194	Michele Alboreto	(ITA)
188	Lewis Hamilton	(GBR)
187	Nigel Mansell	(GBR)
185	Nick Heidfeld	(GER)
180	Ralf Schumacher	(GER)
179	Sebastian Vettel	(GER)

176	Graham Hill	(GBR)
175	Jacques Laffite	(FRA)
171	Niki Lauda	(AUT)
165	Jacques Villeneuve	(CDN)
163	Thierry Boutsen	(BEL)
162	Mika Hakkinen	(FIN)
	Johnny Herbert	(GBR)
161	Ayrton Senna	(BRA)
159	Heinz-Harald Frentzen	(GER)
158	Martin Brundle	(GBR)
	Olivier Panis	(FRA)
152	John Watson	(GBR)
149	Rene Arnoux	(FRA)
147	Eddie Irvine	(GBR)
	Derek Warwick	(GBR)
146	Carlos Reutemann	(ARG)
144	Emerson Fittipaldi	(BRA)
135	Jean-Pierre Jarier	(FRA)
132	Eddie Cheever	(USA)
	Clay Regazzoni	(SWI)
128	Mario Andretti	(USA)
	Adrian Sutil	(GER)
126	Jack Brabham	(AUS)

123	Ronnie Peterson	(SWE)
119	Pierluigi Martini	(ITA)
117	Nico Hulkenberg	(GER)
116	Damon Hill	(GBR)
	Jacky Ickx	(BEL)
	Alan Jones	(AUS)
114	Keke Rosberg	(FIN)
	Sergio Perez	(MEX)
	Patrick Tambay	(FRA)
112	Denny Hulme	(NZL)
	Jody Scheckter	(RSA)
111	Heikki Kovalainen	(FIN)
	John Surtees	(GBR)
109	Philippe Alliot	(FRA)
	Daniel Ricciardo	(AUS)
	Mika Salo	(FIN)
108	Elio de Angelis	(ITA)
106	Jos Verstappen	(NED)
104	Jo Bonnier	(SWE)
	Pedro de la Rosa	(SPA)
	Romain Grosjean	(FRA)
	Jochen Mass	(GER)
100	Bruce McLaren	(NZL)

CONSTRUCTORS

929	Ferrari
802	McLaren
721	Williams
593	Renault* (*nee* Toleman then Benetton then Renault II, Lotus II & Renault III)
547	Toro Rosso (*nee* Minardi)
492	Lotus

456	Force India (*nee* Jordan then Midland then Spyker)
418	Tyrrell
423	Sauber (including BMW Sauber)
409	Prost (*nee* Ligier)
394	Brabham
383	Arrows
359	Red Bull (*nee* Stewart then

	Jaguar Racing)
324	Mercedes GP (*nee* BAR then Honda Racing then Brawn GP)
230	March
197	BRM
132	Osella
129	Renault

MOST WINS

DRIVERS

91	Michael Schumacher	(GER)	**15**	Jenson Button	(GBR)	**9**	Mark Webber	(AUS)
53	Lewis Hamilton	(GBR)	**14**	Jack Brabham	(AUS)	**8**	Denny Hulme	(NZL)
51	Alain Prost	(FRA)		Emerson Fittipaldi	(BRA)		Jacky Ickx	(BEL)
42	Sebastian Vettel	(GER)		Graham Hill	(GBR)	**7**	Rene Arnoux	(FRA)
41	Ayrton Senna	(BRA)	**13**	Alberto Ascari	(ITA)		Juan Pablo Montoya	(COL)
31	Nigel Mansell	(GBR)		David Coulthard	(GBR)	**6**	Tony Brooks	(GBR)
27	Jackie Stewart	(GBR)	**12**	Mario Andretti	(USA)		Jacques Laffite	(FRA)
25	Jim Clark	(GBR)		Alan Jones	(AUS)		Riccardo Patrese	(ITA)
	Niki Lauda	(AUT)		Carlos Reutemann	(ARG)		Jochen Rindt	(AUT)
24	Juan Manuel Fangio	(ARG)	**11**	Rubens Barrichello	(BRA)		Ralf Schumacher	(GER)
23	Nelson Piquet	(BRA)		Felipe Massa	(BRA)		John Surtees	(GBR)
	Nico Rosberg	(GER)		Jacques Villeneuve	(CDN)		Gilles Villeneuve	(CDN)
22	Damon Hill	(GBR)	**10**	Gerhard Berger	(AUT)			
20	Mika Hakkinen	(FIN)		James Hunt	(GBR)			
	Kimi Raikkonen	(FIN)		Ronnie Peterson	(SWE)			
16	Stirling Moss	(GBR)		Jody Scheckter	(RSA)			

CONSTRUCTORS

224	Ferrari	**16**	Cooper	**1**	BMW Sauber
181	McLaren	**15**	Renault		Eagle
114	Williams	**10**	Alfa Romeo		Hesketh
79	Lotus	**9**	Ligier		Penske
64	Mercedes GP (including Honda Racing, Brawn GP)		Maserati		Porsche
53	Red Bull (including Stewart)		Matra		Shadow
49	Renault* (including Benetton, Renault II, Lotus II & Renault III)		Mercedes		Toro Rosso
			Vanwall		
35	Brabham	**4**	Jordan		
23	Tyrrell	**3**	March		
17	BRM		Wolf		
		2	Honda		

Felipe Massa reached the end of 2016 still on 11 wins in his F1 career, but if he does return for 2017 with Williams, he might yet beat that.

MOST WINS IN ONE SEASON

Lewis Hamilton, celebrating here at Silverstone in 2016, is the only man ever to enjoy three 10-win seasons; he did it in consecutive years 2014-16.

DRIVERS

13	Michael Schumacher	2004		Damon Hill	1996		Alberto Ascari	1952
	Sebastian Vettel	2013		Michael Schumacher	1994		Jim Clark	1965
11	Lewis Hamilton	2014		Ayrton Senna	1988		Juan Manuel Fangio	1954
	Michael Schumacher	2002	**7**	Fernando Alonso	2005		Damon Hill	1994
	Sebastian Vettel	2011		Fernando Alonso	2006		James Hunt	1976
10	Lewis Hamilton	2015		Jim Clark	1963		Nigel Mansell	1987
	Lewis Hamilton	2016		Alain Prost	1984		Kimi Raikkonen	2007
9	Nigel Mansell	1992		Alain Prost	1988		Nico Rosberg	2015
	Nico Rosberg	2016		Alain Prost	1993		Michael Schumacher	1998
	Michael Schumacher	1995		Kimi Raikkonen	2005		Michael Schumacher	2003
	Michael Schumacher	2000		Ayrton Senna	1991		Michael Schumacher	2006
	Michael Schumacher	2001		Jacques Villeneuve	1997		Ayrton Senna	1989
8	Mika Hakkinen	1998	**6**	Mario Andretti	1978		Ayrton Senna	1990

CONSTRUCTORS

19	Mercedes GP	2016	**9**	Ferrari	2001		Williams	1997
16	Mercedes GP	2014		Ferrari	2006	**7**	Ferrari	1952
	Mercedes GP	2015		Ferrari	2007		Ferrari	1953
15	Ferrari	2002		McLaren	1998		Ferrari	2008
	Ferrari	2004		Red Bull	2010		Lotus	1963
	McLaren	1988		Williams	1986		Lotus	1973
12	McLaren	1984		Williams	1987		McLaren	1999
	Red Bull	2011	**8**	Benetton	1994		McLaren	2000
	Williams	1996		Brawn GP	2009		McLaren	2012
11	Benetton	1995		Ferrari	2003		Red Bull	2012
10	Ferrari	2000		Lotus	1978		Tyrrell	1971
	McLaren	2005		McLaren	1991		Williams	1991
	McLaren	1989		McLaren	2007		Williams	1994
	Williams	1992		Renault	2005			
	Williams	1993		Renault	2006			

MOST POLE POSITIONS

DRIVERS

68	Michael Schumacher	(GER)
65	Ayrton Senna	(BRA)
61	Lewis Hamilton	(GBR)
46	Sebastian Vettel	(GER)
33	Jim Clark	(GBR)
	Alain Prost	(FRA)
32	Nigel Mansell	(GBR)
30	Nico Rosberg	(GER)
29	Juan Manuel Fangio	(ARG)
26	Mika Hakkinen	(FIN)
24	Niki Lauda	(AUT)
	Nelson Piquet	(BRA)
22	Fernando Alonso	(SPA)
20	Damon Hill	(GBR)
18	Mario Andretti	(USA)
	Rene Arnoux	(FRA)
17	Jackie Stewart	(GBR)
16	Felipe Massa	(BRA)
	Stirling Moss	(GBR)

	Kimi Raikkonen	(FIN)
14	Alberto Ascari	(ITA)
	Rubens Barrichello	(BRA)
	James Hunt	(GBR)
	Ronnie Peterson	(SWE)
13	Jack Brabham	(AUS)
	Graham Hill	(GBR)
	Jacky Ickx	(BEL)
	Juan Pablo Montoya	(COL)
	Jacques Villeneuve	(CDN)
12	Gerhard Berger	(AUT)
	David Coulthard	(GBR)
11	Mark Webber	(AUS)
10	Jochen Rindt	(AUT)

CONSTRUCTORS

208	Ferrari
154	McLaren
128	Williams
107	Lotus
73	Mercedes GP (including Brawn GP, Honda Racing, BAR)
59	Red Bull
39	Brabham
34	Renault* (including Toleman, Benetton, Renault II, Lotus II & Renault III)
31	Renault
14	Tyrrell
12	Alfa Romeo
11	BRM
	Cooper
10	Maserati
9	Ligier
8	Mercedes
7	Vanwall
5	March
4	Matra
3	Force India (including Jordan)
	Shadow
	Toyota
2	Lancia
1	BMW Sauber
	Toro Rosso

Michael Schumacher tops the table for pole positions, and this one at the 2002 German GP at Hockenheim is one of 68 in his 19-year F1 career.

FASTEST LAPS

DRIVERS

76	Michael Schumacher	(GER)	18	David Coulthard	(GBR)
43	Kimi Raikkonen	(FIN)	17	Rubens Barrichello	(BRA)
41	Alain Prost	(FRA)	16	Felipe Massa	(BRA)
31	Lewis Hamilton	(GBR)	15	Clay Regazzoni	(SWI)
30	Nigel Mansell	(GBR)		Jackie Stewart	(GBR)
28	Jim Clark	(GBR)	14	Jacky Ickx	(BEL)
	Sebastian Vettel	(GER)	13	Alberto Ascari	(ITA)
25	Mika Hakkinen	(FIN)		Alan Jones	(AUS)
24	Niki Lauda	(AUT)		Riccardo Patrese	(ITA)
23	Juan Manuel Fangio	(ARG)	12	Rene Arnoux	(FRA)
	Nelson Piquet	(BRA)		Jack Brabham	(AUS)
22	Fernando Alonso	(SPA)		Juan Pablo Montoya	(COL)
21	Gerhard Berger	(AUT)	11	John Surtees	(GBR)
20	Nico Rosberg	(GER)	10	Mario Andretti	(USA)
19	Damon Hill	(GBR)		Graham Hill	(GBR)
	Stirling Moss	(GBR)			
	Ayrton Senna	(BRA)			
	Mark Webber	(AUS)			

CONSTRUCTORS

236	Ferrari
153	McLaren
133	Williams
71	Lotus
54	Renault* (including Toleman, Benetton, Renault II & Lotus II)
52	Red Bull
41	Mercedes GP (including Brawn GP + BAR + Honda Racing)
40	Brabham
22	Tyrrell
18	Renault
15	BRM
	Maserati
14	Alfa Romeo
13	Cooper
12	Matra
11	Prost (including Ligier)
9	Mercedes
7	March
6	Vanwall

MOST POINTS (THIS FIGURE IS GROSS TALLY, I.E. INCLUDING SCORES THAT WERE LATER DROPPED)

DRIVERS

2247	Lewis Hamilton	(GBR)	360	Damon Hill	(GBR)
2108	Sebastian Vettel	(GER)		Jackie Stewart	(GBR)
1832	Fernando Alonso	(SPA)	329	Ralf Schumacher	(GER)
1594.5	Nico Rosberg	(GER)	316	Romain Grosjean	(FRA)
1566	Michael Schumacher	(GER)	310	Carlos Reutemann	(ARG)
1360	Kimi Raikkonen	(FIN)	307	Juan Pablo Montoya	(COL)
1235	Jenson Button	(GBR)	289	Graham Hill	(GBR)
1124	Felipe Massa	(BRA)	281	Emerson Fittipaldi	(BRA)
1047.5	Mark Webber	(AUS)		Riccardo Patrese	(ITA)
798.5	Alain Prost	(FRA)	277.5	Juan Manuel Fangio	(ARG)
658	Rubens Barrichello	(BRA)	275	Giancarlo Fisichella	(ITA)
616	Daniel Ricciardo	(AUS)	274	Jim Clark	(GBR)
614	Ayrton Senna	(BRA)	273	Robert Kubica	(POL)
535	David Coulthard	(GBR)	261	Jack Brabham	(AUS)
485.5	Nelson Piquet	(BRA)	259	Nick Heidfeld	(GER)
482	Nigel Mansell	(GBR)	255	Jody Scheckter	(RSA)
420.5	Niki Lauda	(AUT)	253	Max Vertsappen	(NED)
420	Mika Hakkinen	(FIN)	248	Denny Hulme	(NZL)
411	Valtteri Bottas	(FIN)	246.5	Jarno Trulli	(ITA)
385	Gerhard Berger	(AUT)	241	Jean Alesi	(FRA)
367	Sergio Perez	(MEX)	235	Jacques Villeneuve	(CDN)
362	Nico Hulkenberg	(GER)	228	Jacques Laffite	(FRA)

CONSTRUCTORS

6642.5	Ferrari
5093.5	McLaren
3608.5	Red Bull (including Stewart, Jaguar Racing)
3553	Mercedes GP (including BAR, Honda Racing, Brawn GP)
3476	Williams
2553.5	Renault* (including Toleman, Benetton, Renault II & Lotus II)
1514	Lotus
1092	Force India (including Jordan, Midland, Spyker)
854	Brabham
805	Sauber (including BMW Sauber)
617	Tyrrell
439	BRM
424	Prost (including Ligier)
367	Toro Rosso
333	Cooper
312	Renault
278.5	Toyota
171.5	March
167	Arrows
155	Matra

Lewis Hamilton and Nico Rosberg have claimed the last three drivers' titles between them and helped Mercedes to three constructors' crowns.

MOST DRIVERS' TITLES

7	Michael Schumacher	(GER)		Alberto Ascari	(ITA)		Denis Hulme	(NZL)
5	Juan Manuel Fangio	(ARG)		Jim Clark	(GBR)		James Hunt	(GBR)
4	Alain Prost	(FRA)		Emerson Fittipaldi	(BRA)		Alan Jones	(AUS)
	Sebastian Vettel	(GER)		Mika Hakkinen	(FIN)		Nigel Mansell	(GBR)
3	Jack Brabham	(AUS)		Graham Hill	(GBR)		Kimi Raikkonen	(FIN)
	Lewis Hamilton	(GBR)	**1**	Mario Andretti	(USA)		Jochen Rindt	(AUT)
	Niki Lauda	(AUT)		Jenson Button	(GBR)		Keke Rosberg	(FIN)
	Nelson Piquet	(BRA)		Giuseppe Farina	(ITA)		Nico Rosberg	(FIN)
	Ayrton Senna	(BRA)		Mike Hawthorn	(GBR)		Jody Scheckter	(RSA)
	Jackie Stewart	(GBR)		Damon Hill	(GBR)		John Surtees	(GBR)
2	Fernando Alonso	(SPA)		Phil Hill	(USA)		Jacques Villeneuve	(CDN)

MOST CONSTRUCTORS' TITLES

16	Ferrari		**3**	Mercedes GP		Brawn
9	Williams		**2**	Brabham		BRM
8	McLaren			Cooper		Matra
7	Lotus			Renault		Tyrrell
4	Red Bull		**1**	Benetton		Vanwall

NOTE: To avoid confusion, the Lotus stats listed are based on the team that ran from 1958 to 1994, whereas those listed as Renault* are for the team based at Enstone that started as Toleman in 1981, became Benetton in 1986, then Renault II in 2002, Lotus II in 2012 and Renault again in 2016. The Renault listings are for the team that ran from 1977 to 1985, the stats for Red Bull Racing include those of the Stewart Grand Prix and Jaguar Racing teams from which it evolved, and those for Mercedes GP for the team that started as BAR in 1999, then ran as Honda GP from 2006 and as Brawn GP in 2009. Force India's stats include those of Jordan, Midland and Spyker, while Scuderia Toro Rosso's include those of its forerunner Minardi.

Tyre changes have long been choreographed to the fraction of a second. In 2017, the crews will have to handle tyres that are both wider and heavier.

2017 FILL-IN CHART

DRIVER	TEAM	Round 1 – 26 March AUSTRALIAN GP	Round 2 – 9 April CHINESE GP	Round 3 – 16 April BAHRAIN GP	Round 4 – 30 April RUSSIAN GP	Round 5 – 14 May SPANISH GP	Round 6 – 28 May MONACO GP	Round 7 – 11 June CANADIAN GP	Round 8 – 25 June AZERBAIJAN GP
LEWIS HAMILTON	Mercedes								
VALTTERI BOTTAS*	Mercedes								
DANIEL RICCIARDO	Red Bull								
MAX VERSTAPPEN	Red Bull								
SEBASTIAN VETTEL	Ferrari								
KIMI RAIKKONEN	Ferrari								
SERGIO PEREZ	Force India								
ESTEBAN OCON	Force India								
FELIPE MASSA*	Williams								
LANCE STROLL	Williams								
FERNANDO ALONSO	McLaren								
STOFFEL VANDOORNE	McLaren								
CARLOS SAINZ JR	Toro Rosso								
DANIIL KVYAT	Toro Rosso								
ROMAIN GROSJEAN	Haas F1								
KEVIN MAGNUSSEN	Haas F1								
NICO HULKENBERG	Renault								
JOLYON PALMER	Renault								
MARCUS ERICSSON	Sauber								
PASCAL WEHRLEIN*	Sauber								

SCORING SYSTEM: 25, 18, 15, 12, 10, 8, 6, 4, 2, 1 POINTS
FOR THE FIRST 10 FINISHERS IN EACH GRAND PRIX

*UNCONFIRMED AT TIME OF GOING TO PRESS

Round 9 – 9 July AUSTRIAN GP	Round 10 – 16 July BRITISH GP	Round 11 – 30 July HUNGARIAN GP	Round 12 – 27 Aug BELGIAN GP	Round 13 – 3 Sept ITALIAN GP	Round 14 – 17 Sept SINGAPORE GP	Round 15 – 1 Oct MALAYSIAN GP	Round 16 – 8 Oct JAPANESE GP	Round 17 – 22 Oct UNITED STATES GP	Round 18 – 29 Oct MEXICAN GP	Round 19 – 12 Nov BRAZILIAN GP	Round 20 – 26 Nov ABU DHABI GP	POINTS TOTAL

Nico Rosberg ended his title-winning 2016 season with this spectacular celebratory dismount from his Mercedes after the Abu Dhabi GP.

The publishers would like to thank the following sources for their kind permission to reproduce the pictures in this book.

LAT Photographic: 21BR, 31BL, 35BL, 49BR, 60BR, 63L, 121; /Sam Bloxham: 29, 43, 44, 45BL, 46, 54, 59T, 63B, 90-91, 94, 97, 101, 102, 104, 105; /Charles Coates: 22, 38-39, 41BL, 47; /Michael Cooper: 17BL; /Glenn Dunbar: 6-7, 8-9, 20, 24-25, 30, 32, 34, 40, 52, 60T, 64-65, 79, 100, 112, 113, 123; /Jakob Ebrey: 103; /Steve Etherington: 10, 12, 14-15, 27BR, 63R, 95, 96, 107, 111, 114, 115; /Robert Fellowes: 63T; /Andrew Ferraro: 59C, 99, 128; /Andrew Hone: 11BL, 13, 18, 19, 23, 26, 28, 36, 42, 48, 50, 51, 55, 56-57, 76-77, 89, 98, 110, 118; /Zak Mauger: 92-93, 106; /Peter Spinney: 53BR; /Steven Tee: 3, 5, 16, 33, 37, 59B, 60BL, 108, 109, 119, 120, 124-125